'In this powerfully argued book, Duncan Green shows how we can make major changes in our unequal and unjust world by concerted action, taking full note of the economic and social mechanisms, including established institutions, that sustain the existing order. If self-confidence is important for the effective agency of deprived communities, so is a reasoned understanding of the difficult barriers that must be faced and overcome. This is a splendid treatise on how to change the actual world— in reality, not just in our dreams.'

Amartya Sen, Thomas W. Lamont University Professor, and Professor of Economics and Philosophy, Harvard University

'In *How Change Happens*, Duncan Green points to a simple truth: that positive social change requires power, and hence attention on the part of reformers to politics and the institutions within which power is exercised. It is an indispensable guide for activists and change-makers everywhere.'

Francis Fukuyama, Olivier Nomellini Senior Fellow at the Freeman Spogli Institute for International Studies (FSI), and the Mosbacher Director of FSI's Center on Democracy, Development, and the Rule of Law, Stanford University

'It was George Orwell who wrote that "The best books… are those that tell you what you know already." Well in Duncan's book *How Change Happens* I have found something better: A book that made me think differently about something I have been doing for my entire life. He has captured so much in these pages, drawing on global and national and local change and examples from past and present. But what makes this book so insightful is that at all times we are able to see the world through Duncan's watchful eyes: From his time as a backpacker in South America to lobbying the WTO in Seattle and his many years with Oxfam, this is someone who has always been watching and always been reflecting. It is this gift that will most help Duncan's readers—whether they be students or those who think they have seen it all. There is always more to notice about such a complex, changing world. And the more we can see, the better we will be at making change happen.'

Winnie Byanyima, Executive Director, Oxfam International

'Once again, following *From Poverty to Power*, Duncan has given us a remarkable tour de force, wide-ranging, readable, combining theory and practice, and drawing on his extensive reading and rich and varied experience. *How Change Happens* is a wonderful gift to all development professionals and citizens who want to make our world a better place. It confronts contemporary complexity, systems, power, and wealth and builds on an extraordinarily rich treasury of experience and evidence to give us a new, grounded realism for development practice. Only after reading and reflecting have I been able to see how badly we have needed this book. It does more than fill a gap. The evidence, examples, analysis, insights, and ideas for action are a quiet but compelling call for reflection on errors and omissions in one's own mindset and practice. Here then we have vital reading for all development professionals, practitioners, and activists, and all concerned citizens. It is as relevant and important for South as North, for funders as activists, for governments as NGOs, for transnational corporations as campaigning citizens. We are all in this together. *How Change Happens* should stand the test of time. It is a landmark, a must read book to return to again and again to inform and inspire reflection and action. I know no other book like it.'

Robert Chambers, Research Associate,
Institute of Development Studies

'This is a gem of a book. Lucidly written and disarmingly frank, it distils the author's decades of experience in global development practice to share what can work and what may not, in changing power relations and complex systems. Again and again I found myself agreeing with him. All of us—practitioners *and* academics—who want a better world, and are willing to work for it, must read this book.'

Bina Agarwal, Professor of Development Economics and Environment,
Global Development Institute, University of Manchester

'This fascinating book should be on the bedside of any activist—and many others besides. Duncan Green is the rare global activist who can explain in clear yet analytical language what it takes to make change happen. Ranging widely from Lake Titicaca in Peru to rural Tajikistan, from shanty towns to the halls of power, this is a book sprinkled with wisdom and insight on every page.'

Dani Rodrik, Ford Foundation Professor of International Political
Economy, John F. Kennedy School of Government, Harvard University

'*How Change Happens* is a positive guide to activists. It is one of the most helpful, hopeful and thoughtful manual on the process of transformation. It is an optimistic book; to be an activist you need to be an optimist! When one feels despondent and disheartened then reading this book will help to encourage, energise, and inspire one to participate in the creation of a better world. Duncan Green makes the case with vivid examples that significant changes have taken place and continue to take place when social and environmental activists employ skilful means and multiple strategies such as advocacy, campaigning, organising, and building movements. It is a wonderful book. Read it and be enthused to join in the journey of change.'

Satish Kumar, Founder of Schumacher College and
Editor Emeritus, *Resurgence & Ecologist*

'The world committed to global transformative change in 2015, with the 2030 Agenda and targets in the Paris Climate Agreement to stay well below 2°C and achieve carbon neutrality by the second half of the century. We need to understand how change happens in order to accelerate our pathway to a safe future. Duncan Green's book is a timely and badly needed guide to bringing about the necessary social and political change.'

Mary Robinson, Chair of the Institute
for Human Rights and Business

HOW CHANGE HAPPENS

DUNCAN GREEN

HOW CHANGE
HAPPENS

OXFAM

OXFORD
UNIVERSITY PRESS

OXFORD
UNIVERSITY PRESS

Great Clarendon Street, Oxford, OX2 6DP,
United Kingdom

Oxford University Press is a department of the University of Oxford.
It furthers the University's objective of excellence in research, scholarship,
and education by publishing worldwide. Oxford is a registered trade mark of
Oxford University Press in the UK and in certain other countries

First Edition published in 2016

Impression: 1

Published in the United States of America by Oxford University Press
198 Madison Avenue, New York, NY 10016, United States of America

British Library Cataloguing in Publication Data
Data available

Library of Congress Control Number: 2016938236

ISBN 978-0-19-878539-2 (hbk.)

Printed in Great Britain by
Clays Ltd, St Ives plc

For Tito and Jenny who got me started, Cathy who kept me going,
and Calum and Finlay, who can take over from here.

FOREWORD

Ha-Joon Chang

'The philosophers have only interpreted the world, in various ways. The point, however, is to change it', said Karl Marx in one of his most celebrated passages, which eventually became one of his two epitaphs (the other one being, 'Workers of all lands, unite').

Marx was certainly right to argue that social theories should be not just about understanding the status quo but also about offering a vision for its improvement; but he was wrong to imply that no one before him had thought like that.

For the last several thousand years at least, human beings have tried to imagine a different world from the one they live in, and worked together to create it. Human history is littered with countless visions of—and struggles for—an alternative social order. These may have been large-scale social experiments based on elaborate theories, like Marxism, the welfare state, or neo-liberalism. Or they may have involved daily struggles for survival, safety, and dignity by oppressed and underprivileged people, even though they may not have had any sophisticated theory about their alternative world. However, the capacity to imagine an alternative social order and cooperating to create it is what distinguishes humankind from other animals.

Despite the fact that much of human history has been about attempting to create different realities, we do not understand the process of social change very well.

To be sure, we have grand historical narratives that describe social change as the results of interactions between technological forces and economic institutions, such as property rights; Marxism is the best example of this. We know quite a bit about the way in which society is transformed because of the changes in political-legal institutions, such as the court system or international trade agreements. We have interesting and detailed accounts of how certain individuals and groups—whether they are political leaders, business leaders, trade unions, or grassroots groups—have succeeded in realizing visions that initially few others thought realistic.

However, we do not yet have a good theory of how all these different elements work together to generate social change. To put it a bit more dramatically, if someone wanted to know how she could change certain aspects of the community, nation, or the world she lives in, she would be hard pressed to find a decent guidebook.

Into this gap steps Duncan Green, the veteran campaigner for development and social justice, with *How Change Happens*, an innovative and thrilling field guide to—let's not mince words—changing the world.

Many conventional discussions of how change happens focus either on technology (mobile phones can bring the revolution!) or a brutal account of realpolitik—how oligarchs and elites carve up the world. While not ignoring such factors, *How Change Happens* develops a far better framework for understanding social change by focusing on power analysis and systemic understanding; this is called the 'power and systems approach'.

The power and systems approach emphasizes that, in order to generate social change, we first need to understand how power is distributed and can be re-distributed between and within social groups: the emancipation of women; the spread of human rights; the power of poor people when they get organized; the shifting power relationships behind the negotiations around the international economic system. While emphasizing the role of power struggles, the book does not see them as voluntaristic clashes of raw forces, in which whoever has more arms, money, or votes wins. It tries to situate those power struggles within complex systems that are continuously changing in unpredictable ways, affecting and being affected by diverse factors like social norms, negotiations, campaigns, lobbying, and leadership.

Providing a theory of social change that is convincing is already a tall order, but Duncan Green sets himself an even higher bar. The book aims to be a practical field guide to social activism. More than that, it aspires to be a field guide not just for the kinds of people he normally works with, such as NGO campaigners or grassroots organizers. It is meant to be a field manual for activists in the broadest sense: politicians, civil servants, businesspeople, even academics.

This is certainly a hugely ambitious project; how can anyone write a book that can provide sophisticated theories of social change, while providing practical advice to activists?

However, amazingly, *How Change Happens* delivers on its promise. Those who are purely interested in understanding better how societies change will find a treasure trove of theoretical insights and empirical evidence. Those who want to change the world through formal politics will certainly learn a lot from the book in terms of how to establish political consensus and legitimacy, how to build coalitions, and how to use national and international laws to initiate and consolidate changes. Civil servants who want to make things better for citizens, or business leaders who want to do more than simply maximize profits will also find plenty of lessons to draw from the book in devising policies and corporate strategies that can make the world a better place in realistic but innovative ways. The book will even help academics, like myself, who try to engage with real-world issues, to grasp better the role that their research and outreach activities can play in bringing about (or hindering) social change.

Drawing on his impressive knowledge of the relevant areas of the social sciences, his thirty-five years of diverse experience in international development and many first-hand examples from the global experience of Oxfam, one of the world's largest social justice NGOs, Duncan Green has produced a unique and uniquely useful book addressing a hugely important but largely neglected issue. Everyone who is interested in making the world a better place should thank him for it.

ACKNOWLEDGEMENTS

Once again, I am indebted to the editorial dream team of Mark Fried and Anna Coryndon. Mark's unique combination of editorial skill, deep knowledge of development, and phenomenal patience helped steer this book from a messy first draft to (hopefully) something rather better. Anna managed the project throughout with her customary grace and attention to detail.

I would like to thank Oxfam for giving me the time and encouragement to write this book, but while I thank Oxfam for its support, I want to make it clear that *How Change Happens* does not necessarily reflect Oxfam policy positions—the views expressed are those of the author.

A huge number of Oxfam friends and colleagues contributed to various drafts and discussions, including Laurie Adams, Emily Brown, Celine Charveriat, Binay Dhital, Thomas Dunmore-Rodriguez, Lisa Marie Faye, Penny Fowler, Uwe Gneiting, Sally Golding, Mark Goldring, Tim Gore, Irene Guijt, Thomas Heath, Mohga Kamal-Yanni, Eluka Kibona, Gawain Kripke, Max Lawson, Paul O'Brien, Jo Rowlands, Erinch Sahan, Joss Saunders, Kashif Shabir, Barry Shelley, Kaori Shigiya, Mary Sue Smiarowski, Caroline Sweetman, and Andrew Wells-Dang.

The book has been greatly helped by the financial and intellectual support of Australia's Department for Foreign Affairs and Trade, including Kirsten Bishop, Helen Corrigan, Steve Hogg, Sally Moyle, and Sandra Kraushaar.

Colleagues at the Developmental Leadership Program have provided invaluable advice, notably Niheer Dasandi, David Hudson, Linda Kelly, Heather Lyne de Ver, Heather Marquette, Alina Rocha Menocal, and Chris Roche.

Thanks to my long-suffering students at the London School of Economics for allowing me to test various iterations of the arguments in the book on them.

More generally, I am deeply indebted to a wide and supportive network of 'development wonks' scattered across academia, civil society, business, and government, including Jean Boulton, Francesco Caberlin, Nathaniel Calhoun, Robert Chambers, Paul Clough, Steve Commins, Stefanie Conrad, Paddy Coulter, Aidan Craney, James Deane, Alice Evans, Jaime Faustino, Robin Ford, Alan Fowler, Greta Galeazzi, John Gaventa, Calum Green, Finlay Green, Tom Harrison, Maximilian Heywood, David Hillman, Robert Jordan, Nanci Lee, Jeremy Lim, Matthew Lockwood, Siobhan Mcdonnell, Catherine Masterman, Masood UL Mulk, Arnaldo Pellini, Vicky Randall, Raul Sanchez-Urribarri, Ryan Stoa, Heidi Tydemers, Craig Valters, Jorge Velasquez, Steve Waygood, Frauke de Weijer, and Leni Wild.

The OUP team of Kim Behrens, Kate Farquhar-Thomson, Phil Henderson, Adam Swallow, and Aimee Wright have been a delight to work with throughout.

I would also like to thank the many, many people around the world who gave up precious time to answer the questions of a nosy visitor. Many are named in the text, unless they wished to remain anonymous.

And finally, if you helped with the book, have scoured this page, and not found your name, all I can offer is my groveling apology and a heartfelt thank you.

As ever, any errors in the text are mine alone and certainly not the responsibility of the many people who have helped me along the way. The research project 'How Change Happens' is funded by Australian Aid and the University of Birmingham's Developmental Leadership Program. The opinions expressed are those of the author and not necessarily those of DFAT/Australian Aid and DLP.

CONTENTS

CONTENTS

INTRODUCTION

I was moved to write this book by a combination of excitement, fascination, and frustration: excitement at the speed and grandeur of many of the social changes occurring today—continents rising from poverty, multitudes gaining access to literacy and decent healthcare for the first time, women in dozens of countries winning rights, respect, and power. Working at Oxfam gives me an extraordinary and privileged ringside seat from which to appreciate both the bigger picture and the individual stories of inspiring activists across the globe. I have also (miraculously) been given time to read and write, arousing undying envy in many of my colleagues. This book is the result of that dialogue between reflection and practice.

My daily excitement is laced with frustration when I see activists take steps that seem destined to fail. Within months of joining Oxfam in 2004, I witnessed two examples, one big and one small. On a field visit to Vietnam, I was taken to see Oxfam's work with Hmong villagers in the north. As we drove to the remote home of this impoverished ethnic minority, we passed the first, more intrepid backpackers starting to arrive in the area. The Hmong produce wonderful textiles, and it was obvious that a tourist boom was in the offing. Yet our project consisted of training villagers to keep their prized water buffalo warm and well during the winter (involving rubbing them regularly with alcohol, among other things). There is nothing wrong with working on livestock, but what were we doing to help them prepare for the coming influx of tourists? When challenged, our local (non-Hmong, middle class Vietnamese) staff replied that they wanted to 'protect' the villagers' traditional ways against the invasion of the outside world.

On a grander scale, I had growing misgivings about an enormous, global campaign Oxfam was then leading that implied global activism around trade, debt, aid, and climate change could somehow 'Make Poverty History'. The campaign seemed to gravely downplay the primacy of national politics. I developed my argument a couple of years later in a book, *From Poverty to Power: How Active Citizens and Effective States can Change the World*. One of the inputs to that book was a paper we commissioned[1] on the theories of change used by different academic disciplines. It turns out they each operate with separate and often conflicting theories of change, and there is no 'department of change studies' to sort it out. I was intrigued, and set out some rather rudimentary ideas about 'how change happens' in an annex to the book, marking the starting point for the prolonged conversation that led eventually to this book.

This book is for activists who want to change the world. A narrow interpretation would say that means people engaged in protest movements and campaigns around topics as disparate as climate change and disabled peoples' rights, usually on the margins of 'the system', people who from the days of the abolitionists have been making change happen. But the list of 'change agents' (English is sadly devoid of non-clunky descriptors in this field) is much wider. I include reformers inside the system, such as politicians (both elected and unelected), public officials, and enlightened business people. And the civic world beyond formal institutions is far too rich to narrow down to a single category of 'campaigners'. Faith groups, community leaders, and the many self-help organizations that women form are all often influential players. Even within aid organizations, those engaged

---

[1] Roman Krznaric, 2007, 'How Change Happens: Interdisciplinary perspectives for human development', Oxfam Research Report (Oxford: Oxfam GB, 2007) http://policy-practice.oxfam.org.uk/publications/how-change-happens-interdisciplinary-perspectives-for-human-development-112539.

in what we call 'programmes'—funding or running projects to create jobs or improve health and education services, or responding to emergencies such as wars or earthquakes—are just as involved in seeking change as campaigners. When I use the word 'activists' I mean all of the above. (If that all sounds too exhausting, and you would rather be an armchair activist who just wants to understand change better, that's fine too.)

How Change Happens also sheds light on why the relationships between such activists are often fraught. People bring their own worldviews to the question of change. Do we prefer conflict ('speaking truth to power') or cooperation ('winning friends and influencing people')? Do we see progress everywhere, and seek to accelerate its path, or do we see (in our darker, more honest moments) a quixotic struggle against power and injustice that is ultimately doomed to defeat? Do we believe lasting and legitimate change is primarily driven by the accumulation of power at grassroots/individual level, through organization and challenging norms and beliefs? Or by reforms at the levels of laws, policies, institutions, companies and elites? Or by identifying and supporting 'enlightened' leaders? Do we think the aim of development is to include poor people in the benefits of modernity (money economy, technology, mobility) or to defend other cultures and traditions and build an alternative to modernity? Do we want to make the current system function better, or do we seek something that tackles the deeper structures of power? The answer is 'all of the above'—this book tries to show how these different approaches fit into the wider picture of change.

The book takes as its starting point Amartya Sen's brilliant definition of development as the progressive expansion of the freedoms to be and to do.[2] It discusses political and social change, as well as some of development's economic aspects. It focuses on *intended* change, even though a good deal of change is unintended or accidental (the invention of the washing machine made a huge contribution to

---

[2] Amartya Sen, *Development as Freedom* (Oxford: Oxford University Press, 1999).

women's empowerment, even though that probably wasn't in the minds of its inventors).

One of the curious insights I gleaned from writing the book is that the same categories of analysis (power, norms, complex systems, institutions, agency) seem to be helpful at all levels, whether considering change in a single community, a country, or at a global level. Like Russian Dolls, or fractals, the same features reappear at different scales as you zoom in and out. Those ways of thinking also help when defending good things from attack (resisting the wrong kind of change) and when trying to explain why change often *doesn't* happen, the deep rooted resistance of institutions, norms, and individuals that often blocks the way.

How Change Happens is divided into four parts. The first sets out the conceptual underpinning of the book, an effort to understand change through the prism of complex systems, power, and social norms. Perhaps it is the legacy of a long-distant physics degree, but at times in the last few years, it has felt something like a unified field theory of development is emerging from these discussions. Part I also wrestles with the fact that books are inevitably linear creations: you start at the beginning and (if it's any good) read through to the end. That seems terribly inappropriate for a discussion of non-linear complex systems, and runs the risk that readers give up before getting to the 'so what' conclusion. I have therefore tried to boil down the final message of the book into a one-page 'power and systems approach' in Part I, which gives a taste of what is to come.

Part II discusses some of the main institutions that are both the object and subject of most change processes: central government, legal systems, political parties and other channels of accountability, the international system, and large transnational corporations. Some of this may feel like hard work, and certainly a long way from a feel-good celebration of activism. I suspect many activists could use a quick refresher on the history, politics, and internal structures of the institutions they wish to influence if we are to find new ideas and possibilities for promoting change and seizing moments of opportunity.

Part III discusses some of activism's main players: citizen activists, advocacy organizations, and the role of leadership. And the final part explores the implications of my analysis for individual activists and their organizations, fleshing out the power and systems approach.

The book is not a manual. Indeed one of its conclusions is that reliance on checklist toolkits is one of the things that is holding us back. Instead it offers a combination of analysis, questions, and case studies, with the aim of helping readers look afresh at both the obstacles and the enthralling processes of change going on all around them, and to gain some new energy and ideas about how to contribute.

Like most change processes, this book emerged rather than being decided in advance. Hundreds of people contributed their ideas and experiences; when we posted a draft version for comment, more than 600 people downloaded it. I have made every effort to incorporate a range of voices and opinions, but in the end, this is a book written by a white, Western (and rapidly aging) male, and it inevitably echoes my experiences, networks, culture, assumptions, and prejudices. Please don't forget that, while you're reading it.

Not that 'I' am a fixed quantity. Researching and writing this book has changed me in ways I probably won't fully understand for some time. I have always felt a tension between the desire to be a 'finisher'— dotting the i's and crossing the t's—and the urge to move on to new ideas, to grab the next shiny shell on the beach. At university, I studied physics but moonlighted for lectures on Joyce and Eliot, and wrote truly execrable poetry. My personality assessments in things like the Myers Briggs test are a mess. Most of the time, I don't know what I think or, like the Queen in *Alice in Wonderland*, I seem to hold entirely contradictory opinions at the same time.

Somehow, the act of writing made me acknowledge that ambiguity and grow comfortable with it. You would think that writing a book, with its words fixed forever and its pretensions to authority, would be anathema to ambiguity, complexity, and change. Luckily books these days are no longer tablets of stone, rather the more time-consuming part of a wider conversation. In this case, the conversation will continue after publication on my 'From Poverty to Power' blog and on the 'How Change Happens' website. I look forward to hearing your thoughts and arguments on all of the issues raised in this book—and to changing my mind, preferably several times before breakfast.

PART I

A POWER AND SYSTEMS APPROACH

Change may not be linear, but books are. One of the standard frustrations for time-strapped readers is having to wade through a couple of hundred pages before you get to the 'so what' section at the end. Many do not make it, so I have cheated—here's a brief preview of the final chapter of the book, which sets out a 'power and systems approach' (PSA) for those seeking to achieve change in the world around them.

Since no amount of upfront analysis will enable us to predict the erratic behaviour of a complex system, a PSA interweaves thought and action, learning and adapting as we go. The purpose of initial study is to enable us to place our bets intelligently. Crucial decisions come after that, as we act, observe the results, and adjust according to what we learn.

A PSA encourages multiple strategies, rather than a single linear approach, and views failure, iteration and adaptation as expected and necessary, rather than a regrettable lapse. It covers our ways of working—how we think and feel, as well as how we behave as activists. It also suggests the kinds of questions we should be asking (non-exhaustive—the list is as endless as our imagination).

How we think/feel/work: 4 steps to help us dance with the system

- Curiosity—study the history; 'learn to dance with the system'.
- Humility—embrace uncertainty/ambiguity.
- Reflexivity—be conscious of your own role, prejudices, and power.
- Include multiple perspectives, unusual suspects; be open to different ways of seeing the world.

The questions we ask (and keep asking)

- What kind of change is involved (individual attitudes, social norms, laws and policies, access to resources)?
- What precedents are there that we can learn from (positive deviance, history, current political and social tides)?
- Power analysis: who are the stakeholders and what kind of power is involved (look again—who have we forgotten?)
- What kind of approach makes sense for this change (traditional project, advocacy, multiple parallel experiments, fast feedback and rapid response)?
- What strategies are we going to try (delivering services, building the broader enabling environment, demonstration projects, convening and brokering, supporting local grassroots organizations, advocacy)?
- Learning and course correction: how will we learn about the impact of our actions or changes in context (e.g. critical junctures)? Schedule regular time outs to take stock and adapt accordingly.

1

SYSTEMS THINKING CHANGES EVERYTHING

The future is a dance between patterns and events

—Embracing Complexity[1]

Political and economic earthquakes are often sudden and unforeseeable, despite the false pundits who pop up later to claim they predicted them all along. Take the fall of the Berlin Wall, the 2008 Global Financial Crisis, or the Arab Spring (and ensuing winter). Even at a personal level, change is largely unpredictable: how many of us can say our lives have gone according to the plans we had as 16-year-olds?

The essential mystery of the future poses a huge challenge to activists. If change is only explicable in the rear-view mirror, how can we accurately envision the future changes we seek, let alone achieve them? How can we be sure our proposals will make things better, and not fall victim to unintended consequences? People employ many concepts to grapple with such questions. I find 'systems' and 'complexity' two of the most helpful.

A 'system' is an interconnected set of elements coherently organized in a way that achieves something. It is more than the sum of its parts: a body is more than an aggregate of individual cells; a university is not merely an agglomeration of individual students, professors,

---

[1] Jean Boulton, Peter Allen, and Cliff Bowman, *Embracing Complexity: Strategic Perspectives for an Age of Turbulence* (New York: Oxford University Press, 2015), p. 29. By permission of Oxford University Press.

and buildings; an ecosystem is not just a set of individual plants and animals.[2]

A defining property of human systems is complexity: because of the sheer number of relationships and feedback loops among their many elements, they cannot be reduced to simple chains of cause and effect. Think of a crowd on a city street, or a flock of starlings wheeling in the sky at dusk. Even with supercomputers, it is impossible to predict the movement of any given person or starling, but there is order; amazingly few collisions occur even on the most crowded streets.

In complex systems, change results from the interplay of many diverse and apparently unrelated factors. Those of us engaged in seeking change need to identify which elements are important and understand how they interact.

My interest in systems thinking began when collecting stories for my book *From Poverty to Power* (2008). The light-bulb moment came on a visit to India's Bundelkhand region, where the poor fishing communities of Tikamgarh had won rights to more than 150 large ponds. In that struggle numerous factors interacted to create change. First, a technological shift triggered changes in behaviour: the introduction of new varieties of fish, which made the ponds more profitable, induced landlords to seize ponds that had been communal. Conflict then built pressure for government action: a group of twelve brave young fishers in one village fought back, prompting a series of violent clashes that radicalized and inspired other communities; women's groups were organized for the first time, taking control of nine ponds. Enlightened politicians and non-governmental organizations (NGOs) helped pass new laws and the police amazed everyone by enforcing them.

The fishing communities were the real heroes of the story. They tenaciously faced down a violent campaign of intimidation, moved from direct action to advocacy, and ended up winning not only access

---

[2] Donella Meadows and Diana Wright, *Thinking in Systems: A Primer* (Abingdon: Routledge, 2009).

to the ponds but a series of legal and policy changes that benefitted all fishing families.[3]

The neat narrative sequence of cause and effect I've just written, of course, is only possible in hindsight. In the thick of the action, no-one could have said why the various actors acted as they did, or what transformed the relative power of each. Tikamgarh's experience, like that of Bolivia's Chiquitanos discussed in Chapter 3, highlights how unpredictable is the interaction between structures (such as state institutions), agency (by communities and individuals), and the broader context (characterized by shifts in technology, environment, demography, or norms).[4]

Unfortunately, the way we commonly think about change projects onto the future the neat narratives we draw from the past. Many of the mental models we use are linear plans—'if A, then B'—with profound consequences in terms of failure, frustration, and missed opportunities. As Mike Tyson memorably said, 'everyone has a plan 'til they get punched in the mouth'.[5]

Let me illustrate with a metaphor. Baking a cake is a linear 'simple' system. All I need do is find a recipe, buy the ingredients, make sure the oven is working, mix, bake, et voila! Some cakes are better than others (mine wouldn't win any prizes), but the basic approach is fixed, replicable, and reasonably reliable. However bad your cake, you'll probably be able to eat it.

Baking a cake is also a fairly accurate metaphor for the approach of many governments, aid agencies, and activist organizations. They

---

[3] Neelkanth Mishra and Mirza Firoz Beg, *Strength in Numbers: Fishing Communities in India Assert their Traditional Rights over Livelihoods Resources* (Oxford: Oxfam GB on behalf of Oxfam India, 2011).

[4] In *From Poverty to Power* I developed this concept into a simple model for analysing processes of change. This book builds on those initial ideas. Duncan Green, *From Poverty to Power: How Active Citizens and Effective States Can Change the World* (Oxford: Oxfam International, 2008), Annex A: How Change Happens, p. 432.

[5] Mike Berardino, 'Mike Tyson Explains One of his Most Famous Quotes', *Sun Sentinal*, 9 November 2012, http://articles.sun-sentinel.com/2012-11-09/sports/sfl-mike-tyson-explains-one-of-his-most-famous-quotes-20121109_1_mike-tyson-undisputed-truth-famous-quotes.

decide on a goal (the cake), pick a well-established method (the recipe), find some partners and allies (the ingredients), and off they go.

The trouble is that real life rarely bakes like a cake. Engaging a complex system is more like raising a child. What fate would await your new baby if you decided to go linear and design a project plan setting out activities, assumptions, outputs, and outcomes for the next twenty years and then blindly followed it? Nothing good, probably.

Instead, parents make it up as they go along. And so they should. Raising a child is iterative, an endless testing of assumptions about right and wrong, a constant adaptation to the evolving nature of the child and his or her relationship with their parents and others. Despite all the 'best practice' guides preying on the insecurity of new parents, child-rearing is devoid of any 'right way' of doing things. What really helps parents is experience (the second kid is usually easier), and the advice and reassurance of people who've been through it themselves—'mentoring' in management speak. Working in complex systems requires the same kind of iterative, collaborative, and flexible approach. Deng Xiaoping's recipe for China's take off epitomizes this approach: 'We will cross the river by feeling the stones under our feet, one by one'.[6]

Systems are in a state of constant change. Jean Boulton, one of the authors of *Embracing Complexity*, likes to use the metaphor of the forest, which typically goes through cycles of growth, collapse, regeneration, and new growth.[7] In the early part of the cycle's growth phase, the number of species and of individual plants and animals increases quickly, as organisms arrive to exploit all available ecological niches. The forest's components become more linked to one another, enhancing the ecosystem's 'connectedness' and multiplying the ways the forest regulates itself and maintains its stability. However, the forest's very connectedness and efficiency eventually reduce its capacity to cope with severe outside shocks, paving the way for a collapse and

[6] Arthur Sweetman and Jun Zhang, *Economic Transitions with Chinese Characteristics*, (Montreal: McGill-Queen's University Press, 2009), p. 1.

[7] Thomas Homer-Dixon, 'Our Panarchic Future', *World Watch* 22, no. 2 (March/April 2009), http://www.worldwatch.org/node/6008.

eventual regeneration. Jean argues that activists need to adapt their analysis and strategy according to the stage that their political surroundings most closely resemble: growth, maturity, locked-in but fragile, or collapsing.

I was not a quick or easy convert to systems thinking, despite the fact that my neural pathways were shaped by my undergraduate degree in physics, where linear Newtonian mechanics quickly gave way to the more mind-bending world of quantum mechanics, wave particle duality, relativity, and Heisenberg's uncertainty principle. Similarly, my experience of activism has obliged me to question linear approaches to campaigning, for example, as I hesitantly embraced the realization that change doesn't happen like that.

Once I began thinking about systems, I started to see complexity and unpredictable 'emergent change' everywhere—in politics, economics, at work, and even in the lives of those around me. The rest of this chapter suggests ways systems thinking may transform our understanding and approach.

Systems, economics, and development

Several great books helped me flesh out the ideas behind systems thinking and apply them to economics. They included Hernando de Soto's *Mystery of Capital*,[8] a brilliant description of how property rights in successful economies emerge organically from gold rushes and other economic events, and *The Origin of Wealth*[9] by Eric Beinhocker,[10] who argues that the discipline that became mainstream economics took a tragic wrong turn in the nineteenth century when its adherents chose physics rather than evolution as the basis for its thinking.

---

[8] Hernando de Soto, *The Mystery of Capital: Why Capitalism Triumphs in the West and Fails Everywhere Else* (New York: Basic Books, 2000).

[9] Eric Beinhocker, *The Origin of Wealth: Evolution, Complexity, and the Radical Remaking of Economics* (London: Random House Business Books, 2007).

[10] See also David Hamilton, *Evolutionary Economics: A Study of Change in Economic Thought* (Albuquerque: University of New Mexico Press, 1970).

Mental models that stress stability and equilibrium (balls in bowls disturbed, then rolling back to rest) hardly capture the profound instability of real economies, which grow and evolve as technologies rise and fall, firms start up or go bust, countries wax and wane.

Replace Isaac Newton with Charles Darwin, and economies start to make much more sense. Firms, ideas, and institutions obey the basic mechanisms of evolution. First comes variation (or differentiation), the endless frenetic churn of human activity, as we attempt to come up with the next big idea, new technology, trendier restaurant, catchier tune. Then comes selection: people either like/buy your idea, or they don't. Next comes amplification: if your app is popular, more and more people buy your product, the company grows and becomes more powerful. And a new round of variation occurs within the bounds of your successful experiment or as competitors try to wipe you out. Evolution lies at the heart of what economist Joseph Schumpeter called the 'creative destruction' of capitalism, and its dynamism partly explains why the centrally planned economies of the last century could not compete.

If companies want to survive in such a system, says *The Origin of Wealth*, they should 'bring evolution inside and get the wheels of differentiation, selection and amplification spinning within a company. Rather than thinking of strategy as a single plan built on predictions of the future, we should think of strategy as a portfolio of experiments that competes and evolves over time.'[11] The same reasoning should apply to activist organizations, and in Chapter 12, I venture some thoughts as to how they might do so.

Systems thinking raises some awkward questions for me regarding economic policy. In my years doing policy advocacy on trade and globalization, the work of economists like Ha-Joon Chang and Dani Rodrik had fully convinced me of the need for the state to play a hands-on role in economic development through some form of

---

[11] Eric Beinhocker, *The Origin of Wealth: Evolution, Complexity, and the Radical Remaking of Economics* (London: Random House Business Books, 2007).

industrial policy. Put in its crudest form, industrial policy boils down to 'picking winners'—as the South Korean state did when it decided to shift its economy into shipbuilding and then electronics. That worked in South Korea and a handful of other 'developmental states', but failed in many others to produce modern, competitive companies because businesses used their connections to lobby for unwarranted state subsidies and protection from imports. Critics of industrial policy love to quote the aphorism 'governments are hopeless at picking winners, but losers are really good at picking governments'.

It is a short step from accepting the systems thinking mantra that 'evolution is cleverer than you are'[12] to arguing in favour of laissez-faire policies that leave it entirely up the market what will be produced and where. Is systems thinking inherently pro-liberalization and anti-state intervention? In order to embrace Eric must I abandon Ha-Joon?

Thinking about how power operates within systems (the topic of Chapter 2) helped me resolve the dilemma. Even if markets start off with a 'level playing field', they self-organize into complex structures that reward winners and punish losers in the 'positive feedback loops' that are a common feature of systems. In the absence of countervailing forces such as state regulation or trade unions, the powerful can use their political and economic clout to get even richer—survival of the fattest, rather than the fittest—and so create growing polarization and unfairness, leading to monopoly and stagnation.[13]

In complex systems, institutions are needed to keep the playing field level enough to encourage the dynamism at its heart—for example, through competition policy, access to information, enhancing general technological skills, or credit and other support for small firms. And since markets should be at the service of society, not the other way around, the state and other institutions must find ways to push

---

[12] Known as Orgel's Second Rule, after evolutionary biologist Leslie Orgel. 'Leslie Orgel', Wikipedia entry, https://en.wikipedia.org/wiki/Leslie_Orgel.
[13] Jean Boulton, Peter Allen, and Cliff Bowman, *Embracing Complexity: Strategic Perspectives for an Age of Turbulence* (New York: Oxford University Press, 2015).

markets to pursue socially desirable goals, such as greater equality, human rights, or long-term sustainability, without undermining the dynamism of the market system. A tall order, but many states have managed to balance power such that public institutions are able to respond rapidly to feedback from the real economy, while remaining sufficiently autonomous to avoid capture by vested interests.[14] To my relief, it turns out that Eric and Ha-Joon are compatible, after all.

Crises as critical junctures

Change in complex systems occurs in slow steady processes such as demographic shifts and in sudden, unforeseeable jumps. Nothing seems to change until suddenly it does, a stop–start rhythm that can confound activists. When British Prime Minister Harold Macmillan was asked what he most feared in politics, he reportedly replied in his wonderfully patrician style, 'Events, dear boy'. Such 'events' that disrupt social, political, or economic relations are not just a prime ministerial headache. They can open the door to previously unthinkable reforms.

In Tikamgarh, in 1995, a protest in which three people were seriously injured and fishing families' houses were burned down became a rallying point for further organization. I have heard dozens of similar accounts around the world—most community change processes include a turning point that becomes iconic and inspirational.

What worked in Tikamgarh also works on a greater scale. Such 'critical junctures', as the economists Daron Acemoglu and James A. Robinson[15] call them, force political leaders to question their long-held assumptions about what constitutes 'sound' policies, and

---

[14] Peter Evans, *Embedded Autonomy: States and Industrial Transformation* (Princeton: Princeton University Press, 1995).

[15] Daron Acemoglu and James Robinson, *Why Nations Fail: The Origins of Power, Prosperity, and Poverty* (New York: Crown Publishers, 2012), p. 101.

make them more willing to take the risks associated with innovation, as the status quo suddenly appears less worth defending.

Much of the institutional framework we take for granted today was born of the trauma of the Great Depression and the Second World War. The disastrous failures of policy that led to these twin catastrophes profoundly affected the thinking of political and economic leaders across the world, triggering a vastly expanded role for government in managing the economy and addressing social ills, as well as precipitating the decolonization of large parts of the globe.

Similarly, in the 1970s the sharp rise in oil prices (and consequent economic stagnation and runaway inflation) marked the end of the post-war 'Golden Age' and gave rise to a turn away from government regulation and to the idealization of the 'free market'. In Communist systems, at different moments, political and economic upheaval paved the way for radical economic shifts in China and Viet Nam.

Milton Friedman, the father of monetarist economics, wrote:

> Only a crisis—actual or perceived—produces real change. When that crisis occurs, the actions that are taken depend on the ideas that are lying around. That, I believe, is our basic function: to develop alternatives to existing policies, to keep them alive and available until the politically impossible becomes politically inevitable. [16]

Naomi Klein, in her 2007 book *The Shock Doctrine*,[17] argues that the Right has used shocks much better than the Left, especially in recent decades. Klein cites the example of how proponents of private education in the United States managed to turn Hurricane Katrina to their advantage: 'Within 19 months, New Orleans' public school system had been almost completely replaced by privately run charter schools.' According to the American Enterprise Institute 'Katrina

---

[16] Milton Friedman, *Capitalism and Freedom*, 2nd ed. (Chicago: The University of Chicago Press, 1982), p. ix.

[17] Naomi Klein, *The Shock Doctrine: The Rise of Disaster Capitalism* (New York: Metropolitan Books, Henry Holt and Company, 2007).

accomplished in a day what Louisiana school reformers couldn't do after years of trying.'[18]

NGOs are not always so nimble in spotting and seizing such opportunities. Three months into the 2011 Egyptian Revolution, I attended a meeting of Oxfam International's chief executive officers (CEOs), at which they spent hours debating whether the uprising in Tahrir Square was likely to lead to a humanitarian crisis. Only then did the penny drop that the protests, upheaval, and overthrow of an oppressive regime were also a huge potential opportunity, at which point the assembled bosses showed admirable speed in allocating budgets for supporting civil society activists in Egypt, and backing it up with advocacy at the Arab League and elsewhere. But by then valuable time had passed; soon the optimism of revolution gave way to the violence and misery of repression.

Some progressive activists engaged in policy advocacy are better attuned to Friedman's lesson. Within weeks of the appalling Rana Plaza factory collapse in Bangladesh that killed over 1,100 people in April 2013, an international 'Accord on Fire and Building Safety in Bangladesh'[19] was signed and delivered.[20] A five-year legally binding agreement between global companies, retailers, and trade unions, the accord mandates some astounding breakthroughs: an independent inspection programme supported by the brand-name companies and involving workers and trade unions; the public disclosure of all factories, inspection reports, and corrective action plans; a commitment by signatory brands to fund improvements and maintain sourcing relationships; democratically elected health and safety committees in all factories; and worker empowerment through an extensive

---

[18] Naomi Klein, *The Shock Doctrine: The Rise of Disaster Capitalism* (New York: Metropolitan Books, Henry Holt and Company, 2007), p. 6.

[19] 'Accord on Fire and Building Safety in Bangladesh' (ACCORD), http://bangladeshaccord.org/.

[20] Duncan Green, 'Will Horror and Over a Thousand Dead Be a Watershed Moment for Bangladesh?' From Poverty to Power blog, 17 May 2013, http://oxfamblogs.org/fp2p/will-horror-and-over-a-thousand-dead-be-a-watershed-moment-for-bangladesh/.

training programme, complaints mechanism, and the right to refuse unsafe work.

In hindsight, we can point to several factors to explain how this grisly 'shock as opportunity' drove rapid movement toward better regulation:

- A forum on labour rights in Bangladesh (the Ethical Trading Initiative) had already built a high degree of trust between traditional antagonists (companies, unions, and NGOs). Trust allowed people to get on the phone to each other right away.
- Prior work, ongoing since 2011, had sketched the outline of a potential accord; the Rana Plaza disaster massively escalated the pressure to act on it.
- A nascent national process (the National Action Plan for Fire Safety) gave outsiders something to support and build on.
- Energetic leadership from two new international trade unions (IndustriALL and UNI Global Union) helped get the right people in the room.

Perhaps we should add to Friedman's instruction 'to keep alternatives alive and available': progressive activists also need to build trust and connections among the key individuals who could implement the desired change.

I am not suggesting that activists become ambulance chasers, jumping on every crisis to make their point. Rather, we must understand the windows of opportunity provided by 'events, dear boy' as critical junctures when our long-term work creating constituencies for change, transforming attitudes and norms, and so on can suddenly come to fruition.

The world is complex—so what?

Many activists are, above all, doers, keen to change the world, starting today. They instinctively reject the first lesson of systems thinking: look hard before you leap. They get itchy with anything that smacks of ivory tower 'beard stroking' and worry about 'analysis paralysis'. In the development arena, donors often accentuate the penchant for short-termism by demanding tangible results within the timescales of project funding cycles.

My advice would be to take a deep breath, put your sense of urgency to one side for a moment, and become a 'reflectivist' who, in the words of Ben Ramalingam, should 'map, observe, and listen to the system to identify the spaces where change is already happening and try to encourage and nurture them.'[21]

That said, another lesson of systems thinking is that you cannot understand and plan everything in advance. If each situation is different, so must be the response. One of the founders of systems thinking, Donella Meadows, talks of the need to learn to 'dance with systems.'[22] But even that may be too choreographed. Perhaps a better analogy is that activists should switch from being architects and engineers to becoming 'ecosystem gardeners'.

Combining these two lessons makes for some surprising principles for how to bring about change:

Be flexible: You should be willing to shelve the current plan in response to emerging events and your organization's culture should thank the staff who alert it to signals of change. In the world of humanitarian response, this approach is standard, whereas in long-term aid programmes or campaigns people are often reluctant to shift gears, or simply fail to notice that new opportunities have opened up.

Seek fast and ongoing feedback: If you don't know what is going to happen, you have to detect changes in real time, especially when the windows of opportunity around such changes are short lived. That means having (or developing) acute antennae and embedding them in

---

[21] Ben Ramalingam, *Aid on the Edge of Chaos* (New York: Oxford University Press, 2013).
[22] Donella Meadows and Diana Wright, *Thinking in Systems: A Primer*, (Abingdon: Routledge, 2009).

multiple networks to pick up signals of change and transmit them to your organization.

Success is often accidental: 'Fortune favours the prepared mind', according to Louis Pasteur, pioneer of the germ theory of disease.[23] Surprising breakthroughs (often subsequently rewritten as triumphs of planning!) are a recurring feature of innovation and change. One reason you need fast feedback is to spot and respond to accidental successes as early as possible. One approach that builds on success born of chance variation, positive deviance, is discussed in the next section.

Undertake multiple parallel experiments: Activists hate failure. No-one wants to think they've wasted their time, or wake up to newspaper headlines about money lost or 'wasted' on failed projects. Compare this risk aversion to a venture capitalist who backs ten projects knowing that nine will fail, but he or she will make enough money on the tenth to more than compensate for the rest. With a venture approach you would spend less time and money designing the perfect plan, and instead pursue a 'lean start-up' based on best guesses about what will work, followed by a fast and frugal cycle of experimentation and adaptation until you find something that really does.[24]

Learn by doing (and failing): In a complex system, it is highly unlikely you will get things right from the outset, or that they will stay right (think back to raising a child). You and your colleagues have to be ready to discuss and learn from failure, rather than sweep it under the carpet. Fast feedback on your own impact is thus just as important as feedback on the outside world, not least to detect unintended consequences. If people are keeping chickens in the latrines you are building, you probably need to go back to the drawing

---

[23] Lecture, University of Lille (7 December 1854).

[24] Steve Blank, 'Why the Lean Start-Up Changes Everything', *Havard Business Review* (May 2013), pp. 63–72.

board.[25] Alas, my experience is that colleagues are reluctant to admit, let alone discuss, failure. A better way may be to ask 'What have you learned?' during the course of any given effort, which covers the same ground in a less embarrassing fashion.

Identify and discuss your rules of thumb: When the US Marines go into combat (an archetypal complex system), they use rules of thumb (stay in contact, take the high ground, keep moving) rather than detailed 'best-practice guidelines'. Activists do too (Have we thought about gender? What is the government doing?), but these often remain tacit, and so are not questioned, tested or improved upon. Make them explicit and review them regularly.

Convene and broker relationships: Bringing dissimilar local players together to find their own solutions can be a particularly useful role for foreign aid organizations and other activists from outside the community in question. Effective convening and brokering requires understanding who should be invited to the table. Which players have, or could have, their hands on the levers of change? Providing them with a space for dialogue outside of their home institutions can encourage them to think in new ways.

If these principles sound a bit abstract, here are three examples of change that put systems thinking into practice.[26]

Chukua Hatua ('take action' in Swahili) is an Oxfam project in Tanzania explicitly modelled on evolutionary theory, aimed at improving the accountability of local authorities to their citizens. In

---

[25] Tim Harford, in his book *Adapt: Why Success Always Starts with Failure*, proposes a 'three step recipe for successful adapting: try new things, in the expectation that some will fail; make failure survivable, because it will be common; and make sure that you know when you have failed … distinguishing success from failure, oddly, can be the hardest task of all'. Tim Harford, *Adapt: Why Success Always Starts with Failure* (London: Little, Brown, 2011).

[26] For an excellent and much more comprehensive guide to using systems thinking in practice, see Kimberly Bowman, John Chettleborough, Helen Jeans, Jo Rowlands, and James Whitehead, *Systems Thinking: An Introduction for Oxfam Programme Staff* (Oxford: Oxfam GB, 2015), http://policy-practice.oxfam.org.uk/publications/systems-thinking-an-introduction-for-oxfam-programme-staff-579896.

the first phase, lots of different hares were set loose, from 'farmer animators' who encouraged peasant communities to engage with village officials, to 'active musicians' who visited primary school student councils to spread the word about the benefits of community participation. The project plan stipulated that this experiment in variation would be followed at a predetermined date by selection. Communities, partners, and Oxfam staff met to identify the most successful variants, which were then expanded and adapted. Farmer animators proved the most promising; communities nominated non-farmers as animators, including a father who was trying to convince families to send their daughters to school and a woman who was organizing fellow traders at the local market. The first generation of animators was put to work training the new arrivals.[27]

A group of 'development entrepreneurs' in the Philippines,[28] backed by The Asia Foundation, advocates for reforms in education, taxation, civil aviation regulation, and property rights by working in small teams (echoing Amazon's Jeff Bezos: 'If it takes more than two pizzas to feed the team, it is too big').[29] The teams comprise a leader, technical analysts (e.g. lawyers), lobbyists with good political skills and networks, and 'insiders' with deep knowledge and experience in the reform area (e.g. former civil servants). Such teams can respond rapidly to events and new opportunities, making a number of 'small bets' and then dropping the experiments that go nowhere.

Every two months, Oxfam's TajWSS project to improve Tajikistan's dismal water and sanitation systems convenes everybody involved:

---

[27] Duncan Green, *The Chukua Hatua Accountability Programme, Tanzania* (Oxford: Oxfam GB for Oxfam International, 2015). Lisa Marie Faye, personal communication, 31 August 2015.

[28] Duncan Green, 'Is This the Best Paper Yet on Doing Development Differently/Thinking and Working Politically?', From Poverty to Power blog, 14 January 2015, http://oxfamblogs.org/fp2p/is-this-the-best-paper-yet-on-doing-development-differentlythinking-and-working-politically/.

[29] George Anders, 'Jeff Bezos Reveals His No. 1 Secret', *Forbes*, 4 April 2012, http://www.forbes.com/forbes/2012/0423/ceo-compensation-12-amazon-technology-jeff-bezos-gets-it.html.

seventeen government ministries and agencies, several UN bodies, international NGOs, aid agencies, academics, journalists, Tajik civil society organizations, private companies, and parliamentarians. Resisting the urge to forge a master plan, this motley grouping engages in a freewheeling discussion that has given birth to innovative partial solutions. For example, local officials have found companies willing to help with village-level chlorination and Tajik banks to help finance water systems. Its biggest victory so far is a new Water Law that establishes who is in charge, who is responsible for regulation, and who is the service provider. According to TajWSS activist Ghazi Kelani, 'We didn't draft it—it had been there for years in somebody's drawer. The network raised the importance of having a law, someone dug it up and we decided it was good enough for a start.'[30]

Positive deviance

These principles for working in complex systems can help activists improve our day-to-day work, but they can also prompt a radical rethink. One of the most exciting alternatives to business as usual goes by the name of 'positive deviance'.

In December 1991, Jerry and Monique Sternin arrived in Viet Nam to work for Save the Children in four communities with under-three-year-olds, most of whom were malnourished. The Sternins asked teams of volunteers to observe in homes where children were poor but well-fed. In every case they found that the mother or father was collecting a number of tiny shrimps, crabs, or snails—making for a portion 'the size of one joint of one finger'—from the rice paddies and adding these to the child's diet. These 'positive deviant' families also instructed the home babysitter to feed the child four or even five times a day, in contrast to most families who fed young children only before parents headed to the rice fields early in the morning and in the late afternoon after returning from a working day. Results were shared on

---

[30] Author interview, September 2012.

a board in the town hall, and the charts quickly became a focus of attention and buzz. By the end of the first year, 80 per cent of the children in the programme were fully rehabilitated.

In their book, *The Power of Positive Deviance*,[31] the Sternins, with Richard Pascale, describe how the approach was subsequently applied in fifty countries, on everything from decreasing gang violence in inner city New Jersey to reducing sex trafficking of girls in rural Indonesia. The starting point is to 'look for outliers who succeed against the odds'. But who is doing the looking also matters. If external 'experts' investigate the outliers and turn the results into a toolkit, little will come of it. When communities make the discovery for themselves, behavioural change can take root—providing what the authors call 'social proof'.

Positive deviance capitalizes on a hugely energizing fact: for any given problem, someone in the community will have already identified a solution. It focuses on people's assets and knowledge, rather than their lacks and problems. The Sternins recount their experience in Misiones Province, Argentina, where dropout rates were awful. Teachers and principals were hostile to criticism and put the blame on the parents. All that started to change when facilitators asked the 'somersault question': why were dropout rates much lower in some schools? Teachers then agreed to ask the parents at those schools, who rapidly identified teacher attitudes toward parents as the key. The positive deviant teachers were negotiating informal annual 'learning contracts' with parents. When many teachers adopted that approach, dropout rates in test schools fell by 50 per cent.

Despite its success, positive deviance remains an outlier in the aid business. The 'standard model' of identifying gaps, devising initiatives to fill them, and disseminating the guidance is incredibly hard to

---

[31] Richard Pascale, Jerry Sternin, and Monique Sternin, *The Power of Positive Deviance: How Unlikely Innovators Solve the World's Toughest Problems* (Cambridge, MA: Harvard Business Press, 2010).

budge. Perhaps not surprisingly, experts are often part of the problem. The Sternins write:

> Those eking out existence on the margins of society grasp the simple elegance of the PD approach—in contrast to the sceptical consideration of the more educated and/or privileged. Uptake seems in inverse proportion to prosperity, formal authority, years of schooling and degrees hanging on walls.[32]

I can vouch from personal experience how hard it is to give up my learned role and become a facilitator. Holding back from providing your own answer when you ask a group a question is, as the Sternins put it, 'more difficult than trying to stifle an oncoming sneeze'.

Conclusion

In the first film in *The Matrix* series (the only one worth watching), the hero, Neo, suddenly starts to see the matrix of ones and zeroes that lies beneath the surface of his world, at which point he becomes invincible. I feel similarly about systems (aside from the invincibility part). As the title of this chapter says, thinking in systems should change everything, including the way we look at politics, economics, society, and even ourselves, in new and exciting ways.

It also poses a devastating challenge to traditional linear planning approaches and to our ways of working.[33] We activists need to become better 'reflectivists', taking the time to understand the system before (and while) engaging with it. We need to better understand the stop–start rhythm of change exhibited by complex systems and adapt our efforts accordingly. And we need to become less arrogant, more willing to learn from accidents, from failures, and from other people. Finally, we have to make friends with ambiguity and uncertainty,

---

[32] Richard Pascale, Jerry Sternin, and Monique Sternin, *The Power of Positive Deviance: How Unlikely Innovators Solve the World's Toughest Problems* (Cambridge, MA: Harvard Business Press, 2010), p. 8.

[33] Though not in all situations, as we shall see in Chapter 12.

while maintaining the energy and determination so essential to changing the world.

It isn't easy, but it is entirely possible, as I hope I have shown. Once we learn to 'dance with the system', no other partner will do. In the next chapter, we explore the force that binds together disparate systems, the sea in which change and change agents swim: power.

Further Reading

E. Beinhocker, *The Origin of Wealth: The Radical Remaking of Economics and What it Means for Business and Society* (Cambridge, Mass: Harvard Business Review Press, 2007).

J. Boulton, P. Allen, and C. Bowman, *Embracing Complexity: Strategic Perspectives for an Age of Turbulence* (Oxford: Oxford University Press, 2015).

K. Bowman, J. Chettleborough, H. Jeans, J. Rowlands, and J. Whitehead, *Systems Thinking: An introduction for Oxfam Programme Staff* (Oxford: Oxfam GB, 2015).

D. Burns and S. Worsley, *Navigating Complexity in international Development: Facilitating Sustainable Change at Scale* (Rugby: Practical Action Publishing, 2015).

D. Meadows and D.H. Wright, *Thinking in Systems: A Primer* (Abingdon: Routledge, 2009).

R. Pascale, J. Sternin, and M. Sternin, *The Power of Positive Deviance: How Unlikely Innovators Solve the World's Toughest Problems* (Cambridge, MA: Harvard Business Press, 2010).

B. Ramalingam, *Aid on the Edge of Chaos* (Oxford: Oxford University Press, 2013).

Further Viewing

'The Implications of Complexity for Development', lecture by Owen Barder, http://www.cgdev.org/media/implications-complexity-development-owen-barder.

2

POWER LIES AT THE HEART
OF CHANGE

As a rather lost and miserable post-college backpacker, I once found myself in a small village on the shores of Lake Titicaca in Peru, at the home of a charismatic activist with the memorable name of Tito Castro. Tito was a lapsed Christian Brother who had decided to devote himself to raising awareness among Peru's indigenous people. He had arrived in the village with a library of books on politics, economics, sociology, and indigenous rights, and when I met him he was lending out books and running discussion groups for local leaders.

Tito took me to meet the villagers and introduced me to Peru's history of apartheid-like racial discrimination. He patiently explained how, by organizing, indigenous people can win greater control over their lives. By the time I went on my way, I was filled with an exhilarating sense of a big and heroic struggle for justice. My slow process of learning suddenly hit a critical juncture, and soon I was back home working to defend human rights in Chile and Central America. Tito later became mayor of the nearest city, Puno, and eventually a sociology professor at Lima's Catholic University.

What Tito showed me—and I experienced—was empowerment in real time, when light bulbs go on in the heads of people who had previously felt helpless or shackled by their lot, and they begin to take action to change it. Such small, personal events often lie at the heart of the tides of social and political change that are the subject of this book.

Empowerment, the driving force behind Amartya Sen's definition of development as the progressive expansion of the freedoms to do and to be,[1] is one of the most ubiquitous buzzwords in the lexicon of development activists. Many, however, shy away from the word from which the term derives: power. Power, which allows one person or institution to command the resources, actions, or innermost thoughts of another, was central to Tito's understanding of Peruvian society and it should be so for all activists.

The most evident and most discussed form of power is what we might call 'visible power'[2]: the world of politics and authority, policed by laws, violence, and money. It gets bad press, conjuring up images of force, coercion, discrimination, corruption, repression, and abuse. But visible power is also necessary to do good, whether to implement enlightened public policies or to prevent acts of violence by the strong against the weak.

Activists seeking social and political change usually focus their efforts on those who wield visible power—presidents, prime ministers, and chief executive officers (CEOs)—since they hold apparent authority over the matter at hand. Yet the hierarchy of visible power is usually underpinned by subtle interactions among a more diverse set of players. 'Hidden power' describes what goes on behind the scenes: the lobbyists, the corporate chequebooks, the old boys network. Hidden power also comprises the shared view of what those in power consider sensible or reasonable in public debate. Any environmentalist who has sat across the table from government officials or mainstream economists and dared to question the advisability of unlimited economic growth in a resource-constrained world will have met the blank faces that confront anyone breaching those boundaries.

In 2002 Karl Rove, aide to President George W. Bush and an archetypal behind-the-scenes operator, memorably captured the role of hidden power. In an interview with Ron Suskind, Rove pointed out

---

[1] Amartya Sen, *Development as Freedom* (Oxford: Oxford University Press, 1999).

[2] See Lisa VeneKlasen and Valerie Miller, *A New Weave of Power, People & Politics: The Action Guide for Advocacy and Citizen Participation* (Oklahoma City: World Neighbors, 2002). See also Powercube—Understanding Power for Social Change, http://www.powercube.net/.

that the journalist was 'in what we call the reality-based community', made up of people who believe that solutions emerge from the 'judicious study of discernible reality.' But 'that's not the way the world really works any more. We're an empire now, and when we act, we create our own reality.'[3] Hidden power is why amassing research and evidence is rarely sufficient to change government policy. Discussion of the facts usually takes place parallel to a shadowy world of competing narratives that have little basis or interest in evidence.

Hidden power can spring from sources other than Karl Rove's dark arts. On visits to India, I have been struck by the clout of senior activists and public intellectuals who embody Gandhian traditions of personal sacrifice and humility. In Latin America, leaders are often said to possess 'mística' (mystique)—an intangible quality of moral authority.

As important as 'hidden power', and certainly more insidious, is 'invisible power', which causes the relatively powerless to internalize and accept their condition. A Guatemalan Mayan woman summed up the nature of invisible power: 'Why do we not speak now? We did when we were children. We have internalised repression. They gave us the words: "stupid"; "you can't"; "you don't know", "poor thing - you are a woman".'[4] In the words of French philosopher Michel Foucault, 'There is no need for arms, physical violence, material constraints. Just a gaze. An inspecting gaze, which each individual will end up interiorizing to the point that he is his own overseer.'[5]

Invisible power often determines the capacity of change movements to influence visible and hidden power. It shapes the belief systems about what is 'normal' or 'natural', leading some groups to

---

[3] Ron Suskind, 'Faith, Certainty and the Presidency of George W. Bush', *The New York Times Magazine*, 17 October 2004, http://www.nytimes.com/2004/10/17/magazine/faith-certainty-and-the-presidency-of-george-w-bush.html.

[4] Quoted in Jenny Pearce, *From 'Empowerment' to 'Transforming Power': Can a Power Analysis Improve Development Policy, Practice and Impact?* (Madrid: FRIDE, 2006), http://fride.org/uploads/Empowerment_Jenny.Pearce_EN.pdf.

[5] Michel Foucault, *Power/Knowledge: Selected Interviews and Other Writings, 1972–77* (New York: Pantheon Books, 1980), p. 155.

exclude themselves, as when women blame themselves for their abuse, or poor people for their poverty. 'Empowerment', through the sort of awareness-raising Tito Castro promoted to build self-esteem and local leadership, seeks to alter invisible power. Because the targets of such efforts are the inner lives of individuals, cultural initiatives and mass media can be important tools, as has been the case in the rapid progress in respect for women's rights in recent decades. Chapter 3 discusses how such shifts are reflected in the evolution of 'norms'—ideas of what is natural, acceptable, or right—an area that I feel receives far too little attention in development circles.

No such thing as a power vacuum

Rich ecosystems of power exist in the most unpropitious of circumstances. The Democratic Republic of Congo is often seen as a failed state, with the population, particularly in the east, suffering from anarchic violence. But to call that a 'power vacuum' is a highly misleading caricature. Power is everywhere, and it is multifaceted.

During a visit to DRC in 2014, I met one village official, Kabuya Muhemeri, in his 'office': tin roof, floor of volcanic rubble, no glass in the windows, bare plank walls covered with heavily logoed NGO and UN posters on sexual violence, torture, HIV, and land rights, plus a hand-drawn map of the area. On his desk, the classic tools of the functionary: a rubber stamp, a mobile phone, and a pile of files and notebooks.

He had been in the post since 2008. He laughed when asked if the state gives him training: 'We rely on the NGOs for that. They help us with what the law says—don't torture, don't lock people up for unpaid debts. There are lots of rights and laws I didn't know.' In his world, state officials and customary authorities are all part of public administration. 'The *chefferie* (traditional authority) collects the taxes. I report to the *mwami* (traditional leader) as well as to the ministry.'[6]

---

[6] Author interview, Eastern Democratic Republic of Congo, June 2014.

Later, I talked to a traditional leader, on the veranda of his rather smart house at the top of a steep mud path. The chief spoke softly, radiating authority and cradling his two mobile telephones. 'I've been chief for twenty years, my father was chief before me. The state authorities are in charge of roads and bridges, tax is collected from shops, restaurants, and markets by the *chef de cheferie* [his superior in the traditional hierarchy]. I encourage the population to pay.'

Several other poles of power vie with civil and traditional authorities: armed groups, the army, the police, humanitarian agencies, faith organizations, civil society organizations, even sports clubs. Activists, whether local or from outside, need to understand the nature and distribution of the power wielded by these varied bodies (especially the ones that are unfamiliar) to determine who they need to work with (and how) to help bring about change.[7] We'll examine the interactions among such poles of power in more detail in Chapter 4.

Power and change

Contemplating the gamut of visible, hidden, and invisible power that supports the status quo can be dispiriting, inducing feelings of helplessness before the Leviathan.[8] Fresh back from my life-changing moment in Tito's house, I spent many long mornings standing outside the US embassy in London, protesting against Washington's policies in Latin America. Our motley scatter of placards and banners contrasted painfully with the vast and highly visible power encapsulated in the great blank face of the building, topped by a huge gilded eagle glowering down at us. I didn't feel very powerful.

Fortunately, other ways of thinking about power highlight the opportunities and possibilities for change. My colleague Jo Rowlands,

[7] Duncan Green, 'Where Does Power Lie in a Fragile State Like Eastern Congo? What Does it Mean for Aid Organizations?', From Poverty to Power blog, 13 June 2014, http://oxfamblogs.org/fp2p/who-has-power-in-a-fragile-state-like-eastern-congo-what-does-it-mean-for-aid-organizations/.

[8] Thomas Hobbes, *Leviathan* (Oxford: Oxford University Press, 1996).

based on her work on women's empowerment in Honduras,[9] identified a different scheme that encapsulates this more optimistic approach:

- Power *within*: personal self-confidence and a sense of rights and entitlement.
- Power *with*: collective power, through organization, solidarity and joint action.
- Power *to*: meaning effective choice, the capability to decide actions and carry them out.
- Power *over*: the power of hierarchy and domination, as described above.

This 'four powers' model suggests a more comprehensive approach to promoting change than simply addressing visible power and decrying hidden and invisible power. Unless people first develop a sense of self-confidence and a belief in their own rights (power within), efforts to help them organize (power with) and demand a say (power to) may not bear fruit. As Tito showed in his Peruvian idyll, personal empowerment can be the first step on the path to social transformation.

Over the last few years, Jo has been a politely persistent mentor and critic, prodding me to think harder about power and participation in change processes, especially in terms of women's rights, where 'power within' has proved to be a remarkably important and useful concept. In South Asia, *We Can* is an extraordinary campaign on violence against women launched in late 2004. At last count it had signed up some four million women and men to be 'change makers'—advocates for an end to violence in their homes and communities. *We Can* does not target policies, laws, or the authorities (visible power). Instead, it addresses invisible power, using dialogue and example to change attitudes and beliefs at the level of individuals and communities. And it's viral. Each change maker talks to friends and neighbours,

---

[9] Jo Rowlands, *Questioning Empowerment: Working with Women in Honduras* (Oxford: Oxfam UK and Ireland, 1997).

and tries to persuade them to change and become change makers as well. To the organizers' surprise, half of the nearly four million change makers who signed on over the course of seven years were men.[10]

For Selvaranjani Mukkaiah, a *We Can* activist in Badulla, Sri Lanka, acquiring 'power within' is life-changing: 'To me change is the killing of fear. Someone may know how to sing but will not sing. Someone or something needs to kindle the fire in you and kill the fear that stops you from changing. I have killed the fear of talking and that is a change for me.'[11]

'Power within' often morphs rapidly into 'power with' and 'power to'. In Nepal, women taking part in Community Discussion Classes (CDCs) moved swiftly from learning to action. Fed up with their drunken husbands' violence, CDC women in Sorahawa, Bardiya District, decided to impose a 500 Rupee fine (rising for further offences) on any man who beat his wife or other female household members after he had been warned not to do so. 'Now, our husbands fear they may lose face on account of community-level insults and also cough up the fine. They go off quietly to sleep.'[12]

However, I have some qualms about 'power within'. The concept seems to skate rapidly over the deeper waters that determine individual attitudes and beliefs. Thinking about power within is only the first step on what should be a much longer conversation about the role of psychology, empathy, and relationships in bringing about change. Many effective activists are instinctively empathetic and emotionally literate (one academic analysis of the Jubilee 2000 debt campaign was

---

[10] Duncan Green, *The 'We Can' Campaign in South Asia*, Oxfam Active Citizenship Case Study (Oxford: Oxfam GB for Oxfam International, 2015), http://policy-practice.oxfam. org.uk/publications/the-we-can-campaign-in-south-asia-338472.

[11] Quoted in 'Change Making: How we adopt new attitudes, beliefs and practices.' Insights from the We Can Campaign, 2011, http://policy-practice.oxfam.org.uk/~/media/ Files/policy_and_practice/gender_justice/we_can/change_making.ashx.

[12] Duncan Green, *The Raising Her Voice Nepal Programme*, Oxfam Active Citizenship Case Study (Oxford: Oxfam GB for Oxfam International, 2015), http://policy-practice.oxfam. org.uk/publications/the-raising-her-voice-nepal-programme-338476.

memorably titled 'Bono Made Jesse Helms Cry'[13]). But many are not. I have seen too many examples of the finger wagging of angry lobbyists who seem unaware of what is going on in the heads of the people they are talking to and unable to grasp that their hectoring tone alienates the very people they are trying to influence. In his 2007 paper, 'How Change Happens', which got me started on the road to this book, Roman Krznaric concluded that 'Development strategies display an overwhelming focus on individual actors, organised social groups, and institutions, with little acknowledgement that societies and institutions are composed of human relationships. There is much greater scope for development organisations to pursue strategies that encourage mutual understanding, empathy, and trust.'[14] (Since then Roman has become something of an empathy guru, writing books[15] and even opening an 'empathy museum'.)[16]

On the other hand, many non-government organizations (NGOs), faith organizations, and others traditionally leery of 'politics' over-invest in individual empowerment, and fail to support the next step from individual to collective empowerment ('power with') or take on those who oppress the disempowered through their hidden and visible power. Their wariness is understandable: collective action tends to be rather more unruly than the orderly workshops that are NGOs' staple. In fact, before imposing the fine for domestic violence, several of the Nepalese women's groups I mentioned earlier decided

---

[13] Joshua Busby, 'Bono Made Jesse Helms Cry: Jubilee 2000, Debt Relief, and Moral Action in International Politics', *International Studies Quarterly* 51, (2007): pp. 247–75, https://www.rgkcenter.org/sites/default/files/file/research/ISQU_451.pdf.

[14] Roman Krznaric, 'How Change Happens: Interdisciplinary perspectives for human development', Oxfam Research Report (Oxford: Oxfam GB, 2007), http://policy-practice.oxfam.org.uk/publications/how-change-happens-interdisciplinary-perspectives-for-human-development-112539.

[15] Roman Krznaric, *Empathy: Why it Matters, and How to Get It* (London: Penguin Random House, 2014).

[16] The Empathy Museum, http://www.empathymuseum.com/.

that the best way to curb their husbands' alcoholism was to burn down the stores selling them drink.[17]

The territories of 'power to' and 'power over' are more familiar for most activists, since their interaction forms the basis of politics and the economy. In some ways the distinction is a false one—one person's 'power to' can be experienced by another as 'power over'. Activists instinctively hostile to 'power over' should recall that, like 'visible power', it is essential to do good. The 'power over' of police, courts, and *in extremis* armed forces guarantees security, an aspect of wellbeing particularly prized by anyone who has lived where it is absent. The issue is whether 'power over' is subject to checks and balances to ensure it is not wielded in an arbitrary and unjust fashion.

Given power's central role in determining both stasis and change, I find its absence from the development lexicon remarkable. The aid landscape is littered with terms that avoid the uncomfortable truth that seldom is power distributed fairly. Apparently neutral words like 'consultation', 'stakeholders', 'dialogue', and 'inclusivity' paper over the underlying power dynamics between conflicting interests, which can determine people's capacity even to participate, never mind influence outcomes. The landmark Paris Declaration on Aid Effectiveness agreed by government aid donors and recipients in 2005 uses the words partner and partnership ninety-six times, but power not once.[18]

Even though aid donors increasingly accept the futility of pursuing purely technical solutions that ignore political realities, they are still not willing to talk about power. Instead, there seems an inbuilt tendency (I'm not sure whether conscious or unconscious) to reduce every question to economics, as if material incentives alone explained human behaviour. That kind of 'political economy analysis' misses what is distinctively political about politics: a broader understanding of power, agency, ideas,

---

[17] Duncan Green, *The Raising Her Voice Nepal Programme*, Oxfam Active Citizenship Case Study (Oxford: Oxfam GB for Oxfam International, 2015), http://policy-practice.oxfam.org.uk/publications/the-raising-her-voice-nepal-programme-338476.

[18] Robert Chambers, *Provocations for Development* (Rugby: Practical Action Publishing, 2012), p. 108.

leadership, the subtleties of building and sustaining coalitions both inside formal politics and beyond, and the role of shocks and accident.[19]

Is power a zero sum game?

I wonder if the reluctance to address power explicitly in the aid world comes from viewing power as a zero sum game. In some circumstances giving power to some people does mean taking it away from others. Often the role of activists is precisely to support that process, for example, by supporting coalitions that can redistribute power from the haves to the have-nots. Resistance from the haves is one reason why change can be violent and difficult on issues such as who owns land, or how the state levies tax and allocates spending.

Good change strategies pursue something more subtle than outright confrontation (which often plays into the hands of the powerful). Reframing the understanding of self-interest, using divide and rule tactics to split up opposition blocs, or promoting long-term shifts in ideas and norms can help get round the zero sum problem. Moreover, many changes benefit both the have-nots and the haves. Men in the *We Can* programme reported marked improvements in their own quality of life from respecting women's rights in the home; unsurprisingly, the sex improved too, according to some.

To add to the complexity, processes and institutions that initially favour one group are sometimes subverted over time and taken over by another: access to justice by poor communities can turn the law from a bulwark of the status quo to a driver of change; capture of democratic processes by the rich can achieve the exact opposite. Empowerment is not so much a single event as a process taking place in a complex system replete with multiple feedback loops, rather than linear chains of cause and effect.

---

[19] David Hudson and Adrian Leftwich, *From Political Economy to Political Analysis* (Birmingham: Developmental Leadership Program, 2014), http://www.dlprog.org/publications/from-political-economy-to-political-analysis.php.

Using power analysis

Many aid organizations have come to the realization that their cherished projects on the ground are at best producing islands of success in a sea of failure as a result of bad government policies. The futility of promoting 'livelihoods projects' that help poor communities benefit from markets, when those same markets are being battered by government debt crises and spending cutbacks, has provoked understandable frustration, and over the past twenty years efforts to change public policy through advocacy and campaigns have mushroomed.

For these activists, power is a central concern and both the visible-hidden-invisible scheme and the 'four powers' approach can help identify what we do or do not know about a system, prompting an exploration of pertinent questions, be it Why are small farmers poor? or Why doesn't the government spend more on local schools?

By formulating tentative answers to such questions, activists initiate what at Oxfam we call a 'power analysis'. In essence, a power analysis tells us who holds what power related to the matter, and what might influence them to change.

Activists informed by a power analysis can select a more appropriate strategy: Will it be lobbying in the corridors of power, protesting in the street, or providing low profile, long-term support for grassroots organizations or public education? Still more questions will sharpen the strategy: Who does the minister or CEO actually listen to? Is he or she persuaded by a successful demonstration on the ground, research, stories, media coverage, or the opinion of peers? Discussing power in its various forms is helpful in challenging assumptions about citizen apathy: Why don't they protest more?

Power analysis can help activists identify a wider range of potential allies. All too often, we tend to default to working with 'people like us', when alliances with unusual suspects (corporations, faith leaders, academics) can be more effective. Finally, power analysis can help us consider upcoming events that may open the door to change: Is an election in the offing? What influence would a drought or hurricane have on people's attitudes? What happens when the Old Man dies?

To move from a general exploration of power to specific plans for influencing its redistribution on any given issue, we need to identify the key players and map where they stand on the matter at hand: Who are the main actors involved (poor communities, decision makers, private sector companies)? What other individuals or institutions (media, religious institutions, intellectuals, traditional leaders) are relevant and influential? Which are potential allies? Which are blockers? And which are 'shifters', potentially important players who can be convinced to support the change?[20]

A key player, of course, is the activists themselves, and power analysis must include them. Discussion of where they are most likely to exert influence (at the household, local, national, or global level) should help identify promising entry points, tactics, and alliances. Every activist group has strengths and weakness. For example, an international NGO like Oxfam can link up consumers in rich countries to put pressure on companies to improve their impact in poor ones, but it can also be seen as a tool of Western foreign policy.

When activists draw up a list of stakeholders, we often initially describe a sparsely populated landscape ('the state', 'people's organizations'). Closer scrutiny normally uncovers a much more complex ecosystem, as I discovered in 2014 when I asked a group of Tajik activists and aid workers to list the stakeholders on water and sanitation in a typical village. First it was only state authorities and villagers' water associations. Then one added, 'Who you turn to depends on the issue: for policy you go to the village head; for health problems to the doctor; if you have bad dreams, you go to the *mullah*.'

The group ended up plotting the influence and level of interest of appointed and elected village officials, the school principal, *mullah*, doctor, respected village elders, women's groups, community

---

[20] Celine Charveriat, 'Power Analysis Checklist and Methodology' (unpublished paper, Oxfam International, 2005).

organizations, state employees, 'educated people', and 'relatives (and lovers!) of powerful people'. All were seen as potential allies in improving the lamentable provision of water and sanitation.[21]

The conversation in Tajikistan brought home to me the importance of mapping *all* the players who could be part of any given change process, as well as the ease with which we default back to a polarized and often self-defeating 'them and us' mental map.

Once the actors are identified, we need to discuss:

Alliances: What combination of likely and unlikely allies will maximize the chances of success? A traditional partnership between activist organizations, relationships with sympathetic individuals in government ministries, or a joint approach with private-sector companies?

Approach: What is most likely to influence the target individuals and institutions whose support is needed to bring about change? Does the barrier to change lie in laws and policies, or in social norms, attitudes, and beliefs? Or is the issue rooted in conflicting interests and thus requires political mobilization to demonstrate clout?

Events: Is change most likely to occur around a specific event, (e.g. an election campaign, the death of a leader, a natural disaster or an economic crisis)? How do we prepare for and respond rapidly to the opportunities (as well as threats) created by such 'shocks'?

Such a power analysis reflects a strategic mindset which prizes results, as opposed to what I might call a 'principled' mindset that prizes 'speaking truth to power'. I use cartoons a lot on my blog, and one of my favourites shows two medieval peasants walking past a castle wall, on which a severed head sits on a spike. One peasant is saying to the other 'he spoke truth to power'. Open and individual opposition

[21] Duncan Green, 'What Makes a Perfect Short Field Trip (and a Top Village Power Analysis)?', From Poverty to Power blog, 7 February 2014, https://oxfamblogs.org/fp2p/what-makes-a-perfect-short-field-trip-and-a-top-village-power-analysis/.

may be admirable, even heroic, but it is seldom effective without a more subtle understanding of the distribution of power and the potential for change. Similarly, by exhorting politicians simply to show 'political will' and do something that will lose them votes or power, we abdicate our responsibility to find a way to enable them to support the change we seek.[22]

Of course, some of the most effective activists don't spend hours doing power analyses. They have a feel for what works, built up from long experience and natural aptitude. 'Power analysis' is simply a way of codifying what such gurus do instinctively, making it explicit and thus easier to learn and share.

Why change *doesn't* happen

Although this book is about 'how change happens', often the important question is 'Why *doesn't* change happen?' Systems, whether in thought, politics, or the economy, can be remarkably resistant to change, like the mature forests discussed in Chapter 1. I like to get at the root of the 'i-word' (inertia) through three other 'i-words': institutions, ideas, and interests. A combination of these often underlies the resistance to change, even when evidence makes a compelling case.

Institutions: Sometimes the obstacle to change lies in the institutions through which decisions are made or implemented. Even when no-one in particular benefits materially from defending the status quo, management systems and corporate culture can be powerful obstacles to change. Although I love Oxfam dearly, I also wrestle with its institutional blockages, including multi-layered processes of sign-off and a tendency to make decisions in ever-expanding loops of emails

---

[22] Duncan Green, 'Why Demanding "Political Will" is Lazy and Unproductive', From Poverty to Power blog, 5 November 2009, http://oxfamblogs.org/fp2p/why-demanding-political-will-is-lazy-and-unproductive/.

where it is never clear who has the final say. I guess I need to work on my internal power analysis.

Ideas: Often inertia is rooted in the conceptions and prejudices held by decision makers, even when their own material interest is not at risk. In Malawi, researchers found that ideas about 'the poor'—the 'deserving' vs. the 'undeserving' poor—had a significant impact on individuals' readiness to support cash transfers to people living in poverty. The elites interviewed—which included civil society, religious leaders, and academics as well as politicians, bureaucrats, and private sector leaders—all believed that redistributive policies make the poor lazy (or lazier). The overwhelming evidence for the effectiveness of cash transfers made no difference; neither did the fact that the elites stand to lose little from such reforms (and could even gain electorally, in the case of politicians).[23]

I witnessed the obstructive power of ideas during my brief spell working in DFID's International Trade Department. We received a visit from a senior official at the Treasury, worried that we were going off message. Radiating the suave self-assurance of a Whitehall mandarin, he informed us that, while he was happy to discuss UK trade policy, we should first agree that there were certain 'universal truths', namely that trade liberalization leads to more trade; more trade leads to less poverty. Both claims were highly debatable, but no-one was going to change the mandarin's habit of regurgitating what he had learned at university some decades back. I recalled Keynes' wonderful line: 'Practical men who believe themselves to be quite exempt from any intellectual influence, are usually the slaves of some defunct economist. Madmen in authority, who hear voices in the air, are distilling their frenzy from some academic scribbler of a few years back.'[24] Not much room for evidence-based policy making there.

---

[23] Heather Marquette, personal email communications, 2015.

[24] John Maynard Keynes, *The General Theory of Employment, Interest and Money* (London: Palgrave Macmillan, 1936), pp. 383–4.

It is always possible, of course, that madmen in authority can be persuaded to change their minds, but it is uphill work: a steady drip-drip of contrary evidence, public criticism, pressure from their peers, and exposure to failures and crises all help. In the end, I fear that really deep-rooted ideas only change with generational turnover.

Interests: The writer Upton Sinclair once remarked 'It is difficult to get a man to understand something, when his salary depends upon his not understanding it.'[25] Powerful players who stand to lose money or status from reform can be very adept at blocking it. Especially when a small number of players stand to lose a lot, whereas a large number of players stand to gain a little, the blockers are likely to be much better organized than the proponents. Billions of people could benefit from a reduction in carbon emissions that reduces the threat of climate change, but they will have to overcome opposition from a handful of fossil fuel companies first.

Interests are not always malign—after all, a great deal of progressive social change comes from poor people fighting for their own interests. Nor are interests always material. Masood Mulk, who runs the Sarhad Rural Support Programme in Pakistan, told me a wonderful story that harks back to the importance of psychology and personal relations:

> I remember a valley where all the poor united to build the road, which they believed would change their lives totally. Unfortunately the road had to pass through the land of a person who had once been powerful in the valley, and he was totally unwilling to allow it. Frustrated, the villagers asked me to come to the valley and go to his house to resolve the problem. It was a remote place so we flew in a helicopter. For hours I tried to persuade him to be generous and give his permission but he would not budge. He did not like the way the communities behaved now that they were powerful. In the end he said he would relent, but only if we would fly around his house three times in the helicopter. I realised that it was all about egos. The villagers were unwilling to go to him because

[25] Upton Sinclair, *I, Candidate for Governor: And How I Got Licked* (Berkley, CA: University of California Press, 1994).

their pride did not allow it, and he was not willing to concede to them unless he could reemphasise his importance.[26]

In recent years, the glacial pace of progress on climate change illustrates all three i's to a depressing extent: vested interests lobby to frustrate attempts to reduce carbon emissions and support spurious 'science' to throw mud at the evidence that underpins the call for action; an unshakable belief in the value of economic growth limits any attempts to imagine a 'beyond-growth' approach to the economy; and global institutions governed by national politicians with short time horizons are poorly suited to solving the greatest collective action problem in history. In December 2015 that may have changed with the Paris Agreement on climate change—a case study on pages 171–175 explores how that change took place.

Conclusion

Walk into any household, village, boardroom, or government office, and you will enter a subtle and pervasive force field of power that links and influences everyone present. Friends and enemies, parents and children, bosses and employees, rulers and ruled. No matter the political system, power is always present. As the joke from the Soviet era put it: Under capitalism, man exploits man. Under socialism, it's the other way around.

Studying and understanding that force field is an essential part of trying to influence change. Though largely invisible to the newcomer, power sets parameters on how social and political relationships evolve. Who are likely allies or enemies of change? Who are the uppers and lowers in this relationship? Who listens or defers to whom? How have they treated each other in the past?

Starting with power should induce a welcome sense of optimism about the possibilities for change. Many of the great success stories in

---

[26] Masood UL Mulk, personal email communications, January 2016.

human progress—universal suffrage, access to knowledge, freedom from sickness, oppression and hunger, are at their root, a story of the progressive redistribution of power.

Thinking in terms of power brings the true drama of development to life. In contrast to the drab portrayal of poor people as passive 'victims' (of disasters, of poverty, of famine) or as 'beneficiaries' (of aid, of social services), 'empowerment' places poor people's own actions centre stage. In the words of Bangladeshi academic Naila Kabeer, 'From a state of powerlessness that manifests itself in a feeling of "I cannot"; activism contains an element of collective self-confidence that results in a feeling of "We can".'[27]

Readers who are starting to feel addled by the number of frameworks I have thrown at them may wish to consider a crude but extremely useful way to keep power in mind when going about your daily business, devised by Robert Chambers, one of the most interesting and original thinkers in development. In any relationship, ask yourself who are the 'uppers' and who the 'lowers'[28] and how that affects their behaviours. Chambers' schema also captures an awkward fact: What do a congenital wife beater, a devout Christian or Muslim, and a lifelong trade union or NGO activist have in common? They can all be the same person; the same individuals can be uppers in one context and lowers in another.

Now that we have explored the constituent elements of power and systems thinking, some readers may wish to review the power and systems approach I set out in summary form at the start of the book. For those who choose to soldier on, there is a full explanation in the final chapter.

---

[27] Dighe & Jain (1989) 'Women's Development Programme: Some Insights into Participatory Evaluation', *Prashasnika* vol. 18 nos. 1–4, pp. 77–98, quoted in Naila Kabeer (1994) *Reversed Realities: Gender Hierarchies in Development Thought*, London: Verso, p. 262.

[28] Duncan Green, 'Robert Chambers on the Fifth Power (the Power to Empower)', From Poverty to Power blog, 29 November 2012, http://oxfamblogs.org/fp2p/robert-chambers-on-the-fifth-power-the-power-to-empower/.

Further Reading

R. Chambers, *Revolutions in Development Inquiry* (London: Earthscan, 2008).

M. Foucault, *Power/Knowledge: Selected Interviews and Other Writings, 1972–77* (New York: Pantheon Books, 1980).

S. Lukes, *Power: A Radical View* (2nd edition) (London: Palgrave Macmillan, 2004).

G. Mulgan, *Good and Bad Power* (London: Allen Lane, 2006).

A. Rao, R. Stuart, and D. Kelleher, *Gender at Work: Organizational Change for Equality* (West Harford: Kumarian Press, 1999).

J. Rowlands, *Questioning Empowerment: Working with Women in Honduras* (Oxford: Oxfam UK and Ireland, 1997).

Further Surfing

Understanding Power for Social Change: The Power Cube http://www.powercube.net/.

3

SHIFTS IN SOCIAL NORMS
OFTEN UNDERPIN CHANGE

Over a beer in a remote corner of Bolivia, Miguel Rivera, a Chiquitano activist, reflected on his own discovery of 'power within'. 'A sense of our rights came from outside, from political leaders and ILO Convention 169', he told me. 'It was important, it made our indigenous part wake up.'[1] It wasn't the kind of conversation you have every day and, to be honest, I didn't entirely welcome it. I had trekked deep into the Bolivian interior to find out how social change happened in the exotic (to me) world of Latin America's indigenous movement, and here was a grassroots activist quoting the stuffy, Geneva-based International Labour Organization (ILO), telling me his people's success was partly down to those international talking shops of which I had been so dismissive.

At least the setting lived up to expectations. The Chiquitanos are best known outside Bolivia from the 1986 film *The Mission*, which recounts how, in exchange for protection by the Jesuits from Brazilian slavers, the Chiquitanos became (and remain) adept Baroque musicians and built extraordinary white-and-orange churches that still attract tourists.

Of all the stories of change I have witnessed over the last thirty-five years, that conversation with Miguel in the sweltering heat of the summer of 2006, and my subsequent visit to the Chiquitano community, was one of the most influential in shaping my thinking. On page 69, to conclude this first part of the book, I use it to illustrate the power and systems approach.

---

[1] Miguel Rivera, Interview with Duncan Green, Bolivia, 2006.

Miguel educated me about the importance of social norms—the explicit or implicit rules specifying what behaviours are acceptable in society. What people see as normal, desirable, or aberrant determines their sense of right and wrong, and can both drive and hold back the search for social justice.

Norms come in all shapes and sizes, whether social, legal, or moral, and they exhibit a subtle contradiction, which they share with institutions like the state or transnational corporations: they are both static and changing. At any given moment, most norms appear fixed; people see them as a 'given', a pre-existing, eternal, social reality. Without that sense of fixity, norms would not provide what they must, namely stable standards of conduct to guide the choices of those subject to them. Yet, at the same time, norms are a continuously evolving system. Even law—the most codified, formal subset of norms—is constantly changing, as I discuss in Chapter 5.[2]

How norms evolve

For much of human history, norms mostly evolved organically in local and national communities. Over the last century, however, a formal process for debating, agreeing, codifying, and implementing global norms has come into being, housed within a number of international institutions, such as the UN and the ILO so revered by Miguel Rivera.

Today that normative framework advances through a bewildering proliferation of conferences, 'high level panels', international targets such as the Sustainable Development Goals, treaties, and conventions. It's a merry-go-round I often prefer to avoid, due to the prevalence of rhetoric and platitude over substance. I now think my aversion (though understandable) is unwarranted. The merry-go-round is complex and unpredictable, but undoubtedly important. The body of international agreements that has emerged captures and nudges

[2] Wayne Sandholtz and Kendall Stiles, *International Norms and Cycles of Change* (Oxford: Oxford University Press, 2008).

along the world's evolving understanding of its condition, building our sense of belonging to one 'humanity'.

Very little of it is 'hard law', enforceable in the courts. But it sets standards that national movements can use to rally for change in legislation and in public attitudes on everything from whether bribery is acceptable or parents have the right to beat their children, to discrimination against migrant workers, indigenous people, or those living with a disability, or what activity should be considered as 'work'.

At an individual level, norms start to develop from the moment of birth, as children soak up notions of what is 'natural' from the behaviours and words of those around them. As an institution (albeit a hugely varied one), the family is probably the greatest forging ground of the values and norms that shape a person's life. Within a few years, schooling starts to play a central role in transmitting society's wider understanding of norms. When activists ignore these early years, they miss a huge trick. Faith organizations, which invest large amounts in education, have been rather more on the ball. St. Francis Xavier, the founder of the Jesuit order, once said 'Give me the child until he is seven and I will give you the man'.

The extent to which norms have changed over time is extraordinary. Two hundred years ago, slavery and colonization were seen as the natural order of things (at least in Europe); men 'owned' women and slaves. States were unencumbered in their conduct of war; today they are partly circumscribed by rules. Entire bodies of international law— human rights, environment—did not even exist a century ago. As these timelines suggest, normative change is deep and slow, often measured in generations or centuries. For that reason, it sometimes passes relatively unobserved and unappreciated by activists or politicians who think in the three- or four-year cycles of elections and campaigns.

I first became fully aware of the importance of norms in the mid-1990s, when researching for a book for Save the Children.[3] Philippe

---

[3] Duncan Green, *Hidden Lives: Voices of Children in Latin America and the Caribbean* (London: Cassell, 1998).

Aries' paradigm-changing book *Centuries of Childhood*[4] showed me just how much of what I considered 'natural' was in fact historically determined. In 1724, the great British novelist Daniel Defoe saw nothing wrong with saying all children over the age of four or five should earn their own bread.

Hundreds of conversations with children across Latin America further transformed my understanding of the nature of childhood and the roles, rights, and responsibilities of children. Of course, working children complained of exploitation and the difficulties of combining work and school, and street kids were often drugged up and miserable, but what struck me most was their sense of agency. Working children told me how much they valued contributing to their family's welfare; street kids laughed while boasting about their ability to get what they could from the various organizations intent on 'rescuing' them ('the food's better there, but they make you pray'). As the father of two young children of my own at the time, it felt very personal.

When the book was published, I learned that challenging norms about something as deep as our attitudes towards children can provoke very powerful reactions. Trade unions accused me of justifying child exploitation, street child organizations of undermining their work. They preferred a notion of childhood as an innocent 'walled garden' in need of protection even if, as Aries shows, that garden is a recent and Western historical construct.

Norms, gender, and power

Women's expected roles have undergone extraordinary change over the last century. Was the main factor behind this shift the right to vote, employment outside the home, the invention of the washing machine,

---

[4] Philippe Ariès, *Centuries of Childhood: A Social History of Family Life* (New York: Random House USA, 1965).

girls' education, new forms of contraception, access to information, or the women's movement? The answer of course is all of the above and more. In a complex system full of feedback loops and surprises, each of these factors has both shaped and been shaped by evolving norms on women's roles.

Globalization is one such driver of change. At 7.30 am every morning, the streets of Dhaka, the capital of Bangladesh, light up as a Technicolor tide of young women in vivid saris emerge from the slums en route to the many mouldering factories that line the streets of the city. The women remain there until well into the night, cutting and stitching clothes for export.

Observing thousands of these laughing, engaged, and eager women on the move, I struggled to maintain my activist's disapproval of globalization and its 'exploitation' of cheap labour. Subsequent conversations in their shantytown huts confirmed how highly prized jobs in the garment factories were. The women certainly complained about the low wages, long hours, and workplace dangers affecting millions of women in Bangladesh's garment industry. But they also insisted that earning an income brings a redistribution of power at home: women can now leave the house without male permission; they exercise more of a voice in household decisions; girl children are more valued than before.

The factories did not head for Dhaka intent on liberating Bangladesh's women. As is often the case in a complex system such as the global garment trade, the evolution of gender norms was an accidental by-product of structural changes in the economy. Also influential were urbanization and the spread of television, with its soap opera portrayals of 'modern' and largely urban women. The introduction of cable television in rural India in the early 2000s led to significant reported increases in women's autonomy, a fall in the acceptability of domestic violence and decreases in preference for male offspring. Researchers also found increased female school enrolment, decreased dropout rates and fewer births per family. The correlation was striking—between 45 and 70 per cent of the difference between rural and urban areas in these three indicators disappeared within two years of cable's introduction.[5]

'Critical junctures', such as wars or political and economic crises, can help shift norms, when an upheaval in traditional routines opens the door to new thinking. In the US, the experience of blacks and whites fighting alongside each other in the Second World War helped galvanize the civil rights movement. Increased attention to inequality in recent years suggests that the 2008 financial crisis may have changed attitudes.

International agreements like those described by Miguel that evening in Bolivia can both reflect and lead changes in public attitudes. The Convention on the Elimination of All Forms of Discrimination Against Women (CEDAW), adopted in 1979 by the UN General Assembly, is often described as an international bill of rights for women. It defines what constitutes discrimination against women and obliges states to commit themselves to a series of measures, including:

- to incorporate the principle of equality of men and women in the legal system, abolish all discriminatory laws, and adopt appropriate ones prohibiting discrimination against women;
- to establish tribunals and other public institutions to ensure the effective protection of women against discrimination; and
- to ensure elimination of all acts of discrimination against women by persons, organizations, or enterprises.

CEDAW and the agreements that emerged from the 1994 International Conference on Population and Development in Cairo and the 1995 World Conference on Women in Beijing created a normative framework that national movements have used to exert steady upwards pressure on respect for women's rights in public attitudes and in

---

[5] Robert Jensen and Emily Oster, 'The Power of TV: Cable Television and Women's Status in India', NBER Working Paper No. 13305 (Cambridge, MA: The National Bureau of Economic Research, 2007), http://www.nber.org/papers/w13305.

legislation. At the time of writing, 189 countries worldwide have ratified CEDAW.[6]

South Asia's *We Can* campaign (mentioned in Chapter 2) is one such movement that seeks to propagate the norms established in CEDAW by promoting 'power within' and 'power with'.[7]

Norm changes and the state

We Can largely bypasses the formal world of state action, but states too can reinforce emerging norms. In 1993, the Indian government introduced a law calling for one third of village council leader positions in village councils (Panchayat) to be reserved for women. At the time, sceptics argued that influential men would place their wives in the position and manage from behind the scenes. However, researchers subsequently found that adolescent girls in villages with female leaders in two election cycles were more likely to want to marry after age 18, less likely to want to be a housewife or have their occupation determined by their in-laws, and more likely to want a job requiring education. Parents were less likely to believe in-laws should determine girls' occupations. The gender gap in adolescent educational attainment was erased and the gender gap in time spent on household chores closed by eighteen whole minutes, reflecting girls spending less time on these activities.[8]

Part of the art of outstanding political leaders such as Gandhi or Mandela lies in their ability to go beyond merely reflecting public norms and instead influence them for the better. Even the endless repetition of simple messages, which may be one of the most off-putting aspects of politicians' daily lives, helps challenge old norms

---

[6] UN Women, Convention on the Elimination of All Forms of Discrimination against Women, 1979, http://www.un.org/womenwatch/daw/cedaw.

[7] http://policy-practice.oxfam.org.uk/our-work/gender-justice/we-can.

[8] Lori Beaman, Esther Duflo, Rohini Pande, and Petia Topalova 'Female Leadership Raises Aspirations and Educational Attainment for Girls: A Policy Experiment in India', *Science* 335, no. 6068 (2012): pp. 582–6.

and cement new ones. Of course, politicians can also reinforce norms that should change, for example, by whipping up hatred against ethnic or religious minorities or desperate migrants.

Leadership in changing norms is not just the preserve of politicians. Role models, celebrities, any number of public figures can play a part. Acts of individual courage can be pivotal moments, as when Princess Diana stood up against the panic and prejudice towards people living with HIV and AIDS in the early years of the pandemic in the UK.[9]

Governments use norms to try to shape people's personal behaviour. Particularly in the richer countries, this includes a daily avalanche of 'nudges' regarding diet, smoking, drink driving, and more. In the US, telling high users of energy how their consumption compared with that of their neighbours prompted them to use less.[10] In the UK, telling residents that most neighbours had already paid their taxes, led payment rates to rise by around 15 per cent.[11]

But government is rarely the original source of new norms. In fact, the ideas for many of what we now consider the core features of the state (social protection, education, healthcare) were incubated by activists before being taken up by the state, as were the rules of war and the principles of child rights. A similar process is now occurring regarding environmental stewardship, data transparency, and disabled people's rights.[12]

Sometimes norms change because they get backing from a powerful constituency that spots an opportunity to further its own interests, as when businesses became aware of the 'pink pound' and suddenly developed a deep interest in gay rights. For politicians the incentive is

[9] 'What Everyone Should Know about HIV', http://www.hivaware.org.uk/about/princess-diana.

[10] 'Nudge Nudge, Think Think: The Use of Behavioural Economics in Public Policy Shows Promise', The Economist, 24 March 2012, http://www.economist.com/node/21551032.

[11] Leo Benedictus, 'The Nudge Unit – Has it Worked So Far?', The Guardian, 2 May 2013, http://www.theguardian.com/politics/2013/may/02/nudge-unit-has-it-worked.

[12] Duncan Green, 'What's Next for the (Rapidly Growing) Global Disabled People's Movement?', From Poverty to Power blog, 27 August 2014, http://oxfamblogs.org/fp2p/whats-next-for-the-rapidly-growing-global-disabled-peoples-movement/.

votes. After decades of activism on gay rights and equal marriage, polls in 2011 finally showed US public support for same-sex marriage exceeding 50 per cent for the first time. In just one week in April 2013, six US senators performed U-turns and declared their support for marriage equality.[13]

A study of how governments come to adopt and implement new human rights norms identified five stages: repression (of those promoting the norm); denial (refusal to acknowledge the issue); tactical concessions (just enough to keep critics quiet); prescriptive status (starting to adopt the spirit of the new norm by ratifying international treaties, changing domestic laws, or setting up new institutions); and rule-consistent behaviour (putting mechanisms in place to ensure the new norms are respected).[14] Large corporations facing pressures on labour rights or environmental safeguards go through much the same journey. In words attributed to Mahatma Gandhi, 'First they ignore you, then they laugh at you, then they fight you, then you win.'

To try and identify what factors drive change in government policies on violence against women, Laurel Weldon and Mala Htun painstakingly constructed the mother of all databases, covering seventy countries over four decades (1975 to 2005). It included various kinds of state action (legal and administrative reforms, protection and prevention, training for officials), as well as a number of other relevant factors (the presence of women legislators, GDP per capita, and the nature of the political regime).

Their findings bear out the importance of pressure from below: 'Countries with the strongest feminist movements tend, other things being equal, to have more comprehensive policies on violence against

<hr>

[13] Duncan Green, 'How Change Happens: What Can We Learn From the Same-Sex Marriage Movement in the US?', From Poverty to Power blog, 20 August 2014, http://oxfamblogs.org/fp2p/how-change-happens-what-can-we-learn-from-the-same-sex-marriage-movement-in-the-us/.

[14] Duncan Green, 'How Change Happens: What Can We Learn From the Same-Sex Marriage Movement in the US?', From Poverty to Power blog, 20 August 2014, http://oxfamblogs.org/fp2p/how-change-happens-what-can-we-learn-from-the-same-sex-marriage-movement-in-the-us/.

women than those with weaker or non-existent movements. This plays a more important role than left-wing parties, numbers of women legislators, or even national wealth. These movements can make the difference between having a critical legal reform or funding for shelters or training for the police, and not having it.'[15] Htun and Weldon also found that governments, like US energy users and UK taxpayers, are particularly susceptible to unfavourable comparisons with their neighbours.

When combined with leadership from political authorities and the international mechanisms of the UN, activism can form a crucial pincer movement. In the words of one Filipina activist, 'How do you cook a rice cake? With heat from the bottom and heat from the top. The protests, the marches, the uncompromising position that women's rights are human rights, full stop. That's the heat from the bottom. That's Malcolm X and the suffragists and gay pride parades. But we also need the heat from the top.'[16]

Norms, culture, and faith

Norms overlap with another blind spot in the thinking of many activists—culture, both the arts (literature, music, cinema, theatre, painting) and, more broadly, the ideas, customs, and behaviour of a particular people, which plays a vital role in shaping values and internal narratives. I am convinced that in the UK the writers JK Rowling and JRR Tolkien are among the most powerful influences on future generations of activists. Culture also binds society together; starting a conversation about the fates of football teams in the British premiership is a sure-fire bonding exercise in many parts of the world.

---

[15] Mala Htun and S Laurel Weldon, 'The Civic Origins of Progressive Policy Change: Combating Violence against Women in Global Perspective, 1975–2005', *American Political Science Review* 106, no. 3 (August 2012): pp. 548–69, http://journals.cambridge.org/repo_A86U0PVC.

[16] Kavita Ramdas, 'Radical Women, Embracing Tradition', Transcript, TED website, April 2010, https://www.ted.com/talks/kavita_ramdas_radical_women_embracing_tradition/transcript?language=en.

Cultural attitudes vary between and within countries. Research by social psychologist Geert Hofstede and others has used interviews and surveys about attitudes to compare culture across nations. They have identified six 'dimensions' that show variation between national cultures: the extent to which people accept inequality, the tolerance for uncertainty and ambiguity, individualism vs. collectivism, the distribution of emotional roles between genders (interestingly, men's roles appear to vary more than women's), long-term vs. short-term orientation, and indulgence vs. restraint. These dimensions have been applied in business (e.g. for designing marketing campaigns), education, and healthcare.[17]

While culture in no way predetermines actions or attitudes, it can heavily influence such things as the authority of leaders, the desirability of risk taking, or the relative standing of young and older people. We activists should see cultural difference, not as a source of frustration ('why can't he just hurry up and say what he means?'), but as a source of strength, since in any ecosystem diversity is a sign of good health.

Perhaps most central to the realm of culture, and often underestimated by activists, is faith. I am a lifelong atheist, but decades of working in Latin America, including eight years for the Catholic aid agency CAFOD (Catholic Agency for Overseas Development), have left me with an abiding respect for the role of faith in social change. In Latin America, I saw the power of liberation theology to move thousands of church activists, nuns, and priests, to confront military dictatorships, often at huge personal cost. When I worked at CAFOD, I used to receive messages such as 'Sorry [Sister] Pat can't make the meeting—she's been arrested again' (for chaining herself to the railings outside the Ministry of Defence, in protest at nuclear weapons). I acquired a deep respect for indomitable nuns everywhere.

Along with the family and education, religion is one of the most powerful forces in shaping an individual's norms and can be a

---

[17] 'National Culture', the Hofstede Centre, http://geert-hofstede.com/national-culture.html.

powerful catalyst of 'power within' and 'power with'. While secularization has been a notable feature of European life for the past fifty years, in much of the rest of the world religious institutions remain at the centre of community life. In many communities, people trust their local church, mosque, or temple more than any other institution. Numerous countries have seen a rise in religious fervour, perhaps because faith can bring solace and security, especially when livelihoods and cultures are challenged by globalization or emigration from settled rural communities to the chaos of the shantytown.

Although public attention often focuses on conflicts between faiths, perhaps more remarkable is how much they have in common. The so-called 'golden rule', expressed in Islam as 'No man is a true believer unless he desireth for his brother that which he desireth for himself' (Azizullah—Hadith 150), has remarkably close parallels in the scriptures of every major religion. When representatives of nine world faiths—Bahá'ís, Buddhists, Christians, Hindus, Jains, Jews, Muslims, Sikhs, and Taoists—attended a World Faiths and Development Conference in 1998, they revealed a startling degree of consensus about some of life's deepest truths:

- Material gain alone cannot lead to true development: economic activities are inter-related with all other aspects of life.
- The whole world belongs to God. Human beings have no right to act in a harmful way to other living creatures.
- Everyone is of equal worth.
- People's wellbeing and their very identity are rooted in their spiritual, social, and cultural traditions.
- Social cohesion is essential for true development.
- Societies (and the world) must be run on the basis of equity and justice.[18]

---

[18] Wendy Tyndale, *Key Issues for Development. A Discussion Paper for the Contribution by the World Faiths Development Dialogue (WFDD) to the World Bank's World Development Report 2001* (Oxford, World Faiths Development Dialogue, 1998), http://siteresources.worldbank.org/DEVDIALOGUE/Resources/WFDD2001.pdf.

These essential affirmations underlie attitudes, beliefs, and personal behaviour, including activism. In southern Africa, I have come across many powerful and charismatic women who run community projects helping those living with HIV or orphaned by AIDS. Most are active church-goers and draw on their faith for inspiration and comfort in what is often an exhausting and thankless task.

However, a profound ambiguity characterizes the interaction between faith and politics. Marx saw religion as 'the opium of the people', blinding us to the true nature of our oppression (today football probably plays a similar role), and Gramsci saw it as a means through which elites could construct and maintain their domination. Yet Durkheim portrayed it as a way of building a collective identity that promotes social cohesion and stability.[19] Religion can encourage or discourage activism, promote conformity or challenge it, foment love or hatred.

Nowhere is this contradictory role more evident than in relation to women's rights. Fundamentalists of virtually all religions view the emancipation of women as profoundly disturbing, giving rise, for example, to the curious alliance of the Vatican, the Iranian government, and the US government to block international progress on sexual and reproductive rights.

But the traffic is not all one way. Despite the opposition of their respective religious hierarchies, women activists in both Muslim and Christian communities have reinterpreted Islamic and Catholic scriptures in accordance with women's rights, leading to a new approach to the faith. In 2004 women's organizations in Morocco won a remarkable victory when parliament unanimously approved a new Islamic Family Code that radically strengthened the rights of women. The reforms included the right to decide legal matters without the guardianship of a male, equal responsibility over the household and

---

[19] Emma Tomalin, 'Sociology, Religion and Development: Literature Review', *Working Paper* No. 4 (Birmingham: University of Birmingham, 2007), http://epapers.bham.ac.uk/1505/1/Tomalin-_Sociology%2C_Religion_and_Development-_A_Literature_Review.pdf.

children, and the need for consent from both husband and wife to dissolve a marriage.[20]

Throughout the campaign, activists opted to work within the framework of Islam, arguing that the conservative interpretation enshrined in family law ran counter to the true spirit of the Koran. According to activist Rabéa Naciri: 'We chose not to separate the universal human rights framework from the religious framework. We maintained that Islam is not opposed to women's equality and dignity and should not be presented as such ... Islamic law is a human and historical production, and consequently is able to evolve, to fulfil the current needs of Muslim men and women.'[21]

Such examples are inspiring, but largely ignored by many activists. I call this 'the flipchart problem'. When I raise the importance of faith and faith-based organizations in discussions within Oxfam, colleagues nod, but somehow the issue never makes it to the flipchart that becomes the record of the conversation. Some of this is due to the failings of many faith organizations, from gay rights to contraception, but a lot also derives from our personal 'cup half empty' feelings about religion. On a visit to the Philippines a few years ago, Filipino staff were describing Oxfam's fascinating work on women's rights among the Muslim communities of Mindanao. What about working with the Catholic Church as well, I asked (after all, far more Filipinos are Catholic than Muslim)? 'No way', came the response, 'we're all lapsed Catholics and have no intention of going back to the fold!' Surely it's time to get over that one.

Are norms neutral?

Human rights activists often defend themselves against charges of imposing alien values on other cultures by arguing that anything the

[20] Alexandra Pittman and Rabéa Naciri, 'Winning Women's Rights in Morocco', IDS Research Summary, October 2008.

[21] Duncan Green, *From Poverty to Power: How Active Citizens and Effective States Can Change the World* (Oxford: Oxfam International, 2008), p. 67.

UN agrees must, by virtue of its global nature, be a universal norm. I have never found that argument entirely convincing. The process by which new norms are set of course reflects the relative power (visible, invisible, or hidden) of the forces at play. In the UN and elsewhere in the international system, it is largely Western norms that 'trickle down', with little evidence of the reverse taking place. How many Western leaders have been influenced in their understanding of rights by a conversation with someone in Africa, Asia, or Latin America?

In discussing norms, we also need to be self-aware. How would you describe your own normative framework, which shapes everything you think, do, and say? If forced, I guess I would go for 'confused Western liberal torn between a set of "West is Best" norms on rights and democracy, and deep moral relativism.'

Some of the cruder forms of support for democratization and market liberalization by US think-tanks give substance to the charge that Western powers use normative change as an instrument of foreign policy. Such was the case in the so-called 'colour revolutions' in the former Soviet Bloc,[22] experiences that were used to justify crackdowns on grassroots organizations in many countries, which we will examine in Chapter 9.

Norms, however, act like a complex system: the way they evolve is seldom linear or imposed. They are fiercely debated, compromises are struck, modifications are made. The prospect of norm shifts can provoke a violent backlash. When women get paid jobs for the first time they can face greater domestic violence; gay rights activists are brutally persecuted in many countries across Africa, some even suffering murder and the horrors of 'corrective rape'.

Moreover, as the balance of power shifts in the international system, the normative traffic is becoming less one-way. During the prolonged debate on the global 'sustainable development goals' agreed

---

[22] Susan Stewart, ed., *Democracy Promotion and the 'Colour Revolutions'* (online eBook, London: Taylor & Francis, 2013), http://www.tandfebooks.com/doi/book/10.4324/9780203722985.

in 2015, developing countries were able to override opposition from the Western powers and introduce goals on reducing inequality. Similarly, the increased role of regional bodies in norm-setting, as evidenced by the African Union's 2003 Women's Protocol,[23] may help correct power imbalances.

Female genital mutilation

The movement against female genital mutilation (FGM) is a good example of activism to transform a destructive social norm. Female genital cutting, which involves full or partial removal of a girl's external genitals, serves no medical purpose and has many harmful consequences. Yet the practice is widespread. The UN estimates that worldwide 125 million women and girls are currently living with the consequences of FGM. A further thirty million girls are at risk of being cut in the next decade across twenty-nine known practising countries in Africa and the Middle East.[24]

This centuries-old practice now faces a major normative shift driven by pioneering national and grassroots campaigners, such as Efua Dorkenoo, a Ghanaian-British academic and midwife who wrote one of the earliest reports on FGM, published in 1980, and campaigned tirelessly up to her death in 2014.[25]

The World Health Organization (WHO) rejected a UN request to investigate FGM in 1958, arguing that it was a cultural, rather than medical, issue. When campaigners reframed FGM as a health rights issue some decades later, they gained the adherence of a group of

---

[23] Protocol to the African Charter on Human and Peoples' Rights on the Rights of Women in Africa, African Commission on Human and Peoples' Rights, http://www.achpr. org/files/instruments/women-protocol/achpr_instr_proto_women_eng.pdf.

[24] This figure underestimates the real number of girls affected, because other countries (e.g. Indonesia) are not included. 'What is FGC?' Orchid Project website, http://or chidproject.org/category/about-fgc/what-is-fgc/.

[25] Stella Efua Graham and Scilla MacLean, eds., *Female Circumcision, Excision, and Infibulation: The Facts and Proposals for Change* (London: Minority Rights Group Report 47, 1980).

powerful and 'neutral' champions: doctors. In 1997, WHO, UNICEF, and the UN Population Fund issued an influential joint statement calling FGM a violation of the rights of women and girls to 'the highest attainable standard of health', helping to persuade at least fourteen African countries to outlaw FGM. Yet prevalence remains high in half a dozen countries, where over 90 per cent of women are still mutilated.[26]

Researchers Gerry Mackie and John Lejeune[27] studied national movements against FGM in Egypt, Ethiopia, Kenya, Senegal, and Sudan, and compared them to an earlier normative campaign against the Chinese practice of binding women's feet to enforce chastity and fidelity by limiting women's physical mobility.

Like FGM, foot-binding was both medically unjustifiable and deeply entrenched in urban and coastal China at the beginning of the twentieth century. First, reformers spread the word that the rest of the world did not bind women's feet, making the natural-foot alternative seem feasible. Second, they explained the advantages of natural feet and the disadvantages of bound feet. And finally, they formed 'natural foot societies' whose members pledged not to allow their sons to marry women with bound feet, as well as not to bind their daughter's feet. The reformers' strategy brought a thousand years of practice to an end in a single generation.

Anti-FGM movements in Africa face similar obstacles: families carry out FGM in order to ensure the marriageability and status of their daughters, so a family's choices depend on those of other families in their community. If a single family ends FGM, their daughter may

---

[26] Alison Brysk, 'Changing Hearts and Minds: Sexual Politics and Human Rights', in *The Persistent Power of Human Rights: From Commitment to Compliance*, edited by Thomas Risse, Stephen Ropp, and Kathryn Sikkink (Cambridge: Cambridge University Press, 2013), pp. 259–74.

[27] Gerry Mackie and John LeJeune, 'Social Dynamics of Abandonment of Harmful Practices: A New Look at the Theory', Special Series on Social Norms and Harmful Practices, *Innocenti* Working Paper No. 2009–06 (Florence: UNICEF Innocenti Research Centre, 2009), http://www.unicef-irc.org/publications/pdf/iwp_2009_06.pdf.

never be able to marry. In other words, FGM is a classic collective action problem, in which everyone must move together to reach a solution (not unlike climate change requiring all nations to curb carbon emissions).

In Senegal, reformers found a solution. When a relatively small critical mass of first movers conditionally resolved to abandon FGM, these families had a strong incentive to recruit the remaining members of their community to join them, until a tipping point was reached and whole communities abandoned the practice. Four thousand Senegalese villages have declared themselves FGM free.[28]

In Egypt, campaigners adapted the 'positive deviance' approach discussed in Chapter 1. Rather than focus on the 97 per cent of Egyptian women who were being subjected to FGM, the 'somersault question' became what could be learned from the 3 per cent who were not. Getting them to testify on camera unlocked a wave of energy for the anti-FGM movement, and worked far better than being lectured at by 'experts' and outsiders.[29]

Making the commitment public helps: in 2000, the Ethiopian development organization KMG began holding public weddings of couples who chose to break with the tradition. As many as 2,000 people attended the first wedding, where 317 girls who had not undergone the practice served as bridesmaids. During the ceremony, the bride and bridesmaids wore signs that read: 'I will not be circumcised. Learn from me!' The groom wore his own placard saying: 'I am happy to marry an uncircumcised woman.' Thanks to such campaigns, backed by government action, younger mothers in Ethiopia are nearly 80 per cent less likely to have a daughter cut than older mothers.

[28] Alison Brysk, 'Changing Hearts and Minds: Sexual Politics and Human Rights', in *The Persistent Power of Human Rights: From Commitment to Compliance*, edited by Thomas Risse, Stephen Ropp, and Kathryn Sikkink (Cambridge: Cambridge University Press, 2013).

[29] Richard Pascale, Jerry Sternin, and Monique Sternin, *The Power of Positive Deviance: How Unlikely Innovators Solve the World's Toughest Problems* (Boston, MA: Harvard Business Press, 2010).

Reported support for cutting halved from 60 per cent in 2000 to 31 per cent in 2005.[30]

Interestingly, where activists emphasized health concerns, which was so effective at the international level, some parents turned to medical practitioners for a 'safer FGM'. Where activists stressed human rights (in both Senegal and Ethiopia) parents abandoned it altogether.

The researchers concluded that parents decide to perform FGM because failure to do so brings shame and social exclusion to girls and their families. Once an alternative is perceived to be feasible and people realize the community might be better off without FGM, a more basic norm comes to the fore—to do what is best for their children—and communities abandon the harmful practice.

The FGM campaign contains numerous insights for activists: the importance of building power within among both girls and women, and their families and friends; the value of positive deviance and social learning (seeing is believing); the need to find a countervailing norm, such as a daughter's health and, as ever the importance of collective action—power with.

Conclusion

To test these ideas, let's contemplate how norms might shift on one of the most pressing issues of our times—climate change. What would it take for driving a car or exceeding personal emissions of X tonnes of CO_2 per year to become as socially unacceptable as smoking or child abuse? A combination of academic research and UN negotiations could affect public understanding of personal responsibility and exert pressure for governments to act. Public personalities from sports stars to intellectuals could stand up and 'take the pledge'. National

---

[30] Alison Brysk, 'Changing Hearts and Minds: Sexual Politics and Human Rights', in *The Persistent Power of Human Rights: From Commitment to Compliance*, edited by Thomas Risse, Stephen Ropp, and Kathryn Sikkink (Cambridge: Cambridge University Press, 2013).

leaders could respond with laws, regulations, and public messaging, motivating schools to teach about climate change and environmental responsibility. Government regulations might include carbon pricing, which would help drive technological breakthroughs in renewable energy. Faith groups could emphasize stewardship and personal responsibility; in 2015 some of the most encouraging progress on climate change came from a Papal Encyclical on the Environment[31] and an impassioned appeal for action from a network of Islamic scholars.[32]

All this could be backed by activist organizations pursuing a range of tactics from litigation against carbon polluters, to using culture to spread the word, to *We Can*-style viral citizen-to-citizen networking. Major weather events provide obvious and semi-predictable 'critical junctures' that can galvanize interest from both the public and decision makers. Faith groups, businesses, academics, and civil society organizations could join forces in broad coalitions, abandoning the go-it-alone purism that has undermined efforts to date.

Far fetched? It pretty much describes how major norm changes have always come about. Anyone interested in bringing about change should surely pay close attention to the way such norms are established and evolve over time. We campaigners and lobbyists often prefer to focus on the tangible—laws and policies, spending commitments, public statements of this and that. It's understandable: we are driven by the desire to measure our impact (and thus prove our effectiveness), by a frustration with the vagueness of 'talking shops' about rights and norms, or by sheer impatience at the slow pace of normative change. Whatever the cause, neglect of 'invisible power' is a big mistake. We can still focus on the tangible to communicate and to

---

[31] Jimmy Akin, 'Pope Francis's Environmental Encyclical: 13 Things to Know and Share', Catholic Answers website, 18 June 2015, http://www.catholic.com/blog/jimmy-akin/pope-francis%E2%80%99s-environmental-encyclical-13-things-to-know-and-share.

[32] *The Economist*, 'Islam and ecology: In almost perfect harmony', http://www.economist.com/blogs/erasmus/2015/08/islam-and-ecology.

campaign, but norms should lie at the heart of our deeper understanding of how change happens. And the norm changes we contribute to are likely to be our activism's greatest legacy.

Further Reading

P. Ariès, *Centuries of Childhood: A Social History of Family Life* (New York: Random House USA, 1965).

A. Betts and P. Orchard, *Implementation and World Politics: How International Norms Change Practice* (Oxford: Oxford University Press, 2014).

J.W. Busby, 'Bono Made Jesse Helms Cry: Jubilee 2000, Debt Relief, and Moral Action in International Politics', *International Studies Quarterly*, vol. 51 (2007): 247–75.

J.W. Busby, *Moral Movements and Foreign Policy* (Cambridge: Cambridge University Press, 2010).

T. Risse, S. Ropp, and K. Sikkink (eds.), *The Persistent Power of Human Rights: From Commitment to Compliance* (Cambridge: Cambridge University Press, 2013).

CASE STUDY

The Chiquitanos of Bolivia

On 3 July 2007, after twelve years of unremitting and often frustrating struggle, the Chiquitano people of Bolivia—a group numbering some 9,000 people—won legal title to the one million hectare (2.4 million acre) indigenous territory of Monteverde in the eastern department of Santa Cruz. Evo Morales, the country's first indigenous president attended the ceremony with several of his ministers. So did three elected mayors, ten local councillors (six women, four men), a senator, a congressman, and two members of the Constituent Assembly—all of them Chiquitanos.

Such an event would have been unthinkable a generation before. Until the 1980s, the Chiquitanos lived in near-feudal conditions, required to work without pay for local authorities, landowners and the Church, and prevented from owning land. In the words of Chiquitano activist Jeronima Quiviquivi,[1] 'My father never realised about our rights. We just did what the white people told us; only they could be in power, be president. We couldn't even go into the town centre, people swore at us. But then we got our own organisation and elected our own leaders and that's when we realised we had rights.'[2]

---

[1] Author interview 2008, quoted in Duncan Green, *From Poverty to Power* (Oxford: Oxfam International, 2008).

[2] Sources: Eduardo Caceres (2007) 'Territories and Citizenship, the revolution of the Chiquitanos', input paper for Oxfam; Diakonia, La Paz (2006) Género, etnicidad y participación política; García Linera. For a short chronology of the Original Community Territory legal process up to 2001, see *Artículo Primero*, vol. V, no. 19 (2001): pp. 37–41.

To test the power and systems approach, let's explore how this change happened.

Systems, Power, and Norms: The change took place as part of wider evolution of indigenous identity and of Bolivian politics and economy. In the 1980s, inspired in part by Chiquitano language radio programmes, for the first time, the Chiquitanos began to identify themselves as indigenous people. Indigenous identity began to replace the class-based peasant identity promoted by the nationalism of the 1952 revolution.

The dawn of 'power within' rapidly led to 'power with' in the form of cultural associations, which rapidly acquired an explicitly political nature. The Chiquitano Indigenous Organization (OICH), represented more than 450 communities. As one elderly woman explained, 'Only a short while ago did we begin calling ourselves Chiquitano Indians... We look alike, we were all handed over to the bosses... they called us *cambas* or peasants until not long ago.'

The Chiquitano movement was unexpectedly boosted by the structural adjustment policies of the 1980s, which dramatically reversed three decades of state intervention and improvements in social rights, and galvanized protest movements across Bolivia. Sacked miners from the highlands spread out across the country, setting up new organizations and spreading their traditions of activism and protest. The 1990s saw some unorthodox measures within the hard-line Washington Consensus policies, including a new law that greatly facilitated participation in local government, and an acceleration of agrarian reform, all of which helped boost indigenous movements.

The Chiquitanos' recovery and celebration of indigenous identity led them to join in continent-wide alliances to protest the 500th anniversary (and celebration) of Christopher Columbus' arrival in the Americas.[3] The rise in indigenous consciousness was reflected in

---

[3] Phillip Wearne, *Return of the Indian: Conquest and Revival in the Americas* (Philadelphia, PA: Temple University Press, 1996).

Bolivia's constitutional reform of 1994, which redefined the state as 'pluri-ethnic and multicultural'.

The tipping point came in 2005, with the election of Evo Morales as Bolivia's first ever indigenous president. It marked a sea change in the fortunes of Bolivia's indigenous peoples, including the Chiquitanos. Many smaller 'critical junctures' helped galvanize the movement, including a succession of long marches to the capital La Paz. At one point protestors broke into the local mayor's office and found documents showing that forced labour had been banned in Bolivia, even though the Chiquitanos were still being obliged to perform it. Their conclusion? We need our own mayor.

Two further factors eased the path to change. The discovery of large reserves of natural gas from the late 1980s onwards contributed to a general perception that the country was on the threshold of a historic opportunity. Second, the historical memory of the country's indigenous peoples allowed them to draw strength from deep traditions of identity and resistance.

Formal Politics: After protests toppled President Sánchez de Lozada in October 2003, identity documents became easier to obtain and candidates were allowed to run independently of traditional political parties, which led to major gains for indigenous peoples in the 2005 municipal elections. Because Evo Morales' MAS party was unpopular locally (it was seen as being dominated by the more numerous indigenous highland peoples), activists stood as OICh (Chiquitano Indigenous Organization) candidates.

The Law: In addition to marches and protests, the Chiquitanos tried to work within the system, insisting on legal procedures despite the tricks of adversaries and delays of judges. In January 1995, the Chiquitanos presented their first legal demand for title to Monteverde under a new concept, 'Original Community Territory'. A year and a half later, a second indigenous march won parliamentary recognition for the concept. Years of tedious legal procedures followed, with small gains and reversals, but they paved the way for eventual legal recognition for their territorial claim.

The International System: The International Labour Organization (ILO) played a role in the rise of indigenous identity and was also a channel for legal appeals from the Chiquitano movement.

The Private Sector: The local private sector, especially landowners and forestry companies, were the main opponent of the land reform, but in the end were unable to stop the momentum of the Chiquitano movement.

Change Agents: The main actors in the drama were, of course, the Chiquitanos themselves. Following the lead of other social movements, lowland peoples organized a march to the capital La Paz in 1990, which, as one participant put it, 'demonstrated that the indigenous peoples of the East exist'. Literally and politically, indigenous people were on the move.

Alliances: A turning point came when the Chiquitanos decided to join up with Bolivia's far more numerous highland Indians. 'We met with one of the highlands leaders,' recalls Chiquitano leader, now Senator, Carlos Cuasase, 'and we said, "Look brother, you have the same problems that we do, the same needs." We agreed not only on [the law to nationalize] hydrocarbons but also to defend the rights of indigenous people of both highlands and lowlands.'[4] The Roman Catholic Church was divided on social justice issues between traditionalists ('blessed are the poor, for theirs is the kingdom of God'), and more radical liberation theologians among the local priests who were important allies for the Chiquitanos.

Oxfam's Role: The Chiquitano movement was highly 'endogenous', with only a minor role for outside supporters such as NGOs. One of these was Oxfam, which provided small amounts of funding, thanks

---

[4] Eduardo Caceres (2007) 'Territories and Citizenship, the revolution of the Chiquitanos', input paper for Oxfam.

to the imaginative ways local staff came up with to get round Oxfam's internal bureaucracy. When one evaluation asked about the 'mobile workshops' we were funding, a sheepish programme officer confessed that this was funding for the long marches to the capital, which did indeed act as mobile workshops.

PART II

INSTITUTIONS AND THE IMPORTANCE OF HISTORY

Institutions are both the object and subject of most attempts to make change happen. The next five chapters will apply the conceptual framework of systems, power, and norms to the institutions that most activists belong to, ally with, or seek to influence.

People seeking change are often impatient, intent on addressing the problems of the world. In the words of one of the greatest activists of them all, they are consumed by 'the fierce urgency of now'.[1] From the perspective of 'now', institutions appear to be permanent and unchanging; in fact, they often depend on that appearance for their credibility. But 'now' is merely a moment on the continuum of history, and history shows us that the status quo is far less fixed than it appears. Yes, institutions are inherently conservative, but their normal

---

[1] Martin Luther King, Jr 'I Have a Dream', 28 August, 1963.

functioning provokes changes in the world, changes that buffet them and oblige them, over time, to either evolve or fail.

Examining history helps us question the world we take for granted, and understand what long-term trends are shaping it. By learning how today's world has been constructed we can more realistically see how it can change. I recently lent Adam Hochschild's wonderful history of the abolitionist movement, *Bury the Chains*,[2] to my son Finlay. Confirming my view that this is the one book every activist should read, he found it a revelation. 'What climate change, gross inequality, or poverty are for us, slavery was to them—a massive, immovable object. Yet, by being small cogs in a very large machine, driven largely by unexpected and uncontrollable factors, they were able to make a difference. So while it's hard for us to see how we can possibly make a dent in something like inequality, we just have to remember that it's been done before!' He started to see everything differently—the people he passed in the street (whether black or white), the purpose and impact of activism.

History inspires a deep respect for the personal sacrifices and the campaigning acumen of our predecessors. In the UK, Friends of the Earth is running a fascinating exchange between historians and campaigners to learn from the activists of yesteryear.[3] I was startled to learn that the Chartists (nineteenth-century democracy campaigners) at one point delivered a petition that was six miles long, with a third of the UK population signed up. And all without social media.

History can provide the intellectual ammunition to challenge the narrow orthodoxy of now. I vividly remember my 'light-bulb moment' back when I first took up international trade activism in the 1990s. It was provoked by a history book, *Kicking Away the Ladder* by Korean economist Ha-Joon Chang. He showed that the policies of

[2] Adam Hochschild, *Bury the Chains: The British Struggle to Abolish Slavery* (London: Pan Macmillan, 2012).

[3] Duncan Green, 'What can today's activists learn from the history of campaigning?', From Poverty to Power blog, 26 November 2015, http://oxfamblogs.org/fp2p/what-can-todays-activists-learn-from-the-history-of-campaigning/.

rapid liberalization that rich countries were then trying to force on poor ones were the exact opposite of the policies they themselves had used during their own take-offs. Rich countries used protection to build up their industries, and only later opened up their markets; now they were trying to force poor countries to liberalize straight away.

The double standards were breathtaking, and the impact of Ha-Joon's book profound. At the WTO headquarters in Geneva, I saw how his concise presentation of history strengthened the determination of developing country governments and activists to resist the arm-twisting from rich countries, and how it sowed well-justified doubt in the minds of the liberalizers.

In systems terms, history reveals how different institutions emerged and evolved to reach the structure, culture, and practices we see today, offering useful insights on how to influence them. History inspires a healthy acceptance of pluralism, since institutions have taken many different paths.

History provides a kind of temporal positive deviance: by studying the historical outliers on any given issue, we get new insights and ideas. One of my next projects is to examine the politics and policies of redistribution that enabled dozens of countries to reduce inequality over periods of a decade or more.[4] With inequality becoming an ever more pressing concern for activists and decision makers, it seems like a seam well worth mining.

History reinforces both curiosity and humility, an antidote to the hubris that sometimes afflicts the activist bubble. It reminds us that the conscious efforts of activists are usually less influential than accident or political and economic changes or 'unusual suspects'.

Not every lesson of history is positive. The central role of conflict and war in driving change always depresses me. Luckily, history is not a straitjacket. Times change and institutions change. New factors, like technologies, women's rights, or mass literacy, emerge to shake the

---

[4] http://oxfamblogs.org/fp2p/what-do-we-know-about-the-politics-of-reducing-inequality-not-much-its-time-to-find-out/.

kaleidoscope of power and unleash the possible, as do new threats like climate change. History can be an engine of the imagination.

The next five chapters use the power and systems approach (PSA) to explore the historical evolution and current role of the institutions I consider central to achieving change: states, the machinery of law, political parties, the international system, and transnational corporations.

4

HOW STATES EVOLVE

In 2015, I spoke to a director of works in a Pacific island nation who understandably preferred to remain anonymous because he had had enough. A no-nonsense engineer trying to build the roads his country desperately needs, he was instead grappling with a venal political system. His frustration was palpable:

> In a mature system, everything is in place—the rules, the processes. Here, the playing field changes all the time. Development here *is* politics. We can see where we want to go, the vision for 2020. But we have a government that is power-hungry, politicians maintaining their own position. I've been moved, suspended, chucked out, called names. We had a good, cost-effective road programme on one of our islands. Then in comes a new minister, and one of his advisers is from that island, so he makes promises, says he wants to build some ridiculously expensive road. I say it's impossible and am basically told 'I'm the minister, what I says goes—I want you out by 5 pm'.

The director, who survived in the end, is a good example of many unsung heroes in the drama of development: civil servants who soldier on despite the obstacles, because the stakes are so high—the institution they work within will shape the fates and futures of their peoples. That institution is the state.

The German philosopher GWF Hegel described the state as 'the march of God through the world'.[1] I doubt the frustrated Pacific engineer would agree with its divine origins, but to a greater or lesser degree, states ensure the provision of health, education, water, and

---

[1] Shlomo Avineri, *Hegel's Theory of the Modern State* (New York: Cambridge University Press, 1974), p. 176.

sanitation; they guarantee rights, security, the rule of law, and social and economic stability; they arbitrate in the inevitable disputes between individuals and groups; they regulate, develop, and upgrade the economy; they organize the defence of national territory. More intangibly, they are an essential source of identity—the rise of nationalism and the state have gone hand to hand, for good or ill.

My own views on the state have evolved from indifference to hostility to admiration. Growing up in 1970s Britain, I was surrounded by a state languishing in the midst of stagflation, industrial unrest, and an aura of historical decline. Everything exciting (anti-nuclear protests, the burgeoning environmental and feminist movements, the cathartic anarchism of punk) was happening outside the channels of government. The state was boring and I took it for granted. In Chile and Argentina in the early 1980s, I saw a far bleaker side of the state: beribboned dictators in sunglasses, and friends in permanent pain over the whereabouts of their 'disappeared' relatives. Latin America at that time recalled George Orwell's 1984, written at the onset of the Cold War, with its dystopian vision of a 'big brother state' as 'a boot stamping on a human face, forever'.[2]

Later in the decade, I moved to Nicaragua before the sheen came off the Sandinista Revolution and saw the upsurge in social and economic freedoms a progressive state could achieve. Then, as Latin America slid into debt crisis and enacted ill-conceived liberalizing market reforms in the 1980s and 1990s, I was struck by the contrast between the region's economic stagnation and the concurrent state-driven 'Asian Miracle'. Collaboration with Ha-Joon Chang cemented my belief in a positive role for the state in development.[3] Matthew Lockwood's book on the state in Africa[4] convinced me that at the heart of Africa's

[2] George Orwell, *Nineteen Eighty-Four* (London: Secker and Warburg, 1949).

[3] Duncan Green and Ha-Joon Chang, 'The Northern WTO Agenda on Investment: Do As We Say, Not As We Did', South Centre, 2003, www.ids.ac.uk/idspublication/the-northern-wto-agenda-on-investment-do-as-we-say-not-as-we-did.

[4] Matthew Lockwood, *The State They're In: An Agenda for International Action on Poverty in Africa* (London: ITDG Publishing, 2005).

problems lay weak states, more than the international system then being targeted by activists around the world. I then focussed my 2008 book, *From Poverty to Power* on 'effective states' as a central pillar of development. States may be ubiquitous, but they are far from static. A constant process of conflict and bargaining shapes their contours and responsibilities, and a flux of power determines both what changes and what does not. Activists need to look under the bonnet of states, and understand them as complex systems that can be influenced. The dynamics of change in states epitomizes the characteristics of systems discussed in Chapter 1: the combination of steady change and sudden, unpredictable jumps born of personalities and events. So does states' inertia: ideas, institutions, and interests interact to prevent progress and drive well-intentioned civil servants to distraction.

I worked for a brief spell for the British government's development department in the mid-2000s. What had appeared to an NGO activist on the outside as a monolithic institution dissolved into Whitehall's sprawling system of ministries and personalities, each with their own traditions, jargons, and acronyms (*lots* of acronyms). Power was endlessly disputed within the system, as everyone lobbied internally for their preferred policies and budgets, using all the tactics of activists everywhere—coalitions, the search for champions, seizing critical junctures, and the rest.

Officials, especially 'mandarins' (senior civil servants), emerged from the shadows as powerful players and rather more permanent than their political masters. The enduring popularity of the British TV satire *Yes Minister* (which I am told is used to induct French officials into the ways of Whitehall) comes from the pleasure of watching the suave mandarin, Sir Humphrey, run rings round his hapless political master. Beyond the Whitehall bubble, similar scenarios can be found in other tiers of the state, right down to local councils.

States influence the lives of their citizens primarily by agreeing and implementing laws, rules and policies, taxation and spending, and public messaging that influences norms and beliefs. Their most basic role is to guarantee the physical security of the population, offering protection against disaster and preventing what Hobbes called the 'war of all against all',[5] in which citizens are at the mercy of anyone with a weapon and a grudge. Historically, as Orwell described, this role has been a double-edged sword. In the twentieth century some 170 million people were killed by their own governments, four times the number killed in wars *between* states.[6] The picture looks diffcrent today; the worst deprivation and suffering often coincide with states that are weak or almost non-existent.

Freedom to be and to do requires income as well as security. States help create jobs, and regulate and upgrade the economy to deliver the kind of inclusive growth that liberates people from hunger and want and allows them to acquire knowledge, skills, voice, and agency, not least by guaranteeing access to quality healthcare, education, water, and sanitation, along with some form of social protection.

Politically, states guarantee the rights and voice of poor and excluded groups both directly (the right to vote, access to justice) and by creating an enabling environment, for example, through legislation on access to information, media independence, or decentralization and other participatory governance reforms.

Of course a gulf yawns between what states should do in theory and what they actually do in practice. Some readers whose experience suggests the state is a tool for elites and anything but progressive will have found these paragraphs alarmingly naive. State sceptics laud the role non-state institutions can play in providing the essentials of a decent life. Development economist Paul Collier even argued for 'independent service authorities' in countries like Haiti, deliberately bypassing states viewed as corrupt, inept, and unreformable. I asked Paul what his exit strategy would be—how would these authorities eventually hand power back to elected officials—he had no reply.[7]

[5] Thomas Hobbes, *De Cive*, 1641, chapter 1, para 13.

[6] Geoff Mulgan, *Good and Bad Power: The Ideals and Betrayals of Government* (London: Allen Lane, 2006).

[7] Duncan Green, 'Paul Collier on Post Conflict Reconstruction, Independent Service Authorities, How to Manage Natural Resources and the Hidden Logic of the G20 London

I believe there is no substitute for effective, accountable states and whatever we do in the short term should help build toward that goal. Setting up parallel and competing systems seems likely to undermine the process.

Understanding states as systems, rather than monoliths, should help us avoid the cruder characterizations of states as 'successes' or 'failures'. States emerge over time and evolve as they interact with numerous non-state institutions and individuals. It is those interactions that matter for activists seeking to promote change.

How states evolve

In evolutionary terms, states are a comparatively recent addition to the family and kinship groups that have been the basic building block of human society since homo sapiens emerged from Africa some 100,000 years ago. China was the first to create a recognizably modern state, in the shape of a coherent, merit-based bureaucracy in the third century BC. By contrast, modern states did not emerge in Europe until some 2,000 years later, following two centuries of wars that whittled 500 political entities down into a couple of dozen nation states.[8]

States rise and fall; prolonged periods of institutional inertia are punctuated by crises and sudden change. Over time, however, states have expanded, both in remit and size. States that once confined themselves to conscripting and taxing their citizens now seek to influence many aspects of their lives. In 1880, government spending in the UK and US was only about 10 per cent of GDP;[9] by 2013 it was 45 per cent and 39 per cent respectively.[10] State spending tends to

Summit', From Poverty to Power blog, 29 June 2009, http://oxfamblogs.org/fp2p/paul-collier-on-post-conflict-reconstruction-independent-service-authorities-how-to-manage-natural-resources-and-the-hidden-logic-of-the-g20-london-summit/.

[8] Francis Fukuyama, *The Origins of Political Order: From Prehuman Times to the French Revolution* (New York: Farrar, Straus and Giroux, 2011), p. 19 and p. 328.

[9] Ha-Joon Chang, *Economics: The User's Guide* (London: Pelican, 2014).

[10] Organisation for Economic Co-operation and Development (OECD), 'General Government Spending', https://data.oecd.org/gga/general-government-spending.htm.

grow as economies develop—in 2012 governments in low income countries spent only 16.5 per cent of their much lower GDP, compared to 38.3 per cent in the Euro area.[11]

In his monumental history of the state,[12] Francis Fukuyama argues that 'the miracle of modern politics' lies in achieving a precarious balance between three pillars: effective centralized administration (civil service), the rule of law (courts), and accountability mechanisms (elected government and parliamentary oversight). Following this framework, I will discuss the administration in this chapter, while subsequent ones will cover the machinery of law and accountability.

Balance among these three elements is a miracle because they are often in conflict. Central administrations usually seek to maximize their power, while courts and parliaments seek to limit it. When balance is achieved, it doesn't always last: societies have always wrestled with the ability of lobbyists and vested interests ('hidden power') to buy access and influence with decision makers. In trying to influence states, insider activists use many of the same tactics, albeit with considerably less money and different aims.

Fukuyama argues that the UK in the nineteenth century was the first to put in place a balance of all three pillars. He also finds comfort in the history of the US, which suffered mind-boggling levels of patronage and corruption in the nineteenth century, yet in the fifty years prior to the Second World War managed to turn the US government into a relatively effective bureaucracy.

In today's developing countries, successive waves of European colonization wielded a determining influence over the evolution of states. Britain, France, Spain, the Netherlands, and others took over existing states or created new ones where none had previously existed. In Latin America, Spain found the militarist imperial structures of the

---

[11] Central Government Finances, 'Expense', World Development Indicators 2015.

[12] Francis Fukuyama, *The Origins of Political Order: From Prehuman Times to the French Revolution* (New York: Farrar, Straus and Giroux, 2011). Francis Fukuyama, *Political Order and Political Decay: From the Industrial Revolution to the Globalization of Democracy* (New York: Farrar, Straus and Giroux, 2014).

Aztecs and Incas not that dissimilar from its own, and used them to rule over their conquered subjects, leaving a legacy of hierarchical unresponsive bureaucracies.

In lucrative Asian colonies such as India or Singapore, whose wealth and trade underwrote the British Empire and Britain's industrialization, the colonizers invested significantly in the national army and civil service to suit their purposes, institutions that lived on after independence. China and East Asia's legacy of strong states survived European occupation and provided a basis for rebuilding upon decolonization. Africa was another story; the pillage of its people by the slave trade required no state institutions and, with the exception of South Africa, the continent appeared to offer little wealth and myriad difficulties for the colonizers. As a result, the Europeans opted for indirect rule with few settlers and fewer state institutions. The least developed parts of the world today are those that lacked either strong indigenous state institutions or transplanted settler-based ones.[13]

The evolution of modern states has taken centuries, in a tortured and often bloody process far removed from the staid world of technocratic 'state building' promoted by today's aid donors. Typical of the evolution of complex systems, the dynamic has been one of slow change, punctuated by sudden upheavals. Historically, war has been one of the great drivers of state evolution; in the words of social historian Charles Tilly, 'war made the state and the state made war'.[14] The first proper state was forged amid carnage on the battlefields of China, and a similar bloodbath gave birth to modern European states and many others across the globe.

War posed existential threats that forced elites to pool their efforts, accept restraints on their individual power, and embrace change. It led to the introduction and expansion of taxation, which in turn required

[13] Francis Fukuyama, *Political Order and Political Decay: From the Industrial Revolution to the Globalization of Democracy* (New York: Farrar, Straus and Giroux, 2014), p. 33.

[14] Charles Tilly, *Coercion, Capital, and European States, AD 990–1990* (Oxford and Cambridge, MA: Basil Blackwell, 1990), p. 54.

a state bureaucracy to collect and administer the revenue. And it laid the foundation for a social contract between citizen and state based on security: the former provided soldiers and money in return for the latter's protection. As noted in Chapter 1, the two world wars of the twentieth century vastly expanded the obligations of citizens and states to each other.

Wars (or the threat of them) are examples of 'critical junctures', major events that also include financial meltdowns and epidemics (the Black Death transformed Europe in the fourteenth century). Another such juncture is a 'resource shock' that finances either a feeding frenzy (Nigeria's discovery of oil and gas), a period of boom and prosperity (Botswana's diamonds) or a cycle of overspending, indebtedness and financial crisis (as seems to be happening in Ghana after its recent oil finds).

Each of these shocks prompted shifts in the structures and operating values of the state that proved crucial to movements for change. Critical junctures act as catalysts of change, rearranging the patterns of alliances and allegiances that underpin the political order, but also transforming norms on everything from the role of the state in providing welfare to the rights of women or African Americans (both strongly influenced by the Second World War). Activists' thirty-year, apparently unsuccessful, campaign for a 'Tobin Tax' on financial transactions only came to fruition after the 2008 global financial crisis, an example explored in Chapter 11.

Longer-term, less visible processes than war also create evolutionary pressures on the state. Economic growth can create new poles of power: it can throw up new entrants to elites, who demand preferential policies; and it can lay the basis for new social movements, through which middle classes demand civil rights and freedom of expression, or trade unions and urban slum dwellers fight for improved state services and a fairer distribution of wealth. Activists need to engage with new movements as they arise out of such slow processes, and at the same time remain alert to moments that allow for breakthroughs.

In recent years the actions and courage of strong and cohesive non-violent civic coalitions have proven vital to the political transitions that presage state change. Since the 1980s, successive waves of civil society protest have contributed to the overthrow of military governments across Latin America, the downfall of Communist and authoritarian regimes in Eastern Europe and Central Asia, the removal of dictators in the Philippines and Indonesia, the end of apartheid in South Africa, and the upheavals of the Arab Spring. Effective tactics have included boycotts, mass protests, blockades, strikes, and civil disobedience.

Even the most repressive states cannot ignore such movements for long. Confucius wrote that every ruler needs arms, food, and trust, but that if any of these had to be forfeited, the first two should be given up before the last. Even unelected governments need a degree of trust to do their day-to-day work. Without it laws will more often be evaded and broken, taxes harder to raise, and information harder to gather. 'Legitimacy'—when citizens accept the rights of states to rule over them—lies at the heart of the social contract between rulers and ruled.[15] States' desire to maintain or regain legitimacy provides activists with avenues for change even in apparently closed political systems.

In Liberia years of entrenched corruption had so eroded the public trust that even dire warnings about Ebola's lethal contagion were seen as a cynical attempt to solicit and 'eat' international donations.[16] Corruption and political sclerosis are not confined to developing countries of course: Fukuyama ends his history of the state with an impassioned denunciation of today's US 'vetocracy', paralysed by vested interests. Left to fester, such decay resembles the build-up of pressures in the earth's crust preceding an earthquake.

[15] Claire Mcloughlin, 'State Legitimacy', DLP Concept Brief 02 (Birmingham: Developmental Leadership Program, 2014), http://publications.dlprog.org/Statelegit.pdf.
[16] Ashoka Mukpo, 'Ebola Terrified Us a Year Ago. What Did It Teach Us About West Africa?', Monkey Cage blog, *The Washington Post*, 7 August 2015, www.washingtonpost.com/blogs/monkey-cage/wp/2015/08/07/ebolas-rapid-spread-terrified-us-a-year-ago-what-did-it-teach-us-about-west-africa/.

Of course, for every Arab Spring there is often an Arab Winter, as forces of cohesion and disintegration slug it out. Systems are in constant flux and change is highly non-linear. Based on his observations in several Mexican municipalities, political scientist Jonathan Fox found state policy evolving through a cycle of conflict and cooperation: after a conflict would break out, more progressive local state officials would talk to the more approachable protest leaders, and a period of reform would ensue. When those reforms ran out of steam, or new issues emerged, conflict would flare up and the cycle would begin anew.[17] Another political scientist, Sidney Tarrow, sees a similar dynamic of repression, partial victories leading to reform, and demobilization, repeating itself in Europe over the last two centuries.[18]

I use this model a good deal, because it neatly explains why struggles move between periods of conflict and cooperation. It also captures the fact that most political change happens through deals behind closed doors that seek to accommodate change and avert mass violence, even if protests and conflicts understandably draw our attention. The 'political settlement' that ended apartheid in South Africa and brought transition to non-racial democracy involved a wide range of pacts, deals, and 'accords' struck between major political forces, powerful economic interests, the labour movement, and civil society groups. Such deals reflect power, both visible and hidden, and activists need to be aware of the extent of their leverage and also be present, with access to decision makers at critical moments, even when decisions are made behind closed doors. Engaging in this way often provokes charges of legitimizing anti-democratic or untransparent processes, while refusing to engage entails missed opportunities. This issue generates a good deal of argument between 'insider' and 'outsider' activists, and will be discussed in Chapter 11.

[17] Jonathan Fox, *Accountability Politics: Power and Voice in Rural Mexico* (New York: Oxford University Press Inc., 2007).
[18] Sidney Tarrow, *Power in Movement: Social Movements and Contentious Politics*, 2nd edition (Cambridge: Cambridge University Press, 1998).

States in developing countries today

Nearly all developing countries reflect the dynamic interplay of ancient political traditions and those imposed by European colonizers. Each state is unique and any typology is inevitably unsatisfactory because particular states tick more than one box, move between categories over time, or because different elements within a state behave in different ways. Nevertheless, I find it helpful to think of today's developing country states in three broad groupings: developmental states, patrimonial states, and fragile/conflict affected states.

Developmental states have an effective centralized state apparatus, geared primarily to generating economic growth. Many of them emerged where state institutions pre-date European takeover. Over the last fifty years, developmental states like South Korea, Singapore, and Malaysia made huge strides growing the economy and reducing poverty; Ha-Joon Chang says that, for a development economist, growing up in 1960s Korea was like being a physicist present at the birth of the universe. The 'Asian Tigers' are closest to the classical description of the state set out by the German sociologist Max Weber, namely an efficient, merit-based civil service that manages to avoid capture by vested interests and guides the national economy in a process of sustained upgrading. Some observers include Botswana, Rwanda, Ethiopia, and Chile in the category.

As that list suggests, there is a problem. While aid donors laud the successes of developmental states in freeing their populations from poverty, human rights advocates condemn their repression of opposition and free speech. Going back to Amartya Sen's definition, developmental states deliver only some kinds of 'freedoms to do and to be', while actively suppressing others.

Before everyone starts calling for a strong leader to impose order and deliver growth, it should be remembered that while some autocracies are developmental, many are not. Cross-country comparisons show that, on average, there appears to be no growth advantage (or disadvantage) in being authoritarian. Autocracies do account for some of development's success stories, but they have also been responsible for innumerable dismal failures. In Latin America, I saw the hyperinflation inflicted by military rule in the 1980s that went hand in hand with their cruel human rights abuses.

The quality of growth also varies. As systems, autocracies are distinguished from democracies by the paucity of feedback loops and constraints—a dictator dictates, after all. With untrammelled power, a leader can conduct necessary reforms, often leading to growth spurts, but should the situation change, or should they simply get it wrong, there is no-one who can force them to alter course. Economies under autocracies are thus characterized by booms and busts, whereas democracies, with their often exasperating degree of feedback and constraint, have historically proved better at avoiding the extremes, producing a smoother ride.[19]

The states I call 'patrimonial' bear very little resemblance to the Weberian ideal. They are deeply inefficient, with high levels of patronage and corruption, as officials and leaders put self and kin before citizens and country. The Pacific director of public works recalled one minister telling him that he was speaking at that meeting on that island, and that he wanted him to make sure that the diggers arrived while he was speaking. There were no road works under way, but he made sure the big yellow excavators arrived for the show. He has even set aside a small fund to pay for such pointless exercises in order to buy the political elbow room to get on with the real work.

Patrimonial states lie along a spectrum from vampire to ruminant: at one extreme, corrupt governments suck the blood out of the economy and give nothing back; at the other extreme, a degree of 'eating' does not rule out something useful emerging as a by-product.

The third grouping of 'fragile and conflict affected states' can barely control the national territory, or are wracked by conflict and violence.

---

[19] Tim Kelsall, 'State of the Art: Authoritarianism, Democracy and Development', The Developmental Leadership Program, 2014.

There, nothing seems to work, public services are negligible, the rule of law practically nonexistent. Citizens do not even enjoy the basic right not to be shot by marauding gangs. Over the course of this century, such states will be home to an increasing proportion of the world's people living in poverty and therefore a growing focus for aid agencies.

Activists may find the typology useful for identifying the appropriate change strategy. In fragile states, where power resides mostly outside the state, activists may be better off working at a local level, with municipal officials and non-state bodies like traditional leaders and faith groups. In developmental states, engaging directly with efficient bureaucracies, using research and argument rather than street protest, often makes for a better (and safer) influencing strategy than challenging politicians. In my experience, closed political systems are often more responsive to evidence than democracies, where political horse-trading dominates. In more patrimonial systems, the best influencing strategy may be to network directly with those in power, perhaps even joining the local golf club to chat up the civil servants and politicians there, as was recommended by one of Oxfam's country directors in West Africa.

The world in which today's states operate is also changing fast. In some ways, traditional nation states are becoming too small for the big things, and too big for the small things. The 'big things'—problems without passports such as climate change, migration, international criminal networks, or tax evasion—have been pushed upwards to regional and global bodies such as the EU, African Union, or UN. For activists, this means working in international networks and/ or within international organizations. The Paris climate change conference in 2015 succeeded in part because a large and influential network of NGOs and scientists worked well with proactive national delegations. I discuss this in a case study on the Paris Agreement on pages 171–175.

At the same time, 'small things' like public services and policing have been pushed downward to municipal and provincial levels. A few cities in Colombia or South Africa are starting to look like 'municipal developmental states'.[20] Decentralization has opened up enormous possibilities for change, as we saw in Chapter 3 regarding the Chiquitanos of Bolivia. At local level, the balance of power between social movements, activist organizations, and the state is likely to be less unequal.

Aid-financed state reform

Over the last thirty years, aid agencies and international financial institutions have devoted considerable attention to reforming states in developing countries. Their efforts to bring about 'good governance' have restructured budgets and ministries, rewritten laws, and even spawned new institutions, but by and large they made little change to the way states operate. The economist Lant Pritchett talks about governments' increasing skill at 'isomorphic mimicry'—a term borrowed from biology, where it describes different organisms that evolve to look alike without actually being related.[21]

The lively conversation among aid donors, researchers, and activists regarding the failure of aid to bring lasting state reform was one of the prime motivators for this book. The discussion in networks with names like 'Doing Development Differently'[22] and 'Thinking and Working Politically'[23] has been rewarding and frustrating in equal measure: rewarding because I have learned a great deal from the assembled big brains about how states and aid systems do and don't

[20] Hugh Cole, 'Are Progressive Cities the Key to Solving Our Toughest Global Challenges?', From Poverty to Power blog, 2 September 2014, http://oxfamblogs.org/fp2p/are-progressive-cities-the-key-to-solving-our-toughest-global-challenges/.

[21] Lant Pritchett, Michael Woolcock, and Matt Andrews, 'Capability Traps? The Mechanisms of Persistent Implementation Failure', CGD Working Paper No. 234 (Washington DC: Center for Global Development, 2010).

[22] The DDD Manifesto Community, Doing Development Differently website, http://doingdevelopmentdifferently.com/.

[23] Adrian Leftwich, 'Thinking and Working Politically: What Does It Mean, Why Is It Important and How Do You Do It?' Document prepared for the Developmental Leadership Program (DLP) Research Policy Workshop, 10–11 March, 2011, in Frankfurt, http://www.gsdrc.org/document-library/thinking-and-working-politically-what-does-it-mean-why-is-it-important-and-how-do-you-do-it/.

work; frustrating because some of the issues dear to my heart ('power within', citizen activism, gender rights) are often pushed aside in favour of dissecting political deal-making at the top. (It has also been rewarding in a more direct sense—as part of the Thinking and Working Politically conversation, Australia's Department of Foreign Affairs and Trade agreed to support the work that went into this book.)

One recurring theme of these conversations is that aid-financed state reform failed because Western donors tried to graft liberal-democratic and free-market institutions onto countries with very different traditions.[24] Governments became adept at passing rules and creating institutions that look good on paper, but are in practice entirely cosmetic. At one point Uganda had the best anti-corruption laws in the world, scoring 99 out of 100 in one league table, yet came 126th in the 2008 Transparency International Corruption Perceptions Index.

In contrast, countries that successfully reformed state institutions did not follow some Washington or London-decreed 'best practice'. Instead, they created hybrid institutions that combine elements of traditional, nationally specific institutions with good ideas from outside. In fragile states, it seems, the facts that governments were less able or willing to pursue imported reforms and non-state institutions were relatively more powerful favoured the creation of locally-relevant hybrid institutions.[25]

One example comes from French-speaking West Africa, where the secular French-style school systems were losing Muslim students at an alarming rate to private religious schools. After vainly attempting to suppress the flourishing parallel world of private education, the governments of Mali, Niger, and Senegal decided instead to 'go with the grain' by bringing unofficial schools more squarely into the formal

---

[24] David Booth and Diana Cammack, *Governance for Development in Africa: Solving Collective Action Problems* (London: Zed Books, 2013), p. 123.

[25] Michael Woolcock, 'Engaging with Fragile and Conflict-Affected States', CID Working Paper No. 286 (Cambridge, MA: Center for International Development, Harvard University, 2014), www.hks.harvard.edu/centers/cid/publications/faculty-working-papers/engaging-with-fragile-and-conflict-affected-states.

state system and at the same time reforming the official system by introducing religious education in state schools.

Preliminary indications suggest that the hybrid schools are providing as good an education as the previous regime.[26] According to Harvard's Matt Andrews, such hybrid solutions are best devised by local stake holders who understand the issue best. Rather than dictate solutions, outsiders should create opportunities for local actors to find their own.[27]

The success of hybrid institutions is what you would expect from a systems perspective. Systems are path dependent—each stage of evolution shapes the possibilities of the next. Activists working with the grain of systems need both to be keenly attuned to new institutional variants that emerge spontaneously (positive deviance), and to use their knowledge of history or experiences elsewhere to sow new variants in the institutional ecosystem. What does *not* work is trying to shoehorn in 'best practice' institutions from elsewhere.

Conclusion

States are complex systems, made up of families of institutions, each with its own history, procedures, and norms. Even the most apparently monolithic dictatorship is, on closer inspection, nothing of the sort. The solidity of presidential palaces and halls of the people is in fact ephemeral, built upon the shifting sands of legitimacy and events. When I lived in Argentina, the military dictatorship appeared impregnable, yet within two years two 'critical junctures' led to its downfall—hyperinflation eroded its middle class support and military defeat in the Falklands destroyed its aura of power.

---

[26] Duncan Green, 'Harnessing Religion to Improve Education in Africa', From Poverty to Power blog, 6 July 2012, http://oxfamblogs.org/fp2p/harnessing-religion-to-improve-education-in-africa/. The reforms have not exacerbated gender imbalances. At primary school level, for example, girls outnumber boys, sometimes significantly.

[27] Matt Andrews, *The Limits of Institutional Reform in Development: Changing Rules for Realistic Solutions* (New York: Cambridge University Press, 2013).

States exemplify the challenges of complexity. The interactions, alliances, and disputes between politicians and civil servants, between one ministry and another, or between different tiers of government, and how each of them in turn respond to citizen demand and other external pressures, provide the political landscape upon which decisions are made. Learning to 'dance with the system'—understanding how the state in question evolved, how its decisions are made, how formal and informal power is distributed within it and how that distribution shifts over time—are essential tasks for any activist intent on making change happen.

Alongside the world of officials and ministries that constitute the administrative state, there are two additional institutional entry points for activists: the structures that administer justice and those that provide accountability. We turn to them now.

Further Reading

M. Andrews, *The Limits of Institutional Reform in Development: Changing Rules for Realistic Solutions* (New York: Cambridge University Press, 2013).

P. Chabal and J.P. Daloz, *Africa Works: Disorder as Political Instrument* (London: James Currey, 1989).

F. Fukuyama, *The Origins of Political Order: From Prehuman Times to the French Revolution* (New York: Farrar, Straus and Giroux, 2011).

F. Fukuyama, *Political Order and Political Decay: From the Industrial Revolution to the Globalization of Democracy* (New York: Farrar, Straus and Giroux, 2014).

T. Hobbes, *Leviathan* (1651, published Oxford: Oxford University Press, 1996).

A. Leftwich, *States of Development: On the Primacy of Politics in Development* (Cambridge: Polity, 2000).

B. Levy, *Working with the Grain: Integrating Governance and Growth in Development Strategies* (Oxford: Oxford University Press, 2014).

M. Lockwood, *The State They're In: An Agenda for International Action on Poverty in Africa* (London: ITDG Publishing, 2005).

5

THE MACHINERY OF LAW

A couple of years ago, I visited a homeless shelter next to Nigambodh Ghat, the main crematorium in central Delhi, the capital of India. The shelter was built on the banks of the polluted Yamuna River, on land shunned by other residents, due to the clouds of smoke from burning bodies rising from the open-air pyres next door. While those flames lit up the night, 100 men of all ages sat cross-legged on their sleeping mats, talking to charismatic activist Harsh Mander about depression and drug rehab. They all seem to be drunk or high, which made the meeting slightly nerve wracking.

Inhospitable as the shelter seemed, it provided these homeless men with a place to sleep and a fixed address. After the meeting, Harsh, who is also a commissioner to India's Supreme Court, advising it on the right to food, roped me in to hand out passbooks. The next day, clutching their proof of address (even if it does say 'homeless shelter') they would all go down to the bank to open accounts. In a month's time they would get biometric ID cards, the digital gateways to rations, cash transfers, and an official identity.

The shelter exists because in 2011 the Court decreed that there should be one homeless shelter for every 100,000 residents. According to Harsh the Supreme Court is the most effective arm of government on social policy. 'I'd been talking to government for years on homelessness without result. I wrote a letter to the Supreme Court saying people were dying in the Delhi winter, and this is the result.'[1]

---

[1] Author Interview, November 2012.

India made me rethink my attitude to the law (and most lawyers), which had previously seemed a stupefying combination of rote learning of cases, tedious obsession with procedures, and impenetrable jargon. Even before meeting Harsh, another light-bulb moment came when a young Spanish lawyer working on food security explained to me, 'You must understand, the state sees the world through the eyes of the law'. Her words have stuck with me, giving meaning to those endless news items on judicial reviews, test cases, and supreme-court rulings: the state sees the world, learns, and evolves at least partly through the machinery of law. Activists take note.

Beyond the set of rules enforced by litigation, the police, and the courts, the rule of law includes legal procedures that prescribe how state officials do their work and laws are implemented. The law also has a broader role: it encapsulates what we expect of our society and at the same time it contributes to delivering on that expectation.

The law matters for a country's development. Because social, political, and economic change alters the distribution of resources and power, creating winners and losers, development is rife with conflict. A biased legal system will increase the potential for violence and exclusion, while a fair and effective one can harness the participation and voice of diverse groups to achieve a more consensual resolution of conflict and a smoother ride for an evolving society.

When the rule of law is absent, the consequences are dire. No-one described that calamity better than Thomas Hobbes, in *Leviathan*, published in 1651:[2]

> Without Law there is no place for Industry, because the fruit thereof is uncertain; and consequently no Culture of the Earth, no Navigation, nor use of the commodities that may be imported by sea; no commodious Building, no instruments of moving and removing such things as require much force; no Knowledge of the face of the Earth, no account of Time, no Arts, no Letters, no Society; and which is worst of all, continual fear and danger of violent death; and the life of people, solitary, poor, nasty, brutish and short.

[2] Thomas Hobbes, *Leviathan* (Oxford: Oxford University Press, 1996), p. 84.

The law as a driver of change

In theory, the law protects rights, imposes duties, and sets a framework for the conduct of almost every social, political, and economic activity. It punishes offenders impartially, compensates the injured, and enforces agreements. In addition, it endeavours to guarantee justice, promote freedom, and provide security.

But as the French writer Anatole France caustically observed 'The law, in its majestic equality, forbids the rich as well as the poor to sleep under bridges, to beg in the streets, and to steal bread.'[3] In practice, the law reflects disparities of wealth and power: money can hire the best lawyers; white-collar crimes always seem to get off more lightly than blue-collar ones; hidden and invisible power work their magic.

The degree to which impartiality is constrained by power varies widely from country to country. When it comes to using the formal legal system to promote development, it is hard to beat India, which suffers from a sclerotic legislature and an indifferent government. Its hyperactive legal system has stepped into the breach. Social activists like Harsh Mander regularly try to persuade the Supreme Court to rule that the government must do something, and then mobilize people to ensure implementation of the ruling. On the rights to food or education, for example, the Court has been the impetus for some of the country's best known progressive legislation.

That culture filters down to the grassroots. Activist talk is dotted with references to PIL—public interest litigation. Women in slums told me they were bringing claims under India's Right to Information Act to find out what their children's schools should be providing, or who is actually in charge of the community toilets, which had been shut for the last seven years.

But not all activists are as well connected as Harsh, and not all PILs are progressive. Plenty of industry lobbyists use the tactic, leading to

---

[3] Anatole France, *The Red Lily*, 1894, chapter 7.

an overall environment characterized by abrupt and unpredictable policy changes. Judicial activism is also not known for its speed. According to a Ministry of Finance study from the 1990s, to settle the backlog of 25 million cases in India's courts will take 324 years at the current disposal rate.[4] I doubt things have got much better since. From a systems perspective, India's judicial activism may well compensate for the failings of the state and the political system, yet it sacrifices the law's ability to act as a neutral arbiter.

When legal systems work for poor people, they can transform the lives of multitudes. In Bangladesh a 2008 Supreme Court ruling confirmed the citizenship rights of thousands of Urdu speakers still living in camps set up after the 1971 War of Independence, allowing them to obtain identity papers that opened the way to formal jobs, votes, and passports.

An analysis by the Overseas Development Institute[5] of the case identified six factors that make this kind of positive impact possible: progressive legal frameworks; sympathetic or activist judiciaries (like the one that helped Harsh Mander); a support structure for legal empowerment (so that poor people have access to money, legal aid, social contacts); a motivated government (especially in implementing, rather than ignoring, court rulings); potential beneficiaries and their supporters with the incentive and capacity to cooperate; and activists with the right combination of insider and outsider tactics, who can spot windows of opportunity and forge effective alliances. Since many lawsuits last for decades, an additional requirement is staying power. Former British Prime Minister Gordon Brown is said to have once joked 'In establishing the rule of law, the first five centuries are the hardest'.

The courts are one of the few institutions that has stood up to autocracy. Until 1994 apartheid South Africa essentially had no

---

[4] Gurcharan Das, *India Grows at Night: A Liberal Case for a Strong State* (New Delhi: Penguin Books India, 2012).

[5] Tam O'Neil, Craig Valters, and Cynthia Farid, *Doing Legal Empowerment Differently: Learning from Pro-Poor Litigation in Bangladesh* (London: Overseas Development Institute, 2015).

written constitution or bill of rights. The white-ruled parliament was supreme, and no court had the power to strike down its laws, no matter how unjust or unfair. But South Africa's courts did have the power to interpret legislation, which they used to blunt some of the more notorious apartheid laws. The Legal Resources Centre, a public interest law firm, won rulings from the country's highest courts, for example, to reverse the policy that had prevented the families of black urban workers from joining them in 'white' cities. Another human rights organization, Lawyers for Human Rights, provided free defence counsel for hundreds of illiterate people being prosecuted for transgressing the apartheid system's oppressive laws.[6]

South Africa also exemplifies another aspect of the law: while it is not immune to influence by elites (that much we know), it can also be influenced by social mobilization ('power with'). I watched fascinated as women's organizations sang and danced outside a Johannesburg courthouse where cases of domestic violence were being tried. I was told such protests greatly increase the chances of success.

The Legal Resources Centre is one of thousands of small, dedicated legal aid and legal rights organizations around the world. I confess I have sometimes been sceptical of activists lugging huge, tattered statute books full of impenetrable legal jargon to workshops in factories and shantytowns, but the legal rights of the poor do matter. A 2002 survey in Ecuador found that women's use of legal aid clinics to help with separation and divorce reduced the probability of severe physical violence after separation by 17 per cent. Legal aid clients also raised their chances of obtaining a child-support award by 20 per cent.[7]

A World Bank study on the use of the courts to enforce the rights to healthcare and education in Brazil, India, Indonesia, South Africa, and

[6] United Nations Development Programme, *Human Development Report 2002: Deepening Democracy in a Fragmented World* (New York: Oxford University Press, 2002).

[7] World Bank, *World Development Report 2006. Equity and Development* (New York: Oxford University Press, 2005).

Nigeria[8] posed an intriguing question: does resort to the legal system make governments more accountable (because they are forced to fulfil their promises) or less (because courts are often the preserve of the rich)? The trade-offs can be complicated: in Costa Rica, a single decision by the Constitutional Chamber of the Supreme Court, (perhaps Latin America's most powerful Constitutional Court) led to an 80 per cent reduction in mortality rates among AIDS patients, but obliged the health system to spend 8 per cent of its medicines budget to treat just 0.012 per cent of its patients.

The World Bank study reached a broadly optimistic conclusion. Judges tend not to try to force governments to do the impossible (when they do, they meet little success). Instead, they have become a part of an iterative policy-making process in which 'litigation upsets the status quo, creating the context for a joint search for new solutions' to previously unrecognized problems (such as access to medicines for new diseases) and to reflect shifts in public opinion (such as on the right to food or work). The study concluded: 'When the courts work in congress with other branches of the state, legalization is democracy by another means.'[9]

Inequality in access to justice remains profound. A UN Commission in 2008 found that four billion people (over half the world's population) are robbed of the chance to better their lives and climb out of poverty because they are excluded from the rule of law (although that figure is disputed).[10] One of the most painful examples of inequality before the law is the harsh treatment of poor people at the hands of the police, who often act as an occupying army in poor communities.

In some places activists have won significant improvements in police behaviour, as we saw in the Tikamagarh case discussed in

---

[8] Varun Gauri and Daniel Brinks, eds., *Courting Social Justice: Judicial Enforcement of Social and Economic Rights in the Developing World* (New York: Cambridge University Press, 2008).

[9] Varun Gauri and Daniel Brinks, eds., *Courting Social Justice: Judicial Enforcement of Social and Economic Rights in the Developing World* (New York: Cambridge University Press, 2008).

[10] 'Making the Law Work for Everyone. Volume 1. Report of the Commission on Legal Empowerment of the Poor' (New York: Commission on Legal Empowerment of the poor/ United Nations Development Programme, 2008).

Chapter 1. 'Community policing', an approach that integrates police into community life, has gained a toehold in many countries. Brazil's police, for example, once notorious for links to death squads and the assassination of street children and other 'undesirables',[11] spearheaded the innovation of women-only police stations beginning in the 1980s. The stations commonly address family violence, are often staffed by specially trained female personnel, and aim to improve the ability of the police to respond to the unique needs of women. Their success was such they have now spread to fifteen countries in Latin America, Africa, and Asia. In India, a study found that the establishment of 188 women's police stations resulted in a 23 per cent increase in reporting of crimes against women and children and a higher conviction rate.[12]

Customary law

In countries where courts and lawyers are in the pockets of wealthy elites, and the laws themselves are structured to protect the privileged, poor people and communities often seek redress through 'customary law', a community-level justice system not codified by the state.

Customary law regulates important aspects of daily life, such as disputes over access to land and water, and family issues, such as inheritance and marriage. It derives its legitimacy from local mores, values, and traditions. And it is affordable: one activist from a remote area in Pakistan argues that, 'Most people in our part of the world who call for sharia courts and laws do so with the belief that it would save them from litigation spread over a lifetime and the exorbitant costs of lawyers. This has little to do with practising Islam or harsh punishments. People just want to keep everything simple.'[13]

---

[11] Gilberto Dimenstein, *Brazil: War on Children* (London: Latin America Bureau, 1991).

[12] UN Women website, 'Women's Police Stations/Units', www.endvawnow.org/en/articles/1093-womens-police-stations-units.html.

[13] Masood Ul Mulk, personal communication, 4 January 2016.

In many poor countries, customary law is the rule rather than the exception. According to the World Bank, in Sierra Leone about 85 per cent of the population fell under customary law as of 2003, while customary tenure affects 90 per cent of land transactions in Mozambique and Ghana.[14] Such numbers bring home the importance for activists of understanding (and working with) the customary system as well as the formal one, if we are to grasp how poor and marginalized people lead their lives, and help them change things for the better.

I got a crash course in the workings of customary law during a visit to the Pacific archipelago of Vanuatu in 2015, especially when we left the capital, Port Vila, and headed for the village of Epau. Conversations in the capital had all been about government, parliament, and aid; in Epau, that all seemed very distant. Here, the chiefs were in charge; lots of them—primary chief, assistant chief, and the chiefs of the community's four tribes—all chosen by bloodline (as are most chiefs in Vanuatu). When I asked what they do if a chief misbehaves, the villagers looked nonplussed. 'We've never had a problem, but I guess the village would meet to discuss the problem and work it out'. When money arrives from outside organizations, the chiefs ask for volunteers to manage it, rather than do so themselves.

The balance between formal and customary systems is constantly evolving, according to former Minister for Lands Ralph Regenvanu: 'It's organic and fluid. The chiefs have agreed that rape, murder, incest, and theft that is large scale or from foreigners should be dealt with by the police, partly because it is too divisive, and partly because they can no longer apply traditional sanctions (killing the perpetrators)'.[15] In contrast, the management of land seems to be ever more in the chiefs' hands, not least because Ralph pushed through legislation to strengthen the customary system.

---

[14] World Bank, *World Development Report 2006. Equity and Development* (New York: Oxford University Press, 2005).

[15] Author Interview, November 2015.

The formal system of police, courts, government, and parliament is tightly interwoven with the traditional chief system. For example, when riots threatened to break out over the management of the Vanuatu National Provident Fund, the police sent for the local chiefs to calm people down. But they each govern according to different worldviews: the chief system focuses on the collective, whereas the formal system privileges the rights of the individual. Customary law is often about making peace and reconciliation, rather than establishing guilt and redress.

Outsiders tend to over-romanticize customary systems, which are just as prone as any other to imbalances of power. I was told that some of the more 'political chiefs' are using the land reform to grab more land for themselves, and that women's rights are routinely violated. According to Merilyn Tahi of the Vanuatu Women's Center, in reconciliation processes arising from domestic violence cases, compensation 'is often paid to the family rather than the women who have been abused.... We should make peace between communities, but women victims need [formal] courts.'[16]

Combining customary and formal systems

The Mystery of Capital[17] by Peruvian economist Hernando de Soto is where I first learned how porous the border between 'modern' and 'customary' legal systems can be. Its subtitle is 'Why Capitalism triumphs in the West, and fails everywhere else' and the back cover carries an endorsement by Margaret Thatcher. But one of its core arguments is, to my mind, progressive (systems thinking rarely sits easily on the Left–Right spectrum). In the most successful economies, property rights emerged organically from social practice and customary laws, not through imposition by experts or central government. De Soto argues that today's US property laws are essentially based on the 'extralegal' practices of its early settlers and

---

[16] Author Interview, November 2015.
[17] Hernando de Soto, *The Mystery of Capital: Why Capitalism Triumphs in the West and Fails Everywhere Else* (New York: Basic Books, 2000).

wildcat miners, and those roots in the daily reality of its citizens are one reason why they have proved so durable.

More broadly, de Soto points out that English legal traditions, now in use across the English-speaking world, evolved out of customary systems (known as 'common law'). In contrast, Spanish and French legal traditions, (in use throughout their former colonies), were imposed from above, ignoring local customary law or other traditions. Essentially, de Soto is saying we should see the Law as an evolving complex system, rather than a fixed entity.

This kind of systemic approach to the law is starting to show results. Efforts by aid donors to bring peace to the arid pastoralist areas of Northern Kenya, which is dogged by violence, combine elements of formal and customary law in a hybrid approach by creating 'peace committees' to resolve conflicts where the formal legal system has failed. In many pastoralist societies conflicts between individuals are perceived to be the responsibility of larger kin groups, who feel obliged to take matters into their own hands. The payment of compensation is a common means of re-establishing peace, reinforcing the social contract both within and between groups, something the formal courts do not recognize.

Peace Committees, formed with the support of NGOs and donors, have sought to institutionalize and regulate this customary approach to conflict resolution. With the participation of local authorities, the committees have drafted detailed declarations, which act as a local system of regulation for the district—in essence locally generated laws. The committees have proved effective and have spread rapidly across the region, but as in Vanuatu there are downsides, born of disparities of power: one declaration stated that the death of a man should be compensated by 100 cows or camels, while the death of a woman is valued at only fifty cows or camels.[18]

---

[18] Caroline Sage, Nicholas Menzies, and Michael Woolcock, *Taking the Rules of the Game Seriously: Mainstreaming Justice in Development—the World Bank's Justice for the Poor Program*, Justice & Development Working Paper Series, 7/2009 (Washington DC: The World Bank, 2009).

While the change potential of hybrid approaches is huge, activists who wish to engage with such endeavours should take note of both the good and the bad sides of the Kenya story, avoiding both 'West-is-Best' bias and naive romanticism about the workings of customary systems. In either system and in hybrids, the key is to understand how power operates and how it can be redistributed to benefit those currently excluded.

International law

I have always been a little sceptical of the phrase 'international law', because it seems to carry a misleading sense of solidity. How can a set of rules and agreements to regulate the behaviour of states (rather than individuals) be considered 'law' when the international system rarely can muster anything resembling police, courts, or sanctions to force states to comply? Power to and power over seem largely absent.

But even though international law may not often be backed by force, it does shape and constrain behaviour and promote a wider sense of how states should behave. If thousands of interactions between nation states pass without a hitch every day, trade is conducted, contracts and rights respected, we have international law to thank.

Some international law is 'hard law', enforceable in courts with fines or sentences. The International Criminal Court and (to a lesser extent) the WTO have the power to enforce their decisions with fines and sanctions. Other international commitments are enshrined in conventions and treaties that can be subsequently incorporated into enforceable national law. At the softest end of the spectrum are aspirational statements and promises like the Sustainable Development Goals agreed at the UN in 2015, which may have some 'teeth' in the shape of reporting requirements, but do not require changes to national legislation.

Like its national counterpart, international law is often designed for, and used by, the powerful. One example is the proliferation of

Investor-State Dispute Settlement (ISDS) mechanisms.[19] In January 2016, the TransCanada energy company went to court to claim that the Obama administration's failure to approve the Keystone XL pipeline violated US obligations under the North American Free Trade Agreement (NAFTA). The company demanded $15 billion in compensation from US taxpayers.[20]

The fact that the US has never lost a NAFTA case shows how power influences the workings of international law. Not only can the US hire vast teams of the best lawyers, it can bring other pressures to bear on weaker countries and on international tribunals. The rules are not meaningless, but nor are they entirely neutral. ISDS mechanisms are a very contentious issue in recent free trade negotiations, like the Trans-Pacific Partnership (TPP) or the Transatlantic Trade and Investment Partnership (TTIP, between the US and EU).[21]

Activists can also use international law in a variety of more progressive ways, whether to buttress litigation or to press for changes to national legislation and public attitudes. As noted in Chapter 3, international law can help promote norm changes, when it is taken up by grassroots movements.

The 1989 Convention on the Rights of the Child (CRC), also discussed in Chapter 3, obliges ratifying governments to protect children from discrimination, to ensure that their best interests are of primary consideration in policy making, to ensure their survival and development, and remarkably to 'assure to the child who is capable of forming his or her own views the right to express those views freely in all matters affecting the child.' The CRC rapidly proved something of a phenomenon in international law, becoming the most widely and

[19] See http://investmentpolicyhub.unctad.org/ISDS for an interactive map of ISDS cases.
[20] Todd Tucker, 'TransCanada is suing the U.S. over Obama's rejection of the Keystone XL pipeline. The U.S. might lose', Monkey Cage blog, *Washington Post*, 8 January, 2016.
[21] Todd Tucker, 'TransCanada is Suing the U.S. Over Obama's Rejection of the Keystone XL Pipeline. The U.S. Might Lose', Monkey Cage blog, *The Washington Post*, 8 January 2016.

107

rapidly ratified human rights treaty in history. Only three countries, Somalia, South Sudan, and the US, have not ratified.[22]

By the time I arrived in Latin America and the Caribbean a few years later, ratification had triggered a spate of new 'children's codes', such as Brazil's Child and Adolescent Statute (ECA), and child rights bodies like Peru's Demunas (Municipal Ombudsman for Children and Adolescents). Most progress was achieved (both in law and, more importantly, in the lives of children) where domestic movements of children and their supporters were strong enough to put pressure on governments from below, to match the pressure from above exerted by the existence of the Convention. Across the region, I had hundreds of conversations with activists, both children and adults, who were using the CRC as the basis for their campaigns.

The December 2015 Paris Agreement on climate change provoked a fascinating conversation on the capacity of international law to address complex problems such as reducing carbon emissions. Some thought the agreement's lack of binding targets were a sign of its weakness, since only a binding document can be enforced by courts and arbitration tribunals. By contrast, Anne-Marie Slaughter, Hilary Clinton's right-hand woman during her period in the State Department, sees Paris as a 'model for effective global governance in the twenty-first century'.[23]

Slaughter argues that the new agreement 'substitutes transparency for compliance' and that is a good thing. The commitments in a legally binding treaty would be permanent, which in practice would lock in the lowest common denominator. Paris agreed a process of review that opens the door to ratcheting up emissions targets over time, and which can be adapted to new evidence, opinion, and national

---

[22] Human Rights Watch, '25th Anniversary of the Convention on the Rights of the Child', 17 November 2014, www.hrw.org/news/2014/11/17/25th-anniversary-convention-rights-child.

[23] Anne-Marie Slaughter, 'The Paris Approach to Global Governance', Project Syndicate website, 28 December 2015, www.project-syndicate.org/commentary/paris-agreement-model-for-global-governance-by-anne-marie-slaughter-2015-12.

circumstances. I discuss this in a case study on the Paris Agreement as a change process on pages 171–175.

Some legal scholars view the remorseless spread of international law, both in scale and the range of issues it covers, as 'the precursor of international government'.[24] Like Gulliver being tied down by the Lilliputians' threads,[25] the web of international law has grown and already exerts a surprising level of discipline on national governments. It has done so in a de Soto-esque fashion, expanding and evolving from its roots in the conduct of war and diplomacy to include trade, environment, and human rights. Its future will be shaped not only by the powers that be, but also by activists who find ways to use it to promote progressive change.

The law as a system

Like many institutions that at first sight appear fixed and monolithic, the law is a system in constant flux. Not only are old laws replaced by new, but the interpretation of laws evolves, including the weight assigned to customary systems. In the words of renowned US Supreme Court Justice Oliver Wendell Holmes, 'The law embodies the story of a nation's development through many centuries, and it cannot be dealt with as if it contained only the axioms and corollaries of a book of mathematics'.[26]

It seems sometimes evolutionary tides are not bound by national borders. In much of Africa and Latin America, the 1990s saw the end of a twenty-year period in which the state had reigned supreme, largely untroubled by legal constraints, swept aside in part by an international surge in interest in rights-based approaches and inter-national human rights law.

[24] Joel Trachtman, *The Future of International Law: Global Government* (New York: Cambridge University Press, 2013).
[25] Jonathan Swift, *Gulliver's Travels* (London: Benjamin Motte, 1726).
[26] Oliver Wendell Holmes, *The Common Law* (Boston: Little, Brown and Company, 1881), p. 1.

A new generation of rights-based constitutional reforms were enacted, like Costa Rica's in 1989, which gave international human rights treaties the same force as domestic law. Constitutional courts in South Africa, Colombia, and elsewhere were set up to oversee new constitutions, becoming lightning rods for legal activism. Colombia's constitutional court heard 800,000 cases on the right to healthcare between 1999 and 2009 and ended up ordering the systematic restructuring of the country's health system because, despite previous legislation calling for universal coverage and other improvements, the government had failed to act.[27]

Some legal systems remain rigid and inflexible and, like the old forest systems discussed in Chapter 1, exhibit periods of sclerosis punctuated by periods of violent disruption and upheaval. But ever more of them have grown malleable, able to adapt to the evolving distribution of power, interests, and norms in their changing societies. In what some lawyers call a 'legal social justice revolution', progressive lawyers around the world recognized that the law is not an immovable institution, and began the slow process of harnessing the law to promote human rights and equality and to address privilege and discrimination. As a result, the law has evolved from a musty, rigid defender of the status quo (especially those aspects that reinforced power and inequality) to an active player in creating and recreating the society in which we live.

Conclusion

There is a character in Shakespeare's *Henry VI* who declares 'The first thing we do, let's kill all the lawyers.'[28] However tempting, I think he's wrong. I now understand why so many activists, especially in the US, are (or want to become) lawyers.

[27] Alicia Ely Yamin and Siri Gloppen, *Litigating Health Rights* (Cambridge, MA: Harvard University Press, 2011), p. 343.
[28] William Shakespeare, *Henry The Sixth, Part 2*, Act 4, scene 2, 71–8.

The legal system, like any institution, is not a level playing field. The rich and powerful can hire better lawyers, can lobby law makers, and generally get a better deal. But not always—if people organize, build the right coalitions, and pursue the right argument and tactics, laws and lawyers can bite back, governments and Big Men can lose cases.

The law will remain an essential weapon in the armoury of activists around the world. In the ever-expanding realm of national and international law, unexplored avenues abound. Oxfam lawyers are currently investigating whether climate change litigation could follow the path of tobacco, and my guess is that obesity and road traffic accidents will one day follow. The challenge will be to build bridges between legal activism and other efforts to influence the system, since the two worlds are often divided by impatience, different theories of change, or the chasm of language.

Now that we have examined the administrative and legal systems, the next chapter will explore the third area of the state in Fukuyama's schema—the institutions that provide accountability.

Further Reading

T. Bingham, *The Rule of Law* (London: Allen Lane, 2010).

T. Carothers, ed., *Promoting the Rule of Law Abroad: In Search of Knowledge* (Washington DC, Carnegie Endowment for International Peace, 2006).

V. Gauri and D. Brinks, eds., *Courting Social Justice: Judicial Enforcement of Social and Economic Rights in the Developing World* (New York: Cambridge University Press, 2008).

R. Kleinfeld, *Advancing the Rule of Law Abroad: Next Generation Reform* (Washington DC, Carnegie Endowment for International Peace, 2012).

B. Tamanaha, *On the Rule of Law: History, Politics, Theory* (Cambridge: Cambridge University Press, 2005).

UNDP, *Making the Law Work for Everyone*. Volume 1. Report of the Commission on Legal Empowerment of the Poor (New York: Commission on Legal Empowerment of the poor/United Nations Development Programme, 2008).

J.A. Widner, *Building the Rule of Law: Francis Nyalali and the Road to Judicial Independence in Africa* (New York: WW Norton, 2001).

6

ACCOUNTABILITY, POLITICAL PARTIES, AND THE MEDIA

It's hard to imagine a more precious timeslot in a politician's calendar than three days before a general election, yet the May 2015 'Citizens' Assembly' in a cavernous London church hall attracted two of the UK's three main party leaders, while the governing Conservatives fielded a high-level stand-in for David Cameron. The politicians submitted themselves to being grilled before 2,500 activists from Citizens UK, a community organization. The audience was a kaleidoscope of multicultural Britain, drawn from faith groups, schools, networks of asylum seekers and refugees, and other grassroots institutions. There was no favouritism: each politician was allowed just four minutes each to make their pitch and they were then cross-examined in detail. Vague or evasive answers were challenged, promises were extracted, and the politicians ended up making extra commitments under pressure from the crowd.[1]

For Francis Fukuyama, accountability means that 'the rulers believe that they are responsible to the people they govern, and put the people's interests above their own'.[2] I would add that accountability also means that the population and institutions of civil society hold significant power and can exact redress when duties and

---

[1] Duncan Green, 'Active Citizens Holding Britain's Politicians to Account—Why Can't the Rest of the UK Election Campaign be More Like This?', From Poverty to Power blog, 6 May 2015, http://oxfamblogs.org/fp2p/active-citizens-holding-britains-politicians-to-account-why-isnt-the-rest-of-the-uk-election-campaign-more-like-this/.

[2] Francis Fukuyama, *The Origins of Political Order: From Prehuman Times to the French Revolution* (New York: Farrar, Straus and Giroux, 2011), p. 321.

commitments are not met.[3] Accountability is the glue that constitutes the social contract between citizen and state, which is desirable in itself because having a voice contributes to wellbeing, as well as being a practical means to drive progressive change.

In aid and official development, however, accountability is often framed much more narrowly in terms of being accountable for the results promised in a particular project, or 'upwards accountability' to donors, which often takes precedence over 'downwards accountability' to citizens.

Some observers equate accountability with democratic elections, but it is a pressing issue in democratic and non-democratic systems alike. This chapter discusses political parties and the media as two crucial institutions that provide avenues for accountability, as well as the burgeoning field of 'social accountability', in both elected and unelected regimes. All three provide valuable channels for activists to hold those in power to account for their decisions.

Political parties as drivers of change

Citizens UK's deliberate and energetic engagement with political parties, especially Right wing ones, is comparatively rare for activist organizations. Development thinkers pay parties scant attention, and aid organizations tend to discount their importance. Few activists take the time to understand and engage with the labyrinth of committees, networks, and debates through which political parties influence the decisions made by those in office.

I sympathize because, in my experience, even progressive parties can be pretty unappealing. I was briefly a Labour Party member in the late 1980s, but found it focused on procedures and structures, and dominated by local government employees who seemed solely

---

[3] Transparency Initiative website, 'Accountability—Definitions', www.transparency-initiative.org/about/definitions.

concerned with conserving their jobs. When my first baby came, I quietly dropped the mind-numbing tedium of party meetings.

I now think that was short-sighted, because familiarity with the complex world of party histories, cultures, structures, and decision making is an essential part of understanding (and influencing) how change happens. However dull, political parties are the clutch in the engine of politics, linking citizens to government. They reconcile and represent the interests and viewpoints of numerous individuals and groups in society; they recruit and train future leaders; and above all, they hold government accountable and organize opposition.[4] In national parliaments, provincial assemblies, and town councils, parties propose, debate, and scrutinize legislation and the actions of central government. And they really come into their own at election time, fielding candidates and marshalling votes.

Democracy based on universal suffrage and political parties is relatively recent, in historical terms. The American Constitution makes no provision for parties and many of the Founding Fathers were hostile to the idea that they should come to govern the country. George Washington warned in his farewell address of 'the baneful effects of the Spirit of Party; a conflict that would divide and potentially destroy the new nation'. His Successor John Adams argued that 'a division of the republic into two great parties...is to be dreaded as the greatest political evil under our Constitution.'[5]

In 1900, New Zealand was the world's only country with a government elected by all its adult citizens. Since then, democratically elected government has spread in successive waves, most recently since the fall of the Berlin Wall. By 2014, Freedom House, a conservative US think tank, classified 125 of the world's 196 countries as electoral

[4] Vicky Randall, 'Political Parties and Democratic Developmental States', *Development Policy Review* 25, no. 5 (2007): pp. 633–52, http://onlinelibrary.wiley.com/doi/10.1111/j.1467-7679.2007.00389.x/pdf.
[5] Francis Fukuyama, *Political Order and Political Decay: From the Industrial Revolution to the Globalization of Democracy* (New York: Farrar, Straus and Giroux, 2014), p. 140.

democracies, compared to only sixty-nine in 1990.[6] In the first twelve years of this century, elections were held in all but five countries with populations over half a million (the holdouts were China, Eritrea, Qatar, Saudi Arabia, and United Arab Emirates).[7]

The parties that contest power in today's democracies come in a bewildering range of shapes and sizes. Some are 'Toyota' parties, whose leaders and followers could fit into a single car; others are mass-based organizations with thousands of organizers. Some represent the interests of just a few wealthy businessmen; others speak for millions of impoverished and marginalized people.[8] Some grew out of social movements, whether religious (India's Bharatiya Janata Party/ BJP, Europe's Christian Democrats, the Middle East's Islamist parties) or social (Bolivia's Movement to Socialism/MAS, Brazil's Workers Party/PT). Others were set up by a government already in power (Mexico's Partido Revolucionario Institucional and the various phantom opposition parties it created). Some draw on ethnic or regional affiliation (many of Kenya's parties) or are personal vehicles for charismatic leaders (Argentina's Peronists, Thailand's Thai Rak Thai).[9]

Parties that emerge from social movements, trade unions, and other organizations of the poor have been responsible for some inspiring breakthroughs in South Africa, Brazil, Bolivia, India, and elsewhere. A recent example is India's Aam Aadmi Party (AAP, or the 'Common Man's Party'), which grew out of an anti-corruption protest sparked by a 2011 hunger strike by a renowned and self-consciously Gandhian

[6] Arch Puddington, 'Discarding Democracy: A Return to the Iron Fist', Freedom House website, https://freedomhouse.org/report/freedom-world-2015/discarding-democracy-return-iron-fist.

[7] Duncan Green, '10 Killer Facts on Democracy and Elections', From Poverty to Power blog, 12 July 2013, https://oxfamblogs.org/fp2p/10-killer-facts-on-democracy-and-elections/.

[8] Thomas Carothers, *Confronting the Weakest Link: Aiding Political Parties in New Democracies* (Washington DC: Carnegie Endowment for International Peace, 2006).

[9] Vicky Randall, 'Political Parties and Democratic Developmental States', *Development Policy Review* 25, no. 5 (2007): pp. 633–52, http://onlinelibrary.wiley.com/doi/10.1111/j.1467-7679.2007.00389.x/pdf.

protestor named Anna Hazare.[10] His action helped force the introduction of anti-corruption legislation, but the movement lost momentum
and media interest in the energy-sapping labyrinths of parliamentary
procedure. Other leaders then recast the movement as a political party
to mobilize for the longer-term grind of political reform. In 2013,
barely a year after its founding, the AAP came second in the Delhi
Assembly elections, and in 2015 it won sixty-seven out of seventy
assembly seats.

Social movements organize as parties because as movements they
tend to rise and fall in sudden bursts of protest and can rarely muster
the long-term engagement with the state required to achieve lasting
change. What's more, civil society organizations find it hard to make
any legitimate claim to represent the will of the people because no-one
has elected them. However, many activists argue that playing the
electoral game entails compromises that inevitably tarnish the clarity
of the message and the moral legitimacy of a protest movement and
lays it open to betrayal by leaders seduced by political opportunism.
Such tensions obliged leaders to break with Anna Hazare to found the
AAP, and have dogged South Africa's African National Congress/
ANC, Brazil's PT, and Bolivia's MAS, all of which emerged from
coalitions of social movements and came to rule the country.

Political parties often follow a cycle of birth, growth, and decay.
A charismatic new leader bursts onto the scene, or a social movement
turns itself into a clean, inspiring new party, and supporters rally to
the flag of a new kind of politics. The AAP, like Podemos in Spain or
Syriza in Greece, has shown huge mobilizing power and a commitment to a new way of doing politics: non-hierarchical, internally
democratic, financially transparent, and free of big money or dynasty
politics. But it proves remarkably hard to maintain that coherence and

---

[10] Prashant Sharma, 'From India Against Corruption to the Aam Aadmi Party: Social
Movements, Political Parties and Citizen Engagement in India', in *Political Parties and Citizen
Movements in Asia and Europe*, edited by Raul Cordenillo and Sam van der Staak (Singapore:
Asia-Europe Foundation, Hanns Seidel Foundation and International Institute for Democracy
and Electoral Assistance, 2014).

dynamism. Most of them must make difficult choices and undertake compromises that contribute to an eventual decline in their support.

Brazil's Workers Party (PT) was founded by independent trade unions, social movements, and others in 1980, initially to protest against military rule, then to turn civil society demands into a long-term political programme. Led by the charismatic union leader José Ignacio da Silva (known to all as Lula), the party won municipal elections and, after several narrow defeats, the national vote in 2003.

The PT brought an exhilarating burst of energy and legitimacy into an otherwise stagnant political system. Within a few years in power, it achieved real progress for Brazil's poor, including substantial reductions in hunger, poverty, and inequality.[11] But over the next decade the compromises required to pass legislation (e.g. using 'incentives' to steer laws through an opposition-dominated Congress[12]) brought an inevitable loss of mobilizing power. The logic of government took over from that of protest and community mobilization, eroding the very things that made the PT different. By 2014, Lula had stepped down, citizens were protesting against the PT government and its approval ratings were plummeting.

The churn of the political party system is both an opportunity and a threat for activists and our organizations. Understand and engage with it, and we can influence current and future governments, reaching far more people than an activist organization can ever hope to alone. Parties can be long-term institutional homes for policies and ideas, in contrast to the peaks and troughs of activist movements. But there are trade-offs. The election of progressive parties often leads to a dip in broader social activism as progressive governments and parties siphon leaders and activists from NGOs and social movements, while urging them to 'leave it to us'. That is often a risky move as

---

[11] Sue Branford and Jan Rocha, *Brazil Under the Workers' Party: From Euphoria to Despair* (Rugby, UK: Practical Action Publishing, 2015).

[12] Mathew M. Taylor, 'Police detained Brazil's ex-president on Friday. Here's what you need to know', *Washington Post*, Monkey Cage blog, 5 March 2016.

even progressive parties need to be kept honest by activists to prevent the compromises and temptations of office from diluting their initial impetus. Like Citizens UK at its London Assembly, activists need to maintain our ability to criticize and oppose if we are to advocate effectively for poor and excluded people.

Patronage and corruption

In the early days of the PT's road to power, in 1986, Chico Mendes, the Brazilian rubber-tappers' leader who became a global environmental hero, ran as a candidate for state deputy. A memorable film shows him strolling down the main street in his home town of Xapuri, greeting his many friends and acquaintances. A stream of local people come up to ask how much he is paying for votes. When he explains he has no money, they wander off, bemused. He lost the election.[13]

The workings of the hidden and invisible power of vested interests and powerful ideas and social norms mean that parties that stand for a particular political, economic, and social programme are obliged to operate in a world dominated by very different beasts: parties designed to achieve power and influence for one or more Big Men, which use patronage to reward supporters and bind them to the leader. Of course, all parties are to some degree both personalist and programmatic, but the distinction remains useful.

Personalist parties are ubiquitous, perhaps reflecting Francis Fukuyama's argument that, in evolutionary terms, kin and family usually come before any other form of personal loyalty.[14] Among many voters (including those in Europe and North America), the strength of ethnic, tribal, regional, or religious identities trumps ideology.[15] Personalist,

---

[13] Duncan Green, *Faces of Latin America* (London: Latin America Bureau, 1991), p. 104.

[14] Francis Fukuyama, *The Origins of Political Order: From Prehuman Times to the French Revolution* (New York: Farrar, Straus and Giroux, 2011).

[15] Matthew Lockwood, however, argues that rapid decolonization meant that the new generation of independence leaders did not have time to build more programmatic parties.

patronage-based parties make a mockery of platforms and policy positions as party hacks shop around for the best deal. According to one study of Kenya: 'nearly all party manifestos look alike, often using the same phraseology, and even identical paragraphs.'[16]

In Argentina Peronist presidents seem to be able to convince their followers to support entirely contradictory policies, from free market liberalization (Carlos Menem) to state intervention (Néstor, then Cristina Kirchner). In Brazil, around a third of legislators in the Chamber of Deputies switch party during each four-year term in search of personal advantage, whether political or financial.[17] Patronage politics also makes it easier for new entrants to create parties, provided they have enough wealth and power to buy support. The developing world in particular has seen an accelerating rate of party 'churn': instead of relatively stable party systems, new parties linked to particular candidates rise and fall each election, a phenomenon encouraged by widespread disenchantment with their more traditional rivals.

The currency of patronage is jobs and cash, memorably summed up by Michela Wrong in the title of her book, *It's Our Turn to Eat*.[18] An election brings a new set of snouts to the trough, as resources are siphoned off from government budgets and unqualified supporters are rewarded with government jobs.

The widespread problems of corruption and patronage are compounded by something I have always found baffling: the apparent inability of countries to establish a fair and transparent system of party and campaign financing. At \$6 billion (\$51 per vote cast), the 2012 US

Matthew Lockwood, *The State They're in: An Agenda for International Action on Poverty in Africa* (London: ITDG Publishing, 2005).

[16] Vicky Randall, 'Political Parties and Democratic Developmental States', *Development Policy Review* 25, no. 5 (2007): pp. 633–52, http://onlinelibrary.wiley.com/doi/10.1111/j.1467-7679.2007.00389.x/pdf.

[17] Vicky Randall, 'Political Parties and Democratic Developmental States', *Development Policy Review* 25, no. 5 (2007): pp. 633–52, http://onlinelibrary.wiley.com/doi/10.1111/j.1467-7679.2007.00389.x/pdf.

[18] Michela Wrong, *It's Our Turn to Eat: The Story of a Kenyan Whistleblower* (London: HarperCollins Publishers, 2009).

elections cost 120 times more than the UK 2010 vote ($50 million, $1.68 per vote cast). Even the violence-scarred 2007 elections in Kenya cost $10 million ($1.01 per vote cast). By some estimates, the total expenditure across all political parties in the 2009 Indian national election was US$3 billion ($7.20 per vote cast).[19] This is big money, and in the absence of state funding for political parties or election campaigns, the prospect of elections sparks a frenetic hustle to raise cash. In such circumstances a relatively small amount of money can buy an inordinate degree of political influence.

In some countries, leaders have apparently perfected the art of organizing superficially competitive elections, without actually letting go of the reins of power.[20] Some are more blatant than others: in 2015 Kazakhstan's President Nursultan Nazarbayev was re-elected with 97.7 per cent of the vote, on a 95 per cent turnout. The 'point 7' is a particularly nice touch, I think.[21]

Since 2000, only fourteen of fifty-one states in Sub-Saharan Africa have seen power transferred between political parties.[22] You might think that the sight of political parties and leaders clinging doggedly to power would boost support for opposition parties. In fact, the opposite appears to be the case. The Afrobarometer public opinion research firm found that while 56 per cent of respondents across eighteen countries said they trusted ruling parties 'somewhat' or 'a lot,' only 36 per cent said the same about opposition parties. Opposition

[19] Prashant Sharma, 'From India Against Corruption to the Aam Aadmi Party: Social Movements, Political Parties and Citizen Engagement in India', in *Political Parties and Citizen Movements in Asia and Europe*, edited by Raul Cordenillo and Sam van der Staak (Singapore: Asia-Europe Foundation, Hanns Seidel Foundation and International Institute for Democracy and Electoral Assistance, 2014).

[20] Vera Songwe, 'From Strong Men to Strong Institutions: An Assessment of Africa's Transition Towards More Political Contestability', Africa in Focus, Brookings, 4 August 2015, www.brookings.edu/blogs/africa-in-focus/posts/2015/08/04-africa-transitions-songwe.

[21] Aditya Tejas, 'Kazakhstan President Nursultan Nazarbayev Reelected with 98% Majority Vote', *International Business Times*, 27 April 2015, www.ibtimes.com/kazakhstan-president-nursultan-nazarbayev-reelected-98-majority-vote-1897642.

[22] Alina Rocha Menocal, 'Ten things to know about democracy and elections', ODI, 2013.

parties were in fact the least trusted institution among the thirteen Afrobarometer asked about.

Moreover, while 71 per cent agreed that the news media 'should constantly investigate and report on corruption and the mistakes made by government', they rejected a similar role for opposition parties. A clear majority (60 per cent) said that after elections, opposition parties should essentially set aside their differences and 'concentrate on cooperating with government and helping it develop the country.' Just 35 per cent thought the opposition should 'regularly examine and criticize government policies and actions' and hold it to account.

Afrobarometer concluded:

> This finding raised questions about how Africans understand the very concept of 'opposition.' There seems to be something of a paradox. Africans clearly support elections as a way of choosing their leaders, and they want to have real choices when they go to the polls. Yet they appear to be uncomfortable with what this means on a daily basis, with the push and pull of politics that is part and parcel of a competitive party system.[23]

Parties and women

To do a decent job of representing citizens, political parties need to reflect their societies, yet the workings of social norms and 'invisible power' meant that they seldom do so. Nowhere is this more true than in the case of women, who have traditionally been marginalized both in internal party power structures, and places in parliaments. As of 2016, women occupied only 22 per cent of parliamentary seats world-wide. Only two countries in the world (Rwanda and Bolivia) had a majority of women in parliament.[24,25]

[23] Carolyn Logan, 'What Ails the Opposition in Africa?', Afrobarometer blog, 4 September 2015, http://afrobarometer.org/blogs/blog-what-ails-opposition-africa.

[24] 'Women in National Parliaments', Situation as of 1 December 2015, Inter-Parliamentary Union website, www.ipu.org/wmn-e/classif.htm.

[25] 'Latest News', Inter-Parliamentary Union website, www.ipu.org/wmn-e/world.htm.

Driven by changing social norms on the roles and rights of women, backed by dedicated activism, that picture has started to change in recent decades. Electoral quotas to try and even up the balance have been introduced in half the countries in the world, with knock-on effects on the internal procedures of many political parties.[26]

One of the pioneers has been India, where in 1992 the Government ruled that at least a third of the seats of all local councils (panchayats) and a third of panchayat leadership seats would be reserved for women. Research a decade later showed that panchayats headed by women were spending more on issues that women had identified as a priority, such as drinking water.[27]

Once elected, women representatives can face isolation and marginalization in male-dominated systems, and can benefit from support and the establishment of networks with other women in similar positions. In Cambodia, Oxfam persuaded a mobile phone operator to equip women community leaders with mobile phones so they could stay in touch with each other (the few women leaders felt very isolated). The neat touch was making sure the phones were pink, so the men wouldn't 'borrow' them.[28]

The Aurat Foundation in Pakistan convenes 'Women's Leadership Groups' in thirty districts across the country, with a total membership of 1,500 women activists. Part of their mandate is to encourage these women to become active in political parties, and in May 2013 six WLG women were elected to provincial assemblies (five in Punjab and one in Sindh), while one became a member of the National Assembly. Working with other civil society organizations, the WLGs and Aurat Foundation developed a 'women's manifesto' for those elections,

[26] Quota Project, 'About Quotas', Global Database of Quotas for Women, www.quotaproject.org/aboutQuotas.cfm.

[27] Lori Beaman, Raghabendra Chattopadhyay, Esther Duflo, Rohini Pande and Petia Topalova, *The Impact of Women Policy Makers on Public Goods in India* (Cambridge, MA: J-PAL, Abdul Latif Jameel Poverty Action Lab), www.povertyactionlab.org/evaluation/impact-women-policy-makers-public-goods-india.

[28] The Pink Phone Project, 'Empowering Cambodian Women Through Mobile Technology', 14 September 2011, www.youtube.com/watch?v=MPEmDXsakBk.

listing the minimum acceptable requirements of political party engagement on women's empowerment. The manifesto and accompanying campaign reached both national media and inner circles of influence, achieving a high level of 'buy in' from political parties.[29]

Parties in non-democratic systems

In one party states, parties are part of the apparatus of command and control, but they are also the eyes and ears of governments that, in the absence of open elections, need alternative feedback systems about their effectiveness (or otherwise) and potential threats to social cohesion or political legitimacy.

Parties thus play an active and constantly evolving role in many non-democracies. The best known is the Chinese Communist Party's role in China's extraordinary transition to 'state capitalism' over the last forty years, but East Asia has other examples. The Communist Party of Viet Nam (CPV) has been the ruling party in the north of the country since 1954 and the only party in power in Viet Nam since unification in 1976.

Since the late 1980s turn towards a market economy, the CPV has gone through significant internal changes, including more open elections for senior members of its leadership. These changes were influenced by an emerging civil society and by the rise of a new social class of wealthy entrepreneurs linked to a segment of high-ranking party officials.

Vietnamese scholar Hai Hong Nguyen argues that 'the CPV is 'motivated more by the desire to survive and avoid Tahrir Square-type events than by a true belief in democratic reform'.[30] Yet party

[29] Duncan Green, 'The Raising Her Voice Pakistan Programme' (Oxford: Oxfam International, 2015).

[30] Hai Hong Nguyen, 'Political Parties, Civil Society and Citizen Movements in Viet Nam', in Political Parties and Citizen Movements in Asia and Europe, edited by Raul Cordenillo and Sam van der Staak (Singapore: Asia-Europe Foundation, Hanns Seidel Foundation and International Institute for Democracy and Electoral Assistance, 2014).

reform has opened opportunities for activists to exert influence, even if Viet Nam remains a one-party state.

The Provincial Governance and Public Administration Performance Index (PAPI)[31] ranks local government performance all over Viet Nam, using local researchers to interview a large, carefully selected sample on their experience in areas such as health and education, the level of petty corruption, and participation. In the words of one of the organizers, Giang Dang, 'When VietNam opened up, the two things that arrived first were beauty contests and Coca Cola. So we decided to organize beauty contests. Most opposition came from the contestants in the beauty contest—the public servants.'[32]

According to Giang Dang, 'higher ranking provinces are keen to keep their position and feature their ranking in all their documents. Some of the lower ranking provinces are starting to set up task forces, and asking us for advice on how to improve performance.'

The secret of PAPI's success lies in the way it actively recruits champions inside the system. Its advisory board has representatives from the National Assembly, ministries, government inspectorates and academia. The Vietnam Fatherland Front (VFF), a mass organization of the CPV, supports the project and opens doors all the way down to commune level.

The CPV's attitude to PAPI underlines the importance of legitimacy and social cohesion in one-party systems. Like most governments, dictatorships are keenly aware of the ups and downs of their legitimacy in the eyes of their citizens and especially their economic elites, and are willing to consider change when loss of legitimacy could threaten their survival. In the case of the CPV, the party knows the poor performance of local government is a threat to its dominance, so

---

[31] The Viet Nam Provincial Governance and Public Administration Performance Index, http://papi.vn/en/index.html.

[32] Presentation to seminar on 'Active Citizenship in Asia', Bangkok, September 2012, http://oxfamblogs.org/fp2p/building-active-citizenship-and-accountability-in-asia-case-studies-from-vietnam-and-india/.

it supports improved accountability via the index, even though it occurs outside party channels.

Party platforms as venues for change

Activists often seek to have their issues incorporated into party platforms, so that if the party is elected they can push for government action. The kinds of questions set out in the power and systems approach, exploring issues of power, precedent, possible strategies, and critical junctures, can be useful in shaping our influencing efforts, as this example from India shows.

India's landmark 2005 National Rural Employee Guarantee Act (NREGA), which guarantees all rural citizens 100 days of unskilled employment per year on public works programmes, came about due to a combination of determined citizen activism and the fortunes of the Congress Party.

In response to drought and rural distress, civil society networks in the state of Rajasthan submitted a petition to the Supreme Court in 2001 on the 'Right to Food', which received favourable interim directives. Encouraged, they drafted a Rajasthan State Employment Guarantee Act in 2003, though it did not garner support from Congress or other parties.

The 2003 legislative assembly elections opened a political window of opportunity, because the Congress Party suffered a demoralizing loss in Rajasthan and other states, leading most to believe it had no chance in the 2004 general election. Impending political defeat weakened the resistance of fiscal conservatives in the Congress leadership and the employment guarantee was included in the 2004 Congress national manifesto.

When the party won a surprise victory that year, the leadership needed to rapidly cobble together a programme. The employment guarantee was not only ready to go, but removing it would have endangered its coalition with Left-wing parties. Still, getting agreement on such a far-reaching initiative still took a determined campaign, involving a fifty-day march across the country's poorest districts, sit-in protests, direct contacts with politicians, and public hearings.[33]

Despite the Congress Party's subsequent loss of power in 2014, the scheme has continued to expand. In 2015, according to the NREGA website, it gave employment to 122 million poor people across India.[34]

The story of the NREGA offers some lessons about working with and through political parties. Activists saw that political travails had made the Congress Party open to new ideas. They developed their proposals well in advance of the critical juncture and they combined insider and outsider tactics to get it onto the platform and finally implemented. The story also demonstrates the importance of accident and luck: if the 2004 elections had gone as expected, Congress would have lost, and NREGA might well have joined the ranks of good, but failed, civil society initiatives.

The media and accountability

States may see the world through the eyes of the law, but politicians often see it through the eyes of the media, and not just any media. During my brief spell working on trade policy at the British aid ministry, DFID, whenever something appeared in the *Financial Times* about the WTO negotiations the minister would send down his special adviser to find out what was going on. Another minister reportedly set a performance target for DFID's long suffering media team for how many photos of himself they were able to place in his favourite (party aligned) newspaper. Rather more honourably, Thomas Jefferson once said (even though he was regularly vilified by the press), 'If I had to choose between government without

---

[33] Ian MacAuslan, 'India's National Rural Employment Guarantee Act: A Case Study for *How Change Happens*' (Oxford: Oxfam International, 2008).

[34] Mahatma Gandhi National Rural Employment Guarantee Act website, http://mnregaweb4.nic.in/netnrega/dynamic2/ReportGenerated.aspx.

newspapers, and newspapers without government, I wouldn't hesitate to choose the latter'.[35]

The media can echo, amplify, or substitute for citizens' voices. Governments monitor (often obsessively) their popularity, detecting unrest and threats to their legitimacy and, eventually, rule. That can be hard to achieve when cocooned in the corridors of power, and the media provides one form of feedback loop to 'what the people are thinking' (as of course does the proliferation of polls and focus groups that inform government decisions). My boss at DFID was using the *Financial Times* partly as a proxy for what was significant in the unfolding global trade talks. The lesson for me as an activist was that I needed to get better at 'using the media' (the title of one indispensable 1980s guide for activists[36]). In other words, find out what paper the minister reads, and try and get it to pick up your press release.

Governments and politicians are often rather better at this than activists, since they wield a lot more formal power and cash and fewer scruples. In the 1990s, Peru's secret-police chief Ivan Montesinos systematically bribed all the democratic checks and balances in the country—the opposition, the judiciary, a free press. Once he had fallen from power, some enterprising scholars managed to get hold of and compare the bribes he paid for different targets. They found that bribing a television channel owner cost about 100 times more than a judge or a politician. One single television channel's bribe was five times larger than the total of all opposition politicians' bribes. By revealed preference, the strongest check on the government's power was the news media (and by some distance).[37]

Since Montesinos' time, the media landscape has been transformed by technology, and with it the role of the media in accountability. In the majority of countries (there are still a few hold-outs like Eritrea and

[35] Thomas Jefferson, letter to Edward Carrington, Paris, 16 January 1787.

[36] Denis MacShane, *Using the Media: How to Deal with the Press, Television and Radio* (London: Pluto Press, 1979).

[37] John McMillan and Pablo Zoido, 'How to Subvert Democracy: Montesinos in Peru', *Journal of Economic Perspectives* 18, no. 4 (2004): pp. 69–92.

Zimbabwe), old media has fragmented and escaped the cruder forms of state ownership. Fragile states have seen the rise of 'warlord radio', media that are controlled by particular political, ethnic, religious, or military leaders and used for factionalist ends. In other fragmented societies local radio has stoked hatred, as in Kenya's post-election violence in 2008 that claimed 1,200 lives, and in the Rwandan geno-cide fourteen years earlier.[38]

Many activists place huge hopes in the power of 'new media' and its role in building accountability. For the optimists, information 'wants to be free' and will unleash a wave of citizen activism to wash away elite control of institutions and wealth on a tide of transparency and online campaigning. But tech-savvy activists often overestimate social media's importance. Old fashioned radio remains the main informa-tion source for adult Kenyans, for example, 89 per cent of whom use the radio weekly for news and information.[39]

However, nasty elites and oppressive states are rather good at monitoring social media activity and using it to track dissidents.[40] Moreover, the fragmentation of both old and new media is leading to an echo chamber effect, producing separate and parallel worlds of information, news, and analysis that can reinforce prejudice, weaken dialogue among groups, and play into the hands of those who use hate and division to consolidate their power.

I may be a tech sceptic, but I am also a compulsive blogger and tweeter, and have seen the strengths and weaknesses of social media for myself. My blog, 'From Poverty to Power',[41] gets about 300,000

---

[38] James Deane, *Fragile States: The Role of Media and Communication*, BBC Media Action Policy Briefing No. 10, (London: BBC Media Action, 2013).

[39] Paddy Coulter and Cathy Baldwin, 'Digital Deprivation: New Media, Civil Society and Sustainability', in *Civil Society in the Age of Monitory Democracy*, edited by Lars Trägårdh, Nina Witoszek, and Bron Taylor (New York and Oxford: Berghahn Books, 2013).

[40] Evgeny Morozov, *The Net Delusion: How Not to Liberate the World* (London: Allen Lane, 2011). Malcolm Gladwell, 'Small Change: Why the Revolution Will Not be Tweeted', *The New Yorker*, 4 October 2010, www.newyorker.com/magazine/2010/10/04/small-change-malcolm-gladwell.

[41] Duncan Green, From Poverty to Power blog, http://oxfamblogs.org/fp2p/.

'unique visitors' a year. That's good for a blog, but tiny compared to audiences for old media. Blogs and Twitter are essentially elitist conversations with 'people like you', but they can exert influence, both directly via the readership (mainly made up of people in the government, political parties, academia, and activist organizations) and indirectly, by influencing old media journalists who trawl blogs and Twitter in search of ideas for their next piece. For activists, social media provides a new and additional link in the web of accountability.

Overall, the evidence supports both optimists and sceptics. A study of the role of the media in four countries—Kenya, Somalia, Afghanistan, and Iraq—concluded that, in all four countries, parts of the media have strengthened ethnic and sectarian identity, especially at key moments such as elections. But some of the vernacular media in Kenya so implicated in fuelling the 2007–8 violence was also instrumental in calling for calm when the violence escalated. Somalis value only those media they can trust, and prove it by switching on or off accordingly. When the Islamist Al-Shabaab group seized power and either operated radio stations or intimidated them into broadcasting their propaganda, it struggled to attract significant audiences.[42]

The media is a complex system, whose behaviour varies over time and place, according to politics, history, culture, technology, and individuals. For activists learning to 'dance' with that system means finding out how the media works in any given setting, learning its language, timetable, and incentives. (I am in awe of Oxfam's media team's ability to put its stories into the public domain at big global moments like the annual Davos meeting of the World Economic Forum.[43])

As noted in Chapter 3, activists have used old media reality shows and soap operas to go beyond issues of short-term accountability to try and influence the underlying system of attitudes and norms.

[42] James Deane, *Fragile States: The Role of Media and Communication*, BBC Media Action Policy Briefing No. 10, (London: BBC Media Action, 2013).

[43] Oxfam press release, '62 people own same as half world – Oxfam', 16 January 2016, www.oxfam.org.uk/media-centre/press-releases/2016/01/62-people-own-same-as-half-world-says-oxfam-inequality-report-davos-world-economic-forum.

In Tanzania, a reality TV show, *Female Food Heroes*, raises awareness of the important, but often overlooked, role of its women food producers. Contestants spend three weeks on the programme, which has become an unlikely national hit, to see which female farmer is chosen as the winner by viewers and others. Fans reportedly include the agriculture minister.[44]

Understanding the role of the media in boosting accountability also means understanding power. Patterns of ownership and party allegiance heavily influence the message in many old media. New media are less obviously subject to such bias, but are hardly a power-free zone either. The most widely read bloggers on aid and development are almost all white Western men (and I'm guilty as charged).

Transparency and accountability initiatives

Most of this chapter has been about what the World Bank calls the 'long route' to accountability:[45] citizens delegate authority to political representatives, usually via political parties, who then govern bureaucracies that deliver services. Long route accountability comes from citizens trying to make sure those politicians are doing their job. But there is also a 'short route' to accountability: rather than asking your MP or local councillor to improve your child's school, why not lobby the headmaster directly?

Attempts to build this short route, often called 'social accountability', have spread like wildfire in recent years, driven both by new technology and the need for solutions when states are weak or unresponsive. These efforts, widely known as 'transparency and accountability initiatives' rely on access to information, citizen monitoring of government performance, and citizen activism to hold officials to account.

---

[44] Oxfam website, 'Bahati Muriga Jacob: Female Food Hero 2014, Tanzania', www.oxfam.org/en/tanzania/bahati-muriga-jacob-female-food-hero-2014.

[45] World Bank, 'World Development Report 2004. Making Services Work for Poor People' (Washington DC: The World Bank, 2003).

In South Africa, the Public Sector Accountability Monitor analysed and publicized budget and service delivery information produced by the health department of one of the weakest provincial governments, the Eastern Cape. While its efforts initially had limited impact, the national government took note and intervened. As a result, the provincial health minister and head of department were replaced, thirty-one officials were criminally charged, and a further 800 officials were dismissed.[46] Needless to say, financial management improved substantially.

The promise of such initiatives is real, but has been oversold. Some talked 'as if all one had to do was to sprinkle mobile phones or internet and the persistent, structural imbalances and power asymmetries that had dogged us for decades would melt away', in the words of one of the movement's most charismatic leaders, Rakesh Rajani of Tanzania.[47]

Rakesh invited me to take part in a soul-searching exercise at Twaweza, the pioneering NGO he founded. Twaweza believed that boosting poor people's access to information could make government more accountable on things like poor schools across East Africa.[48] They took the idea to scale, providing social content for top TV soap operas or radio satire, and advertising on the back page of 40 million school notebooks. It was a challenging, large-scale innovation and donors loved it.

The trouble was it wasn't working. None of the evaluations led by eminent academics from around the world had uncovered evidence that Twaweza's information was registering with citizens on any scale,

---

[46] Duncan Green, 'Ups and Downs in the Struggle for Accountability—Four New Real Time Studies', From Poverty to Power blog, 5 September 2013, https://oxfamblogs.org/fp2p/watching-the-ups-and-downs-of-accountability-work-four-new-real-time-studies/.

[47] Rakesh Rajani, 'Why Transparency and Technology Won't Drive Accountability', in Duncan Green, 'What are the Limits of Transparency and Technology? From Three Gurus of the Openness Movement (Eigen, Rajani, McGee)', From Poverty to Power blog, 7 April 2014, http://oxfamblogs.org/fp2p/what-are-the-limits-of-transparency-and-technology-the-thoughts-of-three-gurus-of-the-openness-movement/.

[48] http://oxfamblogs.org/fp2p/a-fascinating-conversation-with-twaweza-one-of-the-worlds-cutting-edge-accountability-ngos/.

still less triggering increased citizen action. One of the evaluators (echoed by Rakesh) called it a 'bucket of cold water' on the original concept. Hence the invitation because, true to its courageous approach, Twaweza published the findings of its (non) impact and invited people to come and discuss them.

The ensuing three days brought home to me the importance of examining the assumptions and conditions that underlie all theories of change—'looking at the arrows'. My all-time favourite cartoon[49] on how change happens shows two boffins in front of a blackboard, with equations to the left and right and in between the words 'then a miracle occurs' (see Figure 6.1). Twaweza's theory of change was: 'citizens get

"I THINK YOU SHOULD BE MORE EXPLICIT HERE IN STEP TWO."

Figure 6.1 Then a miracle occurs

Source: Sidney Harris, Science Cartoons Plus.com

[49] Sidney Harris, 2016, http://www.sciencecartoonsplus.com/pages/gallery.php.

information about services → citizens take action to improve them'; in between lay the unexplored 'miracle' of accountability.

As one of the evaluators of the programme pointed out, inside that simple a → b theory of change, lay a whole sequence of assumptions and conditions: Do I understand the information? → Is it new information to me? → Do I care? → Do I think that it is my responsibility to do something about it? → Do I have the skills to make a difference? → Do I have the sense of efficacy to think that my efforts will have an impact? → Are the kinds of actions I am inspired to take different from what I am already doing? → Do I believe my own individual action will have an impact? → Do I expect fellow community members to join me in taking action?[50] Unless we have a much fuller analysis of the systems through which power works to achieve accountability, we are essentially crossing our fingers and hoping for 'a miracle to occur'.

Twaweza's degree of openness may be exceptional, but the problems it identified were not. Unless we have a much fuller analysis of the systems through which power works to achieve accountability, we are essentially crossing our fingers and hoping for a miracle to occur. What is needed instead is to look at the system as a whole, including political parties and the media, combining demand from activists, access to information, and a better understanding of how those in power make decisions and could become allies in change—what I call a power and systems approach.[51] For the moment, that approach looks like a better bet than waiting for miracles, but I wouldn't be surprised if we are back in Dar es Salaam in a few years examining another set of depressing evaluations, because that's the nature of working in complex systems.

---

[50] Duncan Green, 'So What Should Twaweza Do Differently? How Accountability Work is Evolving', From Poverty to Power blog, 9 October 2013, http://oxfamblogs.org/fp2p/so-what-should-twaweza-do-differently-how-accountability-work-is-evolving/.

[51] Jonathan Fox, 'Social accountability: what does the evidence really say?', GPSA Working Paper Series No. 1, September 2014.

Conclusion

All too often a gulf divides the words of those in positions of power and responsibility from their subsequent deeds. The gulf is partly the result of the workings of ideas, interests, and institutions, and a reflection of the way power is distributed in society. The gap between words and deeds often engenders cynicism about those in power among the public ('all politicians are the same').

However tempting, I think activists who simply endorse that scepticism will miss valuable opportunities for change. Political parties, the media, and social accountability initiatives are vital parts of systems of accountability that can be used, and strengthened, to close the gap.

Countries with stagnant or corrupt party systems do not remain so forever. Instead, they constitute an ever-evolving system, driven by pressure from below, changing norms, new leaders, and critical junctures. Activists need to learn to dance with that system, using the media, and 'short route' approaches, but also working with parties by building alliances, identifying and working with champions, and seizing moments of opportunity, because parties carry the potential to achieve changes on an otherwise impossible scale.

Further Reading

R. Cordenillo and S. van der Staak (eds.) *Political Parties and Citizen Movements in Asia and Europe* (Singapore: Asia-Europe Foundation, Hanns Seidel Foundation and International Institute for Democracy and Electoral Assistance, 2014).

J. Deane, *Fragile States: The Role of Media and Communication*, BBC Media Action Policy Briefing No. 10 (London: BBC Media Action, 2013).

F. Fukuyama, *The Origins of Political Order: From Prehuman Times to the French Revolution* (New York: Farrar, Straus and Giroux, 2011).

V. Randall, *Political Parties in the Third World* (London: SAGE Publications, 1988).

A. Rocha Menocal, *Ten things to know about democracy and elections* (London: Overseas Development Institute, 2013).

7

HOW THE INTERNATIONAL SYSTEM SHAPES CHANGE

'Shame!' roared the bearded activist, pointing an accusing finger as, uncomfortably besuited, I wended my way through the police lines. Attending an international trade conference as a civil society delegate was supposed to be a routine induction to CAFOD's work in international institutions. However, the 1999 WTO ministerial in Seattle was anything but routine. Trapped between tear gas spraying robocops and enraged protesters, we NGO lobbyists from the UK had to take refuge with the British government delegates in their swanky conference centre offices. And that proved a great chance to build relationships and trust. It probably wasn't what my placard-wielding accuser intended, but as it turned out he was very helpful.

For me Seattle marked the beginning of several years of lobbying on global trade rules. Working alongside government delegations from Pakistan, the Philippines, and many other countries, plus a plethora of fellow NGO policy wonks and academics, provided me with a great introduction to the complex dynamics of the international system, and how activism interacts with events, long-term trends, and shifts in norms and ideas.

The key event in those years was the 9/11 attack on New York's World Trade Center, which took place just weeks before the WTO ministerial that followed the debacle in Seattle. Jittery delegates in Doha flinched whenever planes flew near the conference centre. Along with berobed Qatari staff, the delegates and I watched on TV screens in the conference hall as US troops took Kabul in response to the attack. In this febrile atmosphere, governments rallied behind the international system and launched an ambitious 'Doha Development Round' of trade talks.

At the ministerial in Cancun two years later, however, longer-term trends came to the fore. Growing unease in the US and Europe had helped weaken the rich countries' resolve and, more importantly, newly assertive developing country blocs refused to sign on to the rich countries' agendas on agriculture and investment, and the talks fell apart in spectacular fashion.

Ideas also played a key role in the evolution of the trade debate, especially the academic counter-attack against the crude 'if it moves, liberalize it' impulse that had dominated in the late 1990s.[1] With the rich countries in retreat on the intellectual and political realms, the round remains on life support a decade and a half after its launch.

That ecosystem of interacting events, long-term economic and political processes, individuals, and ideas is typical of how change happens in the international system.

The multilateral system evolves

In many ways, the international system is an extraordinary success story. Every day sees huge amounts of largely smooth interchange between nation states: people cross borders; emails, letters, and post-cards arrive at the correct destination; freighters load and unload containers of goods in foreign ports in an ever-expanding cycle of global trade. We only notice when those relatively unencumbered processes are interrupted, as in Europe's migration meltdown, which is dominating the headlines as I write. Remarkably, these smoothly functioning exchanges occur under a fairly loose system of governance—a combination of norms, rules, procedures, and institutions—and without any recognized world government.

---

[1] See, for example, Dani Rodrik, *The Global Governance of Trade as if Development Really Mattered* (Cambridge, MA: Harvard University, 2001), www.sss.ias.edu/files/pdfs/Rodrik/Research/global-governance-of-trade.pdf. Or Ha-Joon Chang, *Kicking Away the Ladder: Development Strategy in Historical Perspective* (London: Anthem Press, 2003).

The first attempt to bring order to international relations came in Europe after the defeat of Napoleon in 1815. The victorious powers set up a 'Concert for Europe' which, though it had no written rules and no permanent institutions, offered a forum for negotiating differences. It successfully limited warfare in Europe for much of the nineteenth century, accommodating the unification and rise of Germany and Italy, before collapsing in the First World War.

Ever since the founding of the Red Cross in 1863, discussions on international governance have been driven by efforts to regulate the use of violence, and the international system has evolved primarily in response to war. The First World War led to the creation of the League of Nations, an idealistic and ill-fated attempt to build a 'world parliament'. The Second World War bequeathed the basic institutions that make up the international system today. The UN, unlike the League, fuses global democracy (the General Assembly) with 'great power' politics (the Security Council). To promote economic coordination between countries and curb the economic nationalism that helped destroy the League, the victorious powers established the predecessor to the WTO and what are known collectively as the 'Bretton Woods Institutions'—the International Bank for Reconstruction and Development (better known as the World Bank), the International Monetary Fund (IMF).

Seventy years on, with increasing signs of sclerosis and strain, the UN, World Bank Group, and IMF, joined by the WTO in 1995, sit atop a burgeoning and complex system of international governance. And I mean complex: during the course of the twentieth century, over 38,000 international organizations were founded, almost half of them in its last two decades.[2]

The UN is a sprawling system unto itself. It consists of three core bodies set up in 1945, the General Assembly, the Security Council, and the Secretariat, subsequently joined by numerous 'specialized agencies',

---

[2] Thomas Weiss, *Global Governance: Why? What? Whither?* (Cambridge: Polity Press, 2013), p. 16.

such as the World Health Organization (WHO) (1948), the UN High Commissioner for Refugees (1950), the UN Conference on Trade and Development (1964), the UN Development Programme (1965), and UN Women (2010).[3]

In response to events (especially failures and crises) as well as the political sclerosis and glacial pace of reform in existing institutions, new elements continue being grafted onto the basic architecture of the international system. The failure of UN peacekeeping to prevent massacres in Bosnia and Rwanda in the 1990s led to the founding of the International Criminal Court in 2002 and an increasingly assertive role for UN peace keepers in crises, backed by a 2005 agreement on the 'responsibility to protect' civilians from genocide, war crimes, ethnic cleansing, and crimes against humanity. The inability of the IMF and World Bank to reflect the long-term decline of Europe's power in their governance structures prompted China, India, Brazil, and other rising economic powers to create the Asian Infrastructure Investment Bank in 2014.

My own highly peripheral engagement is also a sign of another evolution in the international system, the rise of non-state networks. States remain the main players, but they are increasingly surrounded by, and forced to engage with, representatives of the private sector, NGOs, philanthrocapitalists such as Bill and Melinda Gates, and policy-savvy academics. Networks among these new players have given rise to public-private initiatives such as the Global Fund to Fight AIDS, Tuberculosis, and Malaria or the Global Alliance for Vaccines and Immunization.

While constitutionally part of the UN system, the IMF and the World Bank were set up in a radically different manner. The UN works largely on the principle of 'one country, one vote' (with the notable exception of the Security Council), whereas decisions at the multilateral financial organizations are generally taken on the basis of

[3] Anthony Payne, *The Global Politics of Unequal Development* (London and New York: Palgrave Macmillan, 2005), chapter 5.

'one dollar, one vote', guaranteeing the dominance of the US and other major donors.[4] At US insistence, the organizations were located in Washington, within walking distance of the White House, rather than with the UN in New York. Put crudely, the UN system is weighted towards the developing countries (although they are often themselves divided in terms of ideology and positions), whereas the Bretton Woods Institutions are more likely to reflect the views of the rich countries.

Ideology and politics are not the only differences. I have always been struck by the divide between the seedy offices and frustrating bureaucracy of the UN and the swanky digs and smart efficiency of the Bank and Fund. I received a graphic demonstration of this in 2013, when I gave talks about blogging to staff at the UN Development Program (UNDP) and World Bank. At the UN, cowed staff debated whether they were even allowed to blog, for fear of offending one or other member state. At the World Bank, the self-confident and amused response to my request to meet its bloggers was 'tricky, there are 300 of them'.[5]

The particular culture of each organization matters because global activism by NGOs and others often relies on alliances with one international institution to influence the rest. Building alliances with the UN system ought to be a no-brainer, given its orientation and commitment to progressive change. Alas it is often a frustrating bureaucratic nightmare.

And adopting a simplistic 'UN good, World Bank bad' view of the world is too simplistic. There are endless turf wars, but also genuine

---

[4] One exception is the arm of the World Bank that lends to low-income countries, the International Development Association (IDA). Technically, this has a different structure to the main board of the Bank, and poor countries get 41 per cent of the vote in decisions made by the IDA board. However, only a few of these countries are involved in setting the agreements that decide the IDA's policies, a process that takes place every three years. Here, as everywhere at the International Finance Institutions (IFIs), it is the large donors who really make all the significant decisions.

[5] Duncan Green, 'Blogging in Big Bureaucracies Round Two: The View From the World Bank', From Poverty to Power blog, 10 May 2013, http://oxfamblogs.org/fp2p/blogging-in-big-bureaucracies-round-two-the-view-from-the-world-bank/.

differences of opinion and ideology within the UN system and the Bretton Woods Institutions, as well as between them. After the 1998 Asian financial crisis, for example, the IMF wanted to pressure countries to cut spending, while the World Bank thought they should reflate.

'Hard' and 'soft' power

Given that most of the decisions that matter in the lives of ordinary people are ultimately taken by national governments, it is not surprising that many officials at international institutions (and not a few activists) yearn for the international system to acquire the 'hard power' to compel governments to act. Only a few international bodies can exercise such influence: the UN can impose sanctions on oppressive regimes; the IMF can try to impose particular economic policies, such as public spending cuts; the WTO can authorize fines to enforce trade rules; and the International Criminal Court (ICC) can prosecute leaders with blood on their hands.

Activists managed to harness the international system's hard power through a successful campaign on arms control launched in 2003 by Oxfam, Amnesty International, and the International Action Network on Small Arms (IANSA), along with many other organizations across the world. The aim of the Control Arms Campaign was to reduce armed violence and conflict through a new Arms Trade Treaty (ATT), which would be the world's first ever global effort to regulate the transfer of conventional weapons and ammunition from one country to another.

When the campaign began, only three governments (Mali, Costa Rica, and Cambodia) would publicly associate themselves with the call for a treaty. Undeterred, the campaign assembled a wide range of allies, including companies in the defence industry that saw themselves as the 'responsible end' of the arms industry, retired generals and former war correspondents, financial investors, people wounded by small arms, and more. Lining up on the other side, were the US (until 2009 the only country that publicly opposed a treaty) and other weapons-dealing states (Russia, China, and Middle Eastern countries), plus the National Rifle Association and associated pro-gun groups.

The initial strategy was to get one government in each region of the world to champion the ATT, and convince others to follow their lead in a snowball effect. Direct lobbying won individual converts within governments, but it was mass petitions and other public campaigning activities that made support for the ATT politically feasible. By mid-2005, the snowball was rolling: at the Biennial meeting of the UN Programme of Action on Small Arms, fifty-five states voiced support; by the end of 2006, 153 countries voted in favour of moving towards a treaty. The ATT became international law on Christmas Eve, 2014.

The ATT campaign is a great case study in how to use power and systems analysis to drive change in the international system. Campaigners were adept at building alliances with 'unusual suspects', had a deep understanding of the way power operated in the inter-national system and moved adroitly between outsider campaigning and insider lobbying as the negotiations progressed. They also made full use of critical junctures, such as outbreaks of violence in Eastern Congo, Darfur, and later Syria, and China's arms shipment to Zimbabwe in 2008 just before violence-marred elections. (South Afri-can dockworkers refused to unload the ship, and the campaign promptly highlighted both the effectiveness of the action, and the human cost it prevented.)[6]

But the 'hard power' of international law has its limits. Powerful countries can ignore the rulings of international bodies or apply them selectively, while less powerful governments often say yes and do nothing.

An underestimated strength of the international system is its 'soft power': the ideas and norms that filter down to societies and states from the endless round of conferences, conventions, and discussions within the international system. As discussed in Chapter 3, the UN's

---

[6] Duncan Green and Anna Macdonald, 'Power and Change: The Arms Trade Treaty' (Oxford: Oxfam GB for Oxfam International, 2015).

most profound influence may well be its role in agreeing and promoting the evolving norms that govern human society on everything from the treatment of women, children, or indigenous people to attitudes to corruption or warfare. International knowledge networks (comprising academics, policy makers, and the research arms of international institutions) can be highly influential, as the International Panel on Climate Change (IPCC) has shown in the case of global climate negotiations. The IPCC is in many ways a modern expression of a nineteenth-century belief in the power of scientific knowledge to solve humanity's most pressing problems, and its success is heartening for a lapsed scientist like me.

I like to think of the debates in international forums as an ecosystem. New ideas, and variations of old ones, are constantly introduced and chewed over. Some rise and are taken up by the institutions that comprise the system, while others wither away. Churn and change are constant, as intellectual tides shape individuals' understanding of the world, and decisions at all levels.

Activists who despair at the deaf ear turned to them by the international system need patience. When I first encountered the IMF and World Bank in the late 1980s, they were 'the Poverty Brokers',[7] using the debt crisis of the 1980s to impose austerity and 'structural adjustment' across the developing world. Growth was all; the state was always the problem, never the solution; deregulated markets the only way forward.

I started off firmly in the 'anti' camp, supporting the '50 years is enough' protests in 1994 that argued for the Bretton Woods Institutions to be scrapped. But as I engaged more and more with staff at the Bank and Fund, my views began to soften. I'd like to believe my shift was due to the institutions improving, but I confess I was also growing older and more conciliatory. These days I even write for the World Bank's governance blog.[8] Even so, when IMF boss Christine Lagarde

---

[7] Martin Honeywell, *The Poverty Brokers: The IMF and Latin America* (London: Latin America Bureau, 1983).

[8] Duncan Green, World Bank blogs, http://blogs.worldbank.org/team/duncan-green.

launched its new paper on gender and inequality at Oxfam's Washington office in 2015,[9] I had to pinch myself. Words like 'gender' and 'inequality' would never have made it past the IMF's internal thought police thirty years ago.

Explaining how the Bretton Woods Institutions have evolved would take a book in itself, but the process shows all the hallmarks of a complex adaptive system. 'Tribes' within each institution from different disciplinary or ideological backgrounds slug it out over vital issues such as the role of the state, the importance and origins of inequality, or whether health and education services should charge user fees.[10] Events and real life move debates along: the terrible human cost of those 1980s structural adjustment dictums sowed doubt and confusion over the 'rightness' of the policies known as the 'Washington Consensus'. Some brilliant, visionary critics in the UN system led the counterattack—UNICEF's book *Adjustment with a Human Face*[11] highlighted the human cost of IMF and World Bank policies, while the annual 'Human Development Report', first published by the UNDP in 1990, pioneered a rethinking of poverty and development away from narrow definitions of income and economic performance; its broader focus on the multiple aspects of well/ill-being guides the work of most of the aid and development sector today.

Those critics and many other activists and intellectuals within and close to the UN system articulated both the failures of the old thinking and a more progressive alternative. One of them, Ha-Joon Chang, likens the band of heterodox economists to which he belongs to the

[9] Christine Lagarde, Managing Director, IMF, 'Catalyst for Change: Empowering Women and Tackling Income Inequality', speech to Oxfam America, 22 October 2015, Washington DC, www.imf.org/external/np/speeches/2015/102215.htm.

[10] Oxfam has been deeply involved in this debate. See, for example, Anna Marriott and Jessica Hamer, 'Investing for the Few: The IFC's Health in Africa Initiative' (Oxford: Oxfam GB for Oxfam International, 2014), http://policy-practice.oxfam.org.uk/publications/investing-for-the-few-the-ifcs-health-in-africa-initiative-325654.

[11] Giovanni Cornia, Richard Jolly, and Frances Stewart, *Adjustment with a Human Face: Protecting the Vulnerable and Promoting Growth* (Gloucestershire: Clarendon Press, 1987).

heroes in *Lord of the Rings*, standing shoulder to shoulder at Helm's Deep, taking on the oncoming tides of neoclassical orcs.

Events and long-term political and economic processes came to the rescue of these beleaguered heroes: the 1998 Asian Financial Crisis and the 2008 global meltdown forced the IMF to recognize the folly of forcing countries to open their capital markets. The economic rise of the BRIC countries (Brazil, Russia, India, China) weakened the dominance of the US and Britain, as exemplified by the World Bank's appointment of Chinese and Indian experts to the top post of chief economist in 2008 and 2012.

As I watched this battle unfold, I came to realize that one of my most useful roles as a non-economist activist was to use the NGOs' ability to organize and communicate to help the Helm's Deep heroes get their message across. I became something of a cheerleader for the heterodox economists.

Others certainly don't share my optimism, so perhaps I have been too thoroughly co-opted. A study of the World Bank's Development Economics Vice Presidency (DEC) concluded that its role was one of 'paradigm maintenance', defending and perpetuating an orthodox form of neoclassical economics through an interlocking set of 'drivers of inertia', including hiring preferences, promotion, and the selective enforcement of rules. Dissident research generally undergoes stricter external review with occasional rejection, or disappears into a Kafkaesque limbo where it is never signed off for publication. Dissidents are labelled 'idiosyncratic', 'disaffected' and otherwise deemed misfits, while the Bank's External Affairs Department gets behind the 'good guys', showering them with high profile speaking and writing opportunities.[12]

---

[12] Duncan Green, 'Why is Economic Orthodoxy so Resistant to Change? The Art of Paradigm Maintenance', From Poverty to Power blog, 17 September 2014, http://oxfamblogs.org/fp2p/the-art-of-paradigm-maintenance-has-anything-changed-at-the-world-bank/.

But whether you are of the cup-half-full or cup-half-empty persuasion, this battle of ideas has great implications for activists and policy makers around the world, because the UN, Fund, and Bank play a crucial role as 'knowledge brokers'. The research they conduct and publish shapes thinking about development and economic policy in virtually every country (including that of activists).

Because 'soft power' matters, we activists should put our shoulders to the wheel to support the forces of light, providing platforms, building alliances, spotting champions, amplifying messages, and doing our own research. If the new friendly rhetoric on rights or inequality at the Bank or Fund doesn't match what they do in practice, we have a perfect opportunity to highlight implementation gaps and double standards.

The sustainable development goals

I became convinced of the value of a power and systems approach in international advocacy during the three frustrating years of discussion that led to the Sustainable Development Goals (SDGs), the successor to the UN's Millennium Development Goals (MDGs). As far as I could tell, the large group of UN and other technocrats involved were more interested in debating metrics and indicators than in driving change on the ground. And the huge circus of NGO and other lobbyists were only trying to shoehorn 'their' issue onto an ever-expanding agenda. Missing was an understanding that progress toward any global goal relies primarily on national decision makers hemmed in by multiple constraints.

The SDG discussion started badly, dogged by confusion over correlation vs. causation in their predecessor. Because poverty had indeed been halved since the MDGs were agreed in 2000, many argued that the MDGs were a success, sidestepping the awkward truth that the main reason behind global progress on poverty was the extraordinary advance of China. And no-one was claiming that the MDGs were the force driving the Chinese government.

As aid dwindles in importance relative to national government spending, the issue of how international agreements can exert traction over national decision making becomes increasingly important. In a 2012 paper written with Matthew Lockwood and Stephen Hale,[13] we looked at what was known about the impact of different kinds of agreements (e.g. international law, goals and targets, regional league tables) on changes in global norms, national government decisions, and empowerment of local civil society. Concerning the SDGs, we concluded that 'Given the substantial investment of money and brainpower in both the MDGs and the global debate over what should replace them, it is scandalous and astonishing that research seems to tell us so little about the impact of such global instruments on the things that matter—the performance of governments and the development of communities in poor countries.'

Subsequently, when Columbia University's Elham Seyedsayamdost did so, surveying fifty countries' implementation of the MDGs, she found that the goals had no apparent influence on how governments spent their money.[14]

But, as I noted in Chapter 4, research and evidence often plays second fiddle to political horse-trading in democratic systems, and our paper, like Seyedsayamdost's, disappeared into the ether.

The SDG process made me highly sceptical about any sentence beginning with the words 'we can', as in 'we can end poverty/abolish hunger/eradicate this or that disease'. The 'we' is an imaginary construct, an exercise in technocratic 'if-I-ruled-the-world' thinking that ignores the national and local officials who will take and implement

---

[13] Duncan Green, Stephen Hale, and Matthew Lockwood, 'How Can a Post-2015 Agreement Drive Real Change? The Political Economy of Global Commitments', revised edition (Oxford: Oxfam GB for Oxfam International, 2012), http://policy-practice.oxfam. org.uk/publications/how-can-a-post-2015-agreement-drive-real-change-revised-edition-the-political-e-250371.

[14] Duncan Green, 'Have the MDGs Affected Developing Country Policies and Spending? Findings of New 50 Country Study', From Poverty to Power blog, 24 July 2015, http://oxfamblogs.org/fp2p/have-the-mdgs-affected-developing-country-policies-and-spending-findings-of-new-50-country-study/.

the decisions necessary to achieve any given goal, not to mention the constraints those decision makers face.[15]

In fairness, the value of such global discussions also lies in their ability to draw attention to development issues, especially insofar as they influence norms. As I write the discussion on how the SDGs will be implemented is ongoing and could yet produce something that influences national governments. But I fear that what we will get in the end is periodic global updates on social progress, issued in New York, which have negligible impact on how governments treat their citizens.

Conclusion

It is easy to become disillusioned with the international system and its unappealing mix of power politics, legalistic nitpicking, and apolitical technocracy. When I first joined the development NGOs, I stalked the pressrooms and NGO fringe events at summits and international conferences, seduced by their aura of power and importance. Summits generate a kind of Stockholm Syndrome even among we marginal NGO types: too many meetings, too little sleep and endless arguments over the fine print of declarations can convince you that the fate of the world lies in changing 'should' to 'shall' in paragraph 2.b.iii.

I remember how disheartening it was when I finally got to 'speak truth to power' at a UN meeting in Geneva, only to watch my carefully honed speech disappear into the cavernous room full of delegates chatting to each other and occasionally tuning in to the simultaneous translation. It didn't feel like a vibrant, world-changing institution and brought to mind a renowned phrase of UN Secretary-General Dag

[15] Pierre Jacquet, 'Incantations, Inclusive Growth and the Illusory "We": Whatever Happened to Politics in the Post-2015 Process?', From Poverty to Power blog, 25 April 2013, http://oxfamblogs.org/fp2p/incantations-inclusive-growth-and-the-illusory-we-whatever-happened-to-politics-in-the-post-2015-process/.

Hammarskjöld, 'The United Nations was not created to take mankind to heaven, but to save humanity from hell.'[16]

That year, 2005, marked a personal watershed: after Make Poverty History and yet another WTO summit in Hong Kong, I dropped out of the frontline of NGO advocacy. I had become convinced that the real arena for social change was at the national, rather than the international, level. I wrote *From Poverty to Power* to make that case, which I like to think contributed to a wider move by Oxfam and others to spend more time and energy on national influencing, rather than the caravan of international summitry.

Looking back, however, I think I swung too far the other way. The international system has a critical role in shaping society's norms and beliefs. Moreover, many of the most pressing challenges facing humanity are 'collective action problems' that cannot be solved by single countries alone.

National politics more often than not punishes leaders who seek to address the collective problems humanity faces, especially when they engage with the international system to do so. UN stalwart Mark Malloch Brown calls it 'the Gordon Brown problem'. At the onset of the financial crisis in 2008, the UK finance minister (no relation) showed extraordinary leadership at the G7 and G20 in pushing for public investment to avert an even greater global meltdown. Yet his political reward was negligible because, though action had to be global, votes remained national, with little credit (and lots of brickbats) for leaders engaging in foreign policy, even if it involves saving the world economy.[17]

Activists can change that equation. Our movements in the national and local arenas can make it politically feasible for governments, as well as enlightened leaders in the international system, to address

---

[16] Quoted in Thomas Weiss, *Global Governance: Why? What? Whither?* (Cambridge: Polity Press, 2013), p. 3.

[17] Mark Malloch-Brown, *The Unfinished Global Revolution: The Road to International Cooperation* (New York: Penguin Press, 2011), p. 199.

climate change, pandemics, crime, weapons proliferation, migration, or race-to-the-bottom competition between nations on taxation. And by acknowledging the primacy of national politics, our advocacy in the international system could become much more effective.

Growing up in the west of England, national elections in the Bath constituency where I lived were enlivened by a classic English eccentric. Posters would appear saying 'vote for Gilbert Young, World Government Party'. (The party's other proposals included turning Buckingham Palace into a home for old-age pensioners.) Young never won more than a few hundred votes, and his party died with him in 1998, but as global collective action problems become more pressing, he may end up being proved right after all.

Making the international system work better is essential to the survival of our species and the individual and community wellbeing of its members. And yes, that may eventually require a move from global governance to some kind of global government. Perhaps one day, Gilbert Young will be lauded as a prophet in the 1970s wilderness.

In the meantime, we activists have plenty of work to do, sharpening our understanding of power and process in the complexity that is the evolving international system, and working to ensure it addresses the many pressing problems we face.

The next chapter looks at another, increasingly important player in that international system—the transnational corporations.

Further Reading

H.J. Chang, *Kicking Away the Ladder: Development Strategy in Historical Perspective* (London: Anthem Press, 2003).

J. Gaventa and R. Tandon (eds.) *Globalizing Citizens: The New Dynamics of Inclusion and Exclusion* (London: Zed Books, 2010).

Mark Malloch-Brown, *The Unfinished Global Revolution: The Road to International Cooperation* (New York: Penguin Press, 2011).

S. Park, *Owning Development: Creating Policy Norms in The IMF and the World Bank* (Cambridge: Cambridge University Press, 2010).

A. Payne, *The Global Politics of Unequal Development* (Abingdon: Palgrave Macmillan, 2005).

Thomas Weiss, *Global Governance: Why? What? Whither?* (Cambridge: Polity Press, 2013), p. 16.

S. Woolcock and N. Bayne, *The New Economic Diplomacy: Decision-Making and Negotiation in International Economic Relations* (Abingdon: Routledge, 2011).

8

TRANSNATIONAL
CORPORATIONS AS DRIVERS
AND TARGETS OF CHANGE

Brian was in an expansive mood. Relaxing over dinner in the Bangladeshi capital of Dhaka, he explained why he had abandoned a British émigré's retirement in Florida to run a large garment factory, where some 2,000 women stitched sportswear for Nike. 'I'm not doing this for the money, I don't need it', he mused. 'It's providing jobs for all those women that makes it worthwhile.'

I was in an awkward position. Thanks to Brian, I had earlier toured the factory (off limits to most visiting NGOs), now I was bonding with him as a fellow Brit. But I could hardly let this pass. After a quick mental calculation, I made a mischievous suggestion: 'Well, why don't you give your salary to the women? It would double their wages—all 2,000 of them!' 'No way', he retorted. 'It's all about keeping count.' He meant that once you get to his level, salary is more about status and peer competition than mere income.

Staying friends with Brian wasn't the only source of awkwardness that day. I was researching a report for a campaign on exploitative transnationals. Yet the garment workers I interviewed, both onsite and off, told me how much they prized working at the clean, modern factory in one of Dhaka's export processing zones. It was infinitely preferable to a sewing job in one of the dingy, dangerous local factories in downtown Dhaka, the women said, let alone a life of domestic servitude back in the village.

Ubiquitous global brands like Nike epitomize widespread concern about globalization and have become the favoured target of campaigners. Transnational corporations (TNCs) certainly hold significant power. The TNC universe now spans some 103,000 parent companies with over 886,000 foreign affiliates.[1] In 2014, these generated an estimated $7.9 trillion in value added[2] and employed some 75 million workers. The total annual sales of TNCs' foreign affiliates rose from $4.7 to $36.4 trillion between 1990 and 2014.[3]

Anxiety over their sheer size has prompted critics to argue that corporations 'rule the world'.[4] One of the most widely visited posts on my 'From Poverty to Power' blog is a World Bank table that shows the world's top 100 economies:[5] fifty-three are countries (measured by GDP), thirty-four are cities (ditto), and thirteen are corporations (measured by turnover[6]). Strictly speaking, this is comparing apples and pears; value added is a better (and lower) measure than turnover. But it remains a fact that a number of firms rival medium-sized countries in economic might.

This chapter focuses on TNCs, not only as economic heavyweights, but also as influential players (for good *and* ill) in political and social change. Small and medium enterprises (SMEs) account for many more jobs and may well be more important in the daily lives of poor people, but these tend to be less active in consciously pursuing and preventing

---

[1] United Nations Conference on Trade and Development (UNCTAD), 'Web Table 34. Number of Parent Corporations and Foreign Affiliates, by Region and Economy, 2010', www.unctad.org/sections/dite_dir/docs/WIR11_web%20tab%2034.pdf.

[2] 'Value added' is the amount by which the value of an article is increased at each stage of its production, exclusive of initial costs.

[3] United Nations Conference on Trade and Development (UNCTAD), *World Investment Report 2015. Reforming International Investment Governance* (Geneva: United Nations, 2015), p. ix and p. 18.

[4] David Korten, *When Corporations Rule the World*, 2nd edition (Bloomfield and San Francisco: Kumarian Press, Inc. and Berrett-Koehler Publishers Inc., 2001).

[5] Duncan Green, 'The World's Top 100 Economies: 53 Countries, 34 Cities and 13 Corporations', From Poverty to Power blog, 19 October 2011, http://oxfamblogs.org/fp2p/the-worlds-top-100-economies-53-countries-34-cities-and-13-corporations/.

[6] 'Turnover' is the amount of money taken in by a business in a certain period.

change. I see SMEs, like markets in general, more as part of the context within which activists operate than actors in their own right. TNCs, on the other hand, behave more like activists.

This chapter is probably going to get me into trouble with some colleagues. Opinions on TNCs seem to be more polarized than on any other subject in development. These run on a spectrum from contempt for corporations as the shock troops of capitalism, destroying lives and cultures in a frenzy of corporate greed, all the way to a Blairite infatuation with their power, scale, and dynamism. Whether through experience or because I'm getting on in years, I have moved from nearer the former to nearer the latter. But this chapter won't seek to pass judgement, rather to sketch out what we need to know to understand TNCs as a system, their history and incentives, and the range of their behaviour.

Some history

The East India Company, established in 1600 with a trading empire that encircled the globe, was the mother of modern TNCs.[7] While its imports of spices, textiles, and teas wrought a lifestyle revolution in the UK, the company became a byword for corporate malpractice and general skulduggery, conquering nations and ruling over millions with its private army. When China tried to stop the firm from flooding the country with smuggled narcotics, two Opium Wars ensued.

The East India Company pioneered the cycle of corruption, bubbles, and bail-outs that has been an all-too-frequent feature of the corporate landscape in recent years. It also launched the shareholder model of corporate ownership, which allowed companies to burst beyond the bounds set by family wealth and led to an explosion of new corporations in Europe and the US in the last third of the nineteenth century.[8]

---

[7] Nick Robins, *The Corporation that Changed the World: How the East India Company Shaped the Modern Multinational,* 2nd edition (London: Pluto Press, 2012).
[8] Bruce Kogut, 'Multinational Corporations', in *International Encyclopedia of the Social & Behavioral Sciences,* edited by N. J. Smelser and Paul B. Baltes (Oxford: Pergamon),

That was when recognizably modern TNCs spread across the developing world, initially concentrated on transport, building railways to facilitate the extraction of raw materials and the marketing of their manufactures. Soon, TNCs expanded into communications (telephones, radio, movies), energy (oil, gas, electricity),[9] and subsequently manufacturing.[10]

The first wave of TNC expansion peaked just before global markets fragmented in the Great Depression and the Second World War. In the post-war era, TNCs expanded again, even though the larger developing countries in Latin America and later Africa placed limits on their operations in order to protect nascent local industry. Many countries nationalized industries, making TNCs much more wary of investing.[11]

In the wake of the oil shock of the 1970s and the debt crisis that followed, developing-country governments began relaxing restrictions as they competed to attract foreign investment, setting off a renewed wave of TNC expansion. Manufacturing and extractive industries led the way, but the wave really took off in the 1990s in services like finance, management consultancy, tourism, hotels, and fast food. As of 2014, services accounted for 63 per cent of global foreign direct investment, more than twice the share of manufacturing (26 per cent); the primary sector (farms, mines, gas, and oil) accounted for less than 10 per cent.[12]

The past thirty years has also seen the rise of new TNCs from emerging economies in South and East Asia and Latin America. In

pp. 10197–204, https://www0.gsb.columbia.edu/faculty/bkogut/files/Chapter_in_smelser-Baltes_2001.pdf.

[9] Alfred Chandler and Bruce Mazlish, eds., *Leviathans: Multinational Corporations and the New Global History* (Cambridge and New York: Cambridge University Press, 2005).

[10] Alfred Chandler and Bruce Mazlish, eds., *Leviathans: Multinational Corporations and the New Global History* (Cambridge and New York: Cambridge University Press, 2005), p. 20.

[11] Alfred Chandler and Bruce Mazlish, eds., *Leviathans: Multinational Corporations and the New Global History* (Cambridge and New York: Cambridge University Press, 2005), p. 40.

[12] United Nations Conference on Trade and Development (UNCTAD), *World Investment Report 2015. Reforming International Investment Governance* (Geneva: United Nations, 2015), p. 12.

2013, southern TNCs held assets of $460 billion, compared to the $858 billion in assets held by their northern counterparts.[13]

In 2011, nine of the top ten African telecommunications companies were from other developing countries.[14] According to the UN, 'developing Asia' (i.e. excluding Japan) now invests abroad more than any other region.[15] Compared with their developed-country counterparts, more southern TNCs are state- or family-owned and more are based in the primary sector or resource-based manufacturing, such as iron, steel, and cement.[16] Developing-country TNCs make greater use of 'intermediate' technologies that are more labour intensive and so create more jobs.[17] Like their northern counterparts, their performance on social and environmental responsibility varies widely.

While China's growing investment in extractive industries in Africa (and its less publicized surge in Southeast Asia and Latin America) is well known, Chinese companies have also taken on a significant number of infrastructure projects deemed too risky by European or US firms.[18] In Sierra Leone in 2005, within two years of the end of a

---

[13] UNCTAD, 'Trends in outward investments by transnational corporations in 2013 and prospects for 2014–15', 28 April 2014, http://unctad.org/en/pages/newsdetails.aspx?OriginalVersionID=729

[14] Top Ten largest telecoms companies in Africa, *IT News Africa*, 21 August 2012, http://www.itnewsafrica.com/2012/08/top-ten-largest-telecoms-companies-in-africa/.

[15] Other strong economies like Taiwan and northern Italy have relied more on networks of SMEs, and failed to produce many global companies. United Nations Conference on Trade and Development (UNCTAD), *World Investment Report 2015. Reforming International Investment Governance* (Geneva: United Nations, 2015), p. ix.

[16] United Nations Conference on Trade and Development (UNCTAD), *World Investment Report 2006. FDI from Developing and Transition Economies: Implications for Development* (Geneva: United Nations, 2006).

[17] Dilek Aykut and Andrea Goldstein, 'Developing Country Multinationals: South-South Investment Comes of Age', in *Industrial Development for the 21st Century: Sustainable Development Perspectives* (New York: United Nations, Department of Economic and Social Affairs, 2007), pp. 85–116.

[18] Deborah Brautigam, 'China-Africa Post-Doctoral Fellowship Opportunity', The China-Africa Research Initiative blog, 19 January 2016, www.chinaafricarealstory.com/.

bloody civil war, China was already investing $270 million in hotel construction and tourism.[19]

Southern TNCs have also become major investors in northern economies. In the UK, India's Tata Steel now owns Corus while Tata Motors owns Jaguar; Brazil's Vale mining conglomerate bought Canada's second largest mining company, Inco, in 2006; Mexico's dynamic cement company Cemex has built a global network through mergers and acquisitions. Chinese companies' attempts to buy US firms have provoked a nationalist backlash on several occasions.

The rise of southern TNCs challenges activists' traditional approach to advocacy. These firms seem less susceptible to threats to their brands, and the family-owned ones are not susceptible to shareholder pressure. Later in this chapter I look at what a new model of influencing might look like.

Most modern TNCs bear little resemblance to the vertically integrated corporations of yesteryear, where, for example, United Fruit directly owned and managed its banana plantations and Ford its factories. Today TNCs sit atop complex 'global production networks', coordinating a web of interconnected firms in multiple locations, through a mind-boggling combination of subcontracting, outsourcing, offshoring, partnerships, and mergers and acquisitions. Global production networks accounted for 80 per cent of international trade in 2012.[20]

The political significance of TNCs is hotly disputed. The acronym 'TNC' is actually somewhat misleading, since few are genuinely transnational: most retain a high degree of linkage to their home countries, particularly in terms of where decision-making power lies and where the high-value end of research and design is located. That home identity shapes their corporate cultures, sometimes leading to hybrid

[19] Mark Doyle, 'Tourism Boost for Sierra Leone', BBC News website, 7 May 2004, http://news.bbc.co.uk/2/hi/africa/3694043.stm.
[20] United Nations Conference on Trade and Development (UNCTAD), *World Investment Report 2013. Global Value Chains: Investment and Trade for Development* (Geneva: United Nations, 2013).

forms: when Japanese TNCs set up a factory in Europe, they blend Japanese and European work practices.[21] And sometimes causing friction: when I visited the Pacific island nation of Vanuatu, local people expressed annoyance that Chinese construction companies not only import Chinese workers, but those workers even grew their own vegetables, minimizing the benefits to local businesses.[22]

Nevertheless, the top echelons of TNCs (not unlike the top positions at big NGOs) are staffed by an international elite that is largely insulated from local environments. They shop at the same luxury boutiques, send their kids to international schools, and move effortlessly around the globe in a business class bubble (jealous? me?). In the 1980s, a hot topic for leftists across Latin America was whether their countries still possessed a truly 'national bourgeoisie', or whether the region's elites had become so Americanized and rootless that they would rather exploit their compatriots and shop in Miami, than build flourishing economies at home. That question is still an open one everywhere, as far as I can tell.

How TNCs drive change

TNCs drive change both through their normal business operations, and through their behaviour as political players. Using a 'poverty footprint' methodology,[23,24] Oxfam sought to measure the economic impact of Unilever's (a producer of consumer goods that owns brands

---

[21] Peter Dicken, *Global Shift: Mapping the Changing Contours of the World Economy*, 6th edition (London: Sage Publications Ltd, 2011), p. 122.

[22] Author field trip, Vanuatu, November 2015.

[23] Oxfam America, The Coca-Cola Company, and SABMiller, 'Exploring the Links Between International Business and Poverty Reduction: The Coca-Cola/SABMiller Value Chain Impacts in Zambia and El Salvador', www.oxfamamerica.org/static/oa3/files/coca-cola-sab-miller-poverty-footprint-dec-2011.pdf.

[24] Rachel Wilshaw, with Erinch Sahan, Gerry Boyle, Katie Knaggs, and Neil McGregor, *Exploring the Links Between International Business and Poverty Reduction: Bouquets and Beans from Kenya* (Oxford: Oxfam International, 2013), http://policy-practice.oxfam.org.uk/pub lications/exploring-the-links-between-international-business-and-poverty-reduction-bouque-290820.

like Marmite and Domestos) presence in Indonesia. The study arrived at some unexpected conclusions: more than half of the 300,000 jobs that Unilever's operations generate in Indonesia are in the company's 'downstream' distribution and retail chain, and only about one-third in the part that makes inputs for the company's products (campaigners' usual focus).[25] Although direct employment was better paid than most, in the less formal parts of the company's activities, away from the comparatively ordered world of permanent jobs, wages, conditions, and the right to organize were found to be weakest.

Beyond the direct impact of a company's capital investment, jobs, and taxes (when they pay them), there can be spill-over effects on the local economy from training of local staff and the introduction of new technology, both of which can influence local firms, especially when the TNCs source their materials and services from local suppliers.

Many TNCs provide products and services that people living in poverty not only want, but can use to improve their lives.[26] Southern-based companies have proven adept at producing and marketing products for poorer consumers. In Tanzania, the Swahili name for cheap motorbike rickshaws is 'bajaji', a corruption of Bajaj, the Indian firm that makes them. When India's Tata Motors launched its $2,500 'people's car' in 2008 it followed in the footsteps of the Volkswagen Beetle or the Model T Ford, promising to bring automobiles to new generations of consumers in the rest of the developing world.[27]

TNCs not only follow consumers' desires; they also shape them, often to resemble those of the former colonialist powers (think McDonald's) and sometimes in ways that are controversial. Perhaps the most notorious is Nestlé's aggressive effort to persuade mothers in

[25] Jason Clay, 'Exploring the Links Between International Business and Poverty Reduction: A Case Study of Unilever in Indonesia' (Oxford: Oxfam GB, Novib Oxfam Netherlands, and Unilever, 2005).
[26] Coimbatore Prahalad and Stuart Hart, 'The Fortune at the Bottom of the Pyramid', strategy+business no. 26 (2002): pp. 1–14.
[27] 'World's Cheapest Car Goes on Show', BBC News website, 10 January 2008, http://news.bbc.co.uk/2/hi/business/7180396.stm.

poor countries to abandon breast-feeding in favour of formula milk, despite the expense and the risks arising from dirty water. It sparked a global boycott[28] that has done lasting damage to the company's previously impressive reputation.

While many firms are diligent in obeying the law and treating their employees and customers with respect, others abuse their power, causing lasting damage to the environment, public health, and local politics. Some undermine the potential for development in a less visible way, by moving operations from one jurisdiction to another to dodge taxes and state regulation. Organizations like Global Witness publish regular exposes of more blatant forms of corporate malpractice. The top stories on its website in January 2016[29] included: allegations of TNC bribery in Nigeria's notorious oil and gas sector; an exposé on TNC purchases of 'conflict minerals' in the Democratic Republic of the Congo; and 'How Southeast Asia's biggest drug lord used shell companies to become a jade kingpin.' World Bank figures suggest that $1 trillion in bribes is paid annually by international companies to secure lucrative deals.[30]

TNCs as influencers

In early 2016, I interviewed Paul Polman, the CEO of Unilever about his approach to change. Polman is active on social and environmental issues well beyond the boundaries of his company, which is why he spared the time to talk to me. He told me that his firm's business model calls for each individual brand to reach 'mission targets'. 'A brand like Domestos', he said, 'wants to build 25 million toilets.

---

[28] 'Nestlé-Free Zone', Baby Milk Action website, www.babymilkaction.org/nestlefree.
[29] 'Protecting Virunga National Park from Oil Companies', Global Witness website, www.globalwitness.org/en/.
[30] Six Questions on the Cost of Corruption with World Bank Institute Global Governance Director Daniel Kaufmann, World Bank News and Broadcast, http://web.worldbank.org/WBSITE/EXTERNAL/NEWS/0,,contentMDK:20190295~menuPK:34457~pagePK:34370~piPK:34424~theSitePK:4607,00.html.

We want to reach five million people in providing livelihoods. We want to improve the lives of 5.5 million women in our value chain. We want to reach one billion people with health and wellbeing—things like handwashing.'

Polman's view of how change happens echoed many of the arguments in this book:

> The job of a CEO has totally changed. You have to be able to work in partnership with national governments and others. I don't want to work with just businesses any more. We discovered quickly that we can't do everything alone. We need to use the size and scale of Unilever to get transformational (i.e. systemic) change. If you want to move the world out of deforestation or transform the tea or palm oil market, you have to focus on the right 30 players. You get a flywheel going,[31] with all these alliances, getting everyone—governments, business, NGOs—together.

Polman, a natural systemic thinker, emphasized the importance of feedback loops and critical junctures:

> If you're smart you can predict maybe one out of ten things, but in the other nine something happens to which you need to react, new competitors, a natural disaster, a new law is passed—things that happen outside of your control. And the world is getting more volatile everywhere. What you have to do as a company is have quick feedback loops from the market that pick up these signals, and a structure that is very agile and externally focussed. So we have delayered and decentralized to the countries. It's the supertanker to speedboat transition, while you are moving.

Polman's commitment and idealism contrasts with the suspicion in which 'big business' is widely held. TNCs' long track record of blocking progressive changes or actively pursuing regressive ones has made many activists cynical about the professed desire of some CEOs to address the world's problems. Corporations usually welcome the creative bit of the market's 'creative destruction', the constant evolutionary churn as new ideas, products, and companies rise and fall, since it provides the raw material companies can turn into global

---

[31] Jim Collins, 'Good to Great', *Fast Company*, October 2001, www.jimcollins.com/article_topics/articles/good-to-great.html.

empires. (I still remember the first time someone recommended Google's nice clean search engine homepage.) But they do everything they can to avoid the destruction part, including a plentiful resort to 'rigged rules and double standards', in the words of one Oxfam report.[32]

Corporations have lobbied extensively for government handouts, excessive patent protection, exclusive contracts, tax breaks, trade rules, and other state interventions that favour their bottom lines (the net profit or loss on a company balance sheet). As one financial executive admitted to *The Wall Street Journal* at the time of the Latin American debt crisis of the 1980s, 'We foreign bankers are for the free market system when we are out to make a buck and believe in the state when we're about to lose a buck.'[33]

As the banker implied, when it comes to specific regulation that restricts their freedom to operate as they please, most TNCs fight tooth and nail to block it. From laws that protect minimum wages, health and safety or freedom of association to rules on product quality, corporate governance or consumer protection, corporate stonewalling has been nearly universal. In 2015 the erstwhile plucky outsider, Google, was reported to have enlisted members of the US Congress (whose election campaigns the company funded) to pressure the EU to drop a €6 billion antitrust case against it, while it raised seven-fold its EU lobbying budget to €4 million a year.[34]

Often individual TNCs opt to keep their heads down and leave the dirty work to business associations (organizations founded and funded by businesses that operate in a specific industry). In the words of Unilever boss Paul Polman, when it comes to climate change lobbying 'the disparities between trade associations and individual

---

[32] Kevin Watkins and Penny Fowler, *Rigged Rules and Double Standards: Trade, Globalisation, and the Fight Against Poverty* (Oxford: Oxfam International, 2002).

[33] *The Wall Street Journal*, 24 May 1985.

[34] Simon Marks and Harry Davies, 'Revealed: How Google Enlisted Members of US Congress it Bankrolled to Fight $6bn EU Antitrust Case', *The Guardian*, 17 December 2015, www.theguardian.com/world/2015/dec/17/google-lobbyists-congress-antitrust-brussels-eu.

companies are huge. The companies say "Yes yes yes", but the trade associations say "No no no". The oil companies are notorious for it.'[35]

Relative bargaining power shapes the nature of the deals struck between particular governments and TNCs. If the host country has something the TNC wants (natural resources, markets, skilled labour, access to export markets), the government's hand is stronger and it will be able to insist on benefits for local people and firms. The more desperate the government, the harder the bargain a TNC can drive.

Because corporations want reliable infrastructure, a healthy, educated workforce and sizable domestic markets, direct investment is heavily concentrated in richer countries. These are also the ones that can bargain more effectively: Brazil, China, India, Mexico, and the Russian Federation received 52 per cent of foreign direct investment (FDI) inflows to developing countries in 2014.[36] By contrast, the poorest states are easily bullied with threats of moving somewhere else. The painful paradox is that the more a government needs foreign investment, the worse the deal it is likely to get. However, the balance of power tends to shift over time: a TNC is most powerful in initial negotiations, less so once it has invested capital and leaving becomes more expensive.

International institutions (discussed in Chapter 7) often intervene to set the rules and shape the balance of power between states and TNCs. While the relatively weak UN agencies provide training and advice to buttress state negotiating and monitoring capacity, the World Bank and IMF attach riders to their loans that protect TNCs from what they view as interference by the state. Loan conditions have required such measures as eliminating capital controls and export taxes, unilaterally reducing tariffs and privatizing state companies and public services. Since the 1990s, a web of bilateral investment treaties and regional and global (WTO) trade agreements has further constrained states' ability

[35] Author Interview with Paul Polman, CEO of Unilever, January 2016.
[36] Calculated from UNCTAD, World Investment Report 2015, Annex table 1 http://unctad.org/en/PublicationsLibrary/wir2015_en.pdf

to regulate TNC behaviour, for example, by proscribing the basic elements of industrial policy.

Corporate lobbying behind closed doors is a key driver of the way trade agreements have evolved. On one of my first visits to the WTO, I burst out laughing when one besuited gent introduced himself in a meeting with officials by saying 'I'm from British Invisibles'. It turned out he was speaking for a powerful association of finance firms that was an extremely effective lobby; true to its name, the general public was largely oblivious of its existence.

One of the most vigorous lobbyists at both global and national levels is the pharmaceutical industry. In the USA, pharmaceutical companies employ 3,000 lobbyists and spend millions to influence national laws and the US position in trade negotiations.[37] In the Uruguay Round that led to the creation of the WTO in 1995, the pharmaceutical lobby steamrollered through an agreement on intellectual property whose implications were unclear to many of those involved. Only after it came into effect did developing countries realize they had signed up to a major extension of corporate monopolies and high-priced drugs that would amount to a death sentence for thousands of sick and dying people.

One huge controversy was over access to medicines for HIV/AIDS, especially in South Africa, the epicentre of the pandemic in the early 2000s. When the Indian generic drug firm CIPLA offered to supply AIDS medicines at a fraction of the cost charged by the big companies, South Africa's Treatment Action Campaign, MSF and Oxfam pressed for action and won a new South African law allowing the importation of the cheaper generic medicines. Then in 2001 nearly three dozen international pharmaceutical corporations precipitated a PR disaster by suing to overturn it, prompting an upsurge of activism that gave them such a public battering they were forced to drop the case.[38]

---

[37] Joseph Stiglitz, *Making Globalization Work* (London: Allen Lane, 2006).
[38] E.B Kapstein & J.W. Busby, *Aids Drugs for All: Social Movements and Market Transformations*, (Cambridge: Cambridge University Press, 2013).

However, pharmaceutical companies have not given up. They continue to push countries to accept more stringent intellectual property rules that further restrain access to medicines. The opportunities for what economists call 'rent seeking' are colossal. In 2015, the company Turing became notorious when it raised the price of Daraprim, a 62-year-old treatment for a dangerous parasitic infection, to $750 (£488) a pill from $13.50 (£8.79). The medicine once sold for $1 a pill.[39]

How do TNCs change?

Activists seek to influence TNCs with strategies that run from cooperation to confrontation. At one end of the spectrum, NGO types sit with corporate executives, academics and government officials on a proliferating number of 'multistakeholder initiatives' on pressing problems like climate change or food security (the hyperactive Paul Polman seems to be on all of them). At the other, activists use litigation or public shaming to oblige governments to act. In between these poles lies the burgeoning realm of lobbying and campaigns to influence particular aspects of corporate behaviour.

According to Erinch Sahan, one of Oxfam's private sector advocates[40]: 'What I've learned is this: build the case for why this particular change is inevitable. Make corporates worry that they're on the wrong side of history. We alone don't have the gravitas to do this. So we try and make sure companies hear from pension fund managers and industry peers, from shareholders at their AGMs, and hundreds of thousands of their consumers are interested enough to contact them on social media. The surprising number of angles they hear from

[39] Reuters, 'Martin Shkreli Announces Turnaround on 5,000% Price Rise for Drug', *The Guardian*, 23 September 2015, www.theguardian.com/business/2015/sep/23/us-pharmaceutical-firm-to-roll-back-5000-price-hike-on-drug.

[40] Erinch Sahan, 'What Makes Big Corporations Decide to Get on the Right Side of History?', From Poverty to Power blog, 26 February 2014, http://oxfamblogs.org/fp2p/what-makes-big-corporations-decide-to-get-on-the-right-side-of-history/.

generates questions: "Are we missing something here? Has this become a mainstream issue?".'

Such approaches can be effective, but as Erinch suggests, more weighty pressures are exerted by the web of regulation, relationships and responsibilities in which TNCs are immersed. Activist organizations are players in this web—known collectively by the unfortunate term 'stakeholders', which always makes me think of people trying to kill a vampire—but it also includes shareholders, customers, the state and other companies.

Above all, corporate executives are subject to the bottom line; if the company loses money, it will go bust or be bought out. That brutal discipline can be a source of dynamism and innovation, yet it makes businesses inherently conservative. As business strategist Simon Levitt argues, TNCs' default mode is to defend the status quo or at least delay change as long as possible.[41] The greater their capital investment (e.g. oil companies' fixed investments in drilling rigs), the more they will resist change.

Levitt identifies four factors that corporations evaluate before supporting progressive change: protecting their brand (especially important for consumer goods companies); the economic cost; the likelihood of impending change in government policy (companies may decide to jump before they are pushed); and whether the firm stands to gain relative to its current or future competitors. Beyond such cost/benefit calculations, leadership at CEO and senior management levels clearly matters in overcoming inertia and inspiring a commitment to change across the company.[42]

These factors are weighed in light of longer-term tidal shifts. Technology is the most obvious: the expansion of TNCs to their present pre-eminence has been driven by successive waves of technological

[41] Simon Levitt, 'Under What Conditions do TNCs Lobby for Change?' (mimeo, undated).
[42] Simon Levitt, 'Under What Conditions do TNCs Lobby for Change?' (mimeo, undated).

progress in transport, communications and production that first allowed them to trade across geographical distances, then create a global assembly line for their products, and most recently to manage complex global production networks. Economic development is another, as TNCs increasingly see China, India and others as lucrative markets, rather than simply enormous reservoirs of cheap labour.

Other long-term shifts are more subtle. The very idea of what a corporation should be and do has evolved over time. In a 1970 article entitled 'The Social Responsibility of Business is to Increase its Profits', economist Milton Friedman accused promoters of corporate social responsibility of 'preaching pure and unadulterated socialism.'[43] Few companies today would agree. The norms governing corporate behaviour (much like human behaviour) have evolved, partly through peer pressure among executives. At the annual gathering of corporate titans in the Swiss skiing resort of Davos, 'masters of the universe' swap notes and influence each other, providing an annual snapshot of a global conversation to which ordinary mortals are seldom admitted.

Though Friedman's words now seem to emanate from a bygone age, shareholders and owners still hold the most power to shape a company's actions. That may be why some of the more progressive companies on social and environmental issues are owned by families or foundations that are able to take a longer-term view than investors seeking to maximize quarterly returns.[44]

In companies where workers have managed to organize, trade unions can exert significant influence, especially regarding wages and working conditions. However, unions have struggled to 'transnationalize' along with their employers, linking up workers in different

[43] Milton Friedman, 'A Friedman Doctrine – The Social Responsibility of Business is to Increase Its Profits', *The New York Times Magazine*, 13 September 1970.

[44] Erinch Sahan, 'How Businesses Can Save the World (When Their Shareholders Aren't Breathing Down Their Neck)', From Poverty to Power blog, 9 April 2015, http://oxfamblogs.org/fp2p/how-businesses-can-save-the-world-when-their-shareholders-arent-breathing-down-their-neck/.

countries and organizing within global production networks characterized by subcontracting and outsourcing.

Corporations with brand names are highly sensitive to the views of consumers, since bad publicity can quickly destroy brand value painstakingly built up over decades. Activists have found success with high-profile campaigns, such as the Nestlé boycott noted above, and with more nuanced engagement, in which civil society organizations use the threat of consumer pressure to persuade companies to improve their social and environmental record.

Why do different TNCs behave so differently?

Geoff, a senior manager in a major UK supermarket, wandered over to me after the meeting with a startling proposition. 'Do you think you NGOs could campaign a bit harder against us? My board is thinking of cutting my budget.' I sat with Geoff on the board of the multi-stakeholder Ethical Trading Initiative to promote labour rights and decent working conditions in his and other firms' global supply chains. It seems he needed a credible threat (and some dark arts) to keep his company engaged.

That conversation took place in the early 2000s, during a wave of 'corporate social responsibility' (CSR) that has since spread across much of the private sector. CSR is controversial: denounced as corporate spin by opponents, it is held up by supporters as a market-friendly alternative to inefficient government regulation. I was definitely in the supporter camp.

One basic lesson I learned at the ETI was not to lump all corporations together. The corporate world is a system, with positive (and negative) deviants, companies that are unusually progressive and others that are the exact opposite. Differences among TNCs often hark back to the combination of institutions, ideas and interests that underlie inertia, as discussed in Chapter 2. The nature of a firm's business is critical (arms, tobacco or oil companies are uniquely regressive). But within a sector, an individual company's history and culture and the nature of its leadership all weigh heavily in how it reacts to pressure from the public, national governments, international bodies or competitors.[45]

Even within the ETI, there were obvious leaders and laggards (I won't start naming names), and the trick was to use the former to put pressure on the latter, since nothing galvanizes action like being shamed in front of your peers and rivals.

Distinguishing between leaders and laggards is also a staple of public campaigns, which make use of brand reputation, corporate rivalry and public pressure to influence corporate behaviour. Oxfam's 'Behind the Brands' campaign produced a league table assessing the agricultural sourcing policies of the world's ten largest food and beverage companies: (in alphabetical order) Associated British Foods (ABF), Coca-Cola, Danone, General Mills, Kellogg's, Mars, Mondelez, Nestle, PepsiCo and Unilever. The results surpassed all the organizers'- expectations: Between February and October 2014, all of the Big Ten published new policies or assessments relating to the issues covered by the campaign.[46] According to Oxfam's Penny Fowler, the critical success factors included: creating a race to the top between the leading companies, balancing stick and carrot (challenging companies but praising them when they moved; plus insider engagement on solutions), and (echoing Erinch Sahan's point) making sure that the companies didn't just hear from Oxfam but also from consumers, investors/pension fund managers, industry peers. Strong and transparent research and methodology also helped, as did filling a policy gap for the companies by setting out a social sustainability framework for agricultural sourcing (which was previously lacking).[47]

---

[45] Dana Brown, Anne Roemer-Mahler and Antje Vetterlein, 'Theorising Transnational Corporations as Social Actors: An Analysis of Corporate Motivations', Working Paper No. 61 (Copenhagen: International Center for Business and Politics, Copenhagen Business School, 2009).

[46] Transparency, gender rights, farm workers and small-scale producers in the supply chain, land rights and access, water rights and access and sustainability, reducing green house gas emissions and helping farmers adapt to climate change.

[47] Penny Fowler, email, January 2016.

Conclusions

The world of TNCs is seething with expressions of power: one major corporate CEO who preferred not to be quoted in this book recalled how sitting next to the British Prime Minister on a long-haul flight allowed him to successfully lobby for a change of legislation that affected his company—an expression of 'hidden power' unavailable to the average activist. TNCs also have invisible power in the extraordinary influence on consumers exerted by brands and the values they claim to embody, as well as the apparently mesmerizing authority of giant corporations in the eyes of policy makers.

TNCs use that power in a system that is growing ever more complex. In a world with more TNCs from more countries, the traditional campaigning approach of targeting large TNCs based in Europe or North America, risks being wrongfooted. Yet many activists have upped their game, shifting their focus from addressing individual companies and their supply chains, toward creating an enabling environment for change by addressing the incentives that motivate companies.

The to-do list is long: overhauling financial markets to end the culture of short-termism that undermines attempts to build sustainability; increasing transparency and reporting requirements to keep corporations from buying politicians and parties; making sure the polluter pays on issues such as carbon emissions; clamping down on tax dodging. For any of these initiatives to prosper, coordinated action between northern and southern activists, and alliances with progressive governments, not to mention exploiting differences among companies, will be essential.

It is not enough for activists to declare ourselves either 'anti-corporate' or 'pro-business'. Whatever the starting point, we need to learn to dance with the TNC system by understanding the traditions and mindsets of particular companies, the new variants, positive deviants and critical junctures that dot the corporate landscape, and the variety of ways corporations can be influenced.

As for me, perhaps I'll have to beg forgiveness from my more anti-capitalist colleagues, because my time at the Ethical Trading Initiative gave me a lasting respect for the dynamism and seriousness of some of the people who run TNCs. Suited and booted in a central London cafe, I once tried to recruit a new garment retailer to join the initiative. I deployed my best corporate speak, stressing the business case for signing up—you can recruit better people and keep them longer, you'll manage your supply chain better, you'll avoid damaging your reputation and brand. The exasperated executive interrupted me: 'Forget all that, I just want to make the world better for my grandchildren'. I still remember my sense of embarrassment and shame.

Further Reading

A. Chandler and B. Mazlish, eds., *Leviathans: Multinational Corporations and the New Global History* (Cambridge and New York: Cambridge University Press, 2005).

G. Cook & J. Johns (eds), *The Changing Geography of International Business* (London: Palgrave Macmillan, 2013).

A. Flohr et al, *The Role of Business in Global Governance: Corporations as Norm-Entrepreneurs* (London: Palgrave Macmillan, 2010).

G. Jones, *Multinationals and Global Capitalism* (Cambridge: Cambridge University Press, 2005).

R. Locke, *The Promise and Limits of Private Power: Promoting Labor Standards in a Global Economy* (Cambridge: Cambridge University Press, 2013).

N. Robins, *The Corporation that Changed the World: How the East India Company Shaped the Modern Multinational*, 2nd ed. (London: Pluto Press, 2012).

J. Ruggie, *Just Business: Multinational Corporations and Human Rights* (New York: WW Norton, 2013).

L. Stout, *The Shareholder Value Myth: How Putting Shareholders First Harms Investors, Corporations, and the Public* (Oakland: Berrett-Koehler Publishers, 2012).

CASE STUDY

The December 2015 Paris Agreement on climate change

Background

On 12 December 2015, more than 190 countries made pledges to cut emissions of greenhouse gases (GHGs), covering 94 per cent of the world's GHG emissions. They also adopted language calling for efforts towards a 1.5 degree limit to global warming—the upper boundary of safety for many fragile island states and Least Developed Countries.[1] After twenty-one years of hard negotiations and six years after the 2009 Copenhagen climate talks ended in disarray, this was a remarkable turnaround. How did it happen? This short case study uses the various chapters and themes in this book to unpack the story of Paris.[2]

Contextual drivers of change

There were three major changes in the context that made Paris such a contrast to Copenhagen.

---

[1] For more detailed analysis, see 'Oxfam's Initial analysis of the Paris Agreement: What will the Paris Agreement be remembered for?', https://www.oxfam.org/en/research/oxfams-initial-analysis-paris-agreement.

[2] Summary of a longer case study paper by Duncan Green and Tim Gore, to be published on the How Change Happens website.

The first, and single most important factor was a US–China joint announcement on climate change at the end of 2014,[3] pledging new targets to cut emissions—notably in China's case to peak emissions by 2030—and to work together for a successful outcome in Paris. With the two biggest GHG emitters on board, an agreement of some kind started to look inevitable. Domestic factors drove both leaders to sign up: on the Chinese side, a smog crisis in Beijing and other cities had shown the environmental limits of China's development model, and especially its reliance on coal. In addition, as China upgrades its economy, its leaders are now keen to move from dirty, low-tech industry to higher value sectors, including renewables.

In the US, President Obama, who had worked to make Copenhagen a success, received much more public backing in the run-up to Paris. Climate activists had pursued an insider strategy prior to Copenhagen, trying to persuade fossil fuel companies to support domestic cap and trade laws, which failed. Since then, they opted for more outsider tactics, building a grassroots movement, with the Keystone pipeline as its iconic issue, which provided the Obama administration with the political room to manoeuvre. In addition, since President Obama was approaching the end of his period in office, and had largely given up on winning bipartisan action from Congress, he was more willing to pursue reform through executive action.

The second major shift occurred within the private sector. In Copenhagen, the fossil fuel lobby dominated the private sector presence. In Paris, for the first time there was a powerful and credible countervailing force to the blockers of the fossil fuel lobby: Hundreds of companies and CEOs made pledges to reduce their own carbon footprint and called for governments to set more ambitious targets. Business supported a price on carbon and called for an end to fossil fuels subsidies. Credit for the shift goes to the leadership of individual

[3] 'U.S.-China Joint Announcement on Climate Change', 11 November 2014, press release, The White House, https://www.whitehouse.gov/the-press-office/2014/11/11/us-china-joint-announcement-climate-change.

companies and CEOs (Ikea and Unilever among them) swayed by growing concerns about the economic impact of climate change.

The third major shift occurred at the intersection of economics and technology: a dramatic change in prices, with the cost of renewable energy falling much faster than predicted. Through a combination of technological innovation and economies of scale, the price of solar power fell by 50 per cent from 2010 to 2014.[4]

Secondary factors added momentum to the train set moving by the US–China announcement: activist pressure, for example, the September 2014 People's Climate March in New York, reenergized the public; outstanding French diplomacy dealt with 'hot potato issues' well in advance of Paris; a May 2015 Papal Encyclical, 'Care for Our Common Home',[5] galvanized Roman Catholics and other faith communities (and may lead to longer-term shifts in social norms and personal behaviour).

The debate over climate science seemed less significant in Paris than in Copenhagen, perhaps because the deniers had lost the argument, so that debates could shift to the real and thorny problems of implementation.

The main players

In addition to leadership from the US and China, a number of groupings of developed and developing countries shaped the Paris process. These included the 'Climate Vulnerable Forum', led by the Philippines, which was instrumental in winning the reference to a 1.5 degree target, and to establishing action to address the 'loss and damage' experienced by poor countries as a fundamental element in the new climate

---

[4] Irena, *Renewable Power Generation Costs in 2014*, January 2015.
[5] 'Encyclical Letter *Laudato si'* of the Holy Father Francis on Care for our Common Home' Libreria Editrice Vaticana, 2015, http://w2.vatican.va/content/francesco/en/encyclicals/documents/papa-francesco_20150524_enciclica-laudato-si.html.

regime. The Pacific Islands, in particular Tony de Brun, foreign minister of the Marshall Islands, also played a prominent role.

The underlying geopolitics of the transition from Copenhagen to Paris saw the establishment of a new paradigm, replacing the Kyoto Protocol's division of the world into North (Annex 1) and South (Non-Annex 1), in which only Annex 1 countries were obliged to cut emissions. In Paris, by contrast, all countries made commitments, with emerging powers like China and India being some of the most ambitious.

Critical junctures

In the run up to Paris, a number of weather events helped build a consensus for action. In particular, a series of major climate-related disasters affected the big economies (US, Australia, Russia) as well as poor countries, building recognition that 'we are all in this together'. But the most important critical juncture had nothing to do with the climate: the appalling 13 November terrorist attacks in Paris, which killed 130 people, generated worldwide condemnation but also a determination to show solidarity with France who hosted the climate conference only weeks later.[6]

Systems thinking: a 21st century international agreement?

According to Christiana Figueres, the UN's lead climate change official and one of the unsung heroes of the Paris Agreement, 'Climate change is a good example of how we are moving to a completely new social contract from the last century.'[7]

---

[6] http://oxfamblogs.org/fp2p/how-will-the-paris-attacks-affect-the-outcome-of-the-climate-change-talks/.

[7] Suzanne Goldenberg, 'Paris climate deal offers flame of hope, says UN official', *The Guardian*, 17 January 2016, http://www.theguardian.com/environment/2016/jan/17/paris-climate-deal-flame-of-hope-diplomacy-christiana-figueres.

First, the Paris Agreement recognizes that today's international system is much more complex than the inter-state arrangements of previous decades. Unlike other negotiations, the Paris climate talks involved governments, business leaders, city councils, civil society organizations, and others in prominent roles. The 'We Mean Business' private sector coalition claimed to have 100 lobbyists using their script in Paris, while 450 mayors held a parallel summit where they made their own climate commitments.

Second, countries agreed a 'review and ratchet' approach in which they each will take stock every five years and update their efforts: each national target must go further than previous commitments. Action to decarbonize the economy can thus evolve in line with changing evidence, technology, and economic capacity. Binding commitments, in contrast, would have set in stone a set of negotiated (and probably minimum acceptable) commitments that would then have been difficult to renegotiate. (It was the attempt to agree binding targets that destroyed the Copenhagen talks.)

At least that is the optimistic view. The Paris Agreement also provides ample room for foot dragging and bad faith, and it is yet to be seen whether the review and ratchet mechanism produces enough action to keep climate change within acceptable limits.

I

PART III

WHAT ACTIVISTS CAN (AND CAN'T) DO

There is a much-quoted phrase attributed to the anthropologist Margaret Mead (although no original source can be found), namely 'Never doubt that a small group of thoughtful, committed citizens can change the world; indeed, it's the only thing that ever has'.[1]

These words have inspired generations of activists, but they always leave me with mixed feelings. If we focus on 'committed' and lose sight of 'thoughtful', we can fall into the seductive trap of thinking that change comes from a noble and pure band of brothers and sisters, willing to go up into the mountains or onto the streets. I don't think that's how change works.

JK Rowling satirizes that kind of 'committed' campaigning in *Harry Potter and the Goblet of Fire*,[2] when Hermione sets up an 'Elf Liberation Front' to free the house elves who serve the wizard community. The house elves are horrified—no-one had asked them if they wanted to be 'liberated', which to them looks very much like being unemployed.

---

[1] The Institute for Intercultural Studies, 'Frequently Asked Questions About Mead/ Bateson', http://www.interculturalstudies.org/faq.html#quote.

[2] J.K. Rowling, *Harry Potter and the Goblet of Fire* (London: Bloomsury, 2000).

Hermione didn't consult the elves; she merely assumed she knew what was right for them. She really needed a proper theory of change.

In contrast, a 'thoughtful' power and systems approach emphasizes humility and curiosity about the system we are seeking to influence. Passion is essential, of course, but it must be tempered with critical thinking. Activists need to be reflectivists too.

The next three chapters explore how activists of different kinds go about that task. They cover grassroots citizen activism, the often-ignored role of leaders, and advocacy to influence the institutions analysed in Section 2. It is a necessarily partial and personal view, reflecting my own background and drawing on the activists, leaders, and campaigners I have met, worked with, and above all learned from. I said at the outset of the book that there was no 'department of change studies' that activists can turn to for guidance—the history and variety of activism is an excellent substitute.

The book will then conclude with a 'so what?' discussion that fleshes out the power and systems approach and its implications for activists and their organizations.

9

CITIZEN ACTIVISM AND CIVIL SOCIETY

I have come across some extraordinary citizen activists over the last thirty years, among them the Chiquitano people of the Bolivian lowlands, the fisherfolk of India's Bundelkhand, and the members of Citizens UK in central London. For centuries, men and women like them have shrugged off the exhaustion of long days spent earning a living and raising families to join with their communities to discuss, organize, and take action. As we have seen, they courageously risk their lives to confront hired thugs and corrupt officials.

They do so for any number of reasons: to feed their families or improve their neighbourhoods, in response to their sense of what is right and wrong, or because working together in a common cause is fulfilling. Supporting their heroic efforts is what has made working in the development business so personally rewarding (it certainly isn't the meetings).

However, I do have one confession to make: in my personal life, I am one of the most inactive citizens I know. I hate confrontation and conflict; I barely know my own neighbours; I'm not a 'joiner'. Nevertheless, I have long been inspired and fascinated by people who behave very differently from me. First, Latin America's brave community organizers, and then the great activists from around the world I have had the privilege to meet through my work at Oxfam. Hypocrisy? Perhaps. I will just have to live with the gulf that separates their lives from mine. At least my son Calum works as a Citizens UK organizer in Peckham in South London.[1] Does that get me off the hook?

This chapter delves a little deeper into who citizen activists are, how they pursue change, and what outsiders can do to help.

Citizen activism has grown exponentially across the developing world, driven by several factors: rapid increases in literacy and access to education (particularly for women), a greater openness to political activity, and the spread of new norms regarding rights and justice. Urbanization too: with exchanges of opinions and information on every street corner, cities are vividly political places, dense with social movements demanding housing, schools, clinics, or decent water and sanitation. Protest and conflict abound, between workers and employers or service providers and users. (The more I see of urban citizens' movements, the more I am baffled by the rural bias of many aid agencies, who seem to prefer villages to shanty towns, even if that means missing many opportunities to support social change.)[2]

Technology plays a part, most recently through the spread of social media and mobile telephones, which greatly expand the possibilities of networking among large groups. Their impact amid the chaos of street protests, however, is often exaggerated by the digirati. One study found that 93 per cent of communications between activists in Cairo's Tahrir Square at the height of the 2011 protests were face-to-face.[3]

What is citizen activism?

Citizen activism certainly includes political activism, but it can be much more. A good definition would be any individual action with

[1] Tom Henderson, 'Peckham Votes Yes to Launching Peckham Citizens', Citizens UK, 26 November 2014, www.citizensuk.org/peckham_votes_yes_to_launching_peckham_citizens.

[2] Duncan Green, 'India's Slums: How Change Happens and the Challenge of Urban Programming', From Poverty to Power blog, 1 November 2012, http://oxfamblogs.org/fp2p/indias-slums-how-change-happens-and-the-challenge-of-urban-programming/.

[3] Michael Edwards, Civil Society, 3rd edition (Cambridge: Polity Press, 2014), p. 85.

social consequences, and much of it involves collective activity, including participation in faith groups or neighbourhood associations, producer organizations and trade unions, village savings and loan groups, and funeral societies, among others. Such participation is an assertion of 'power with', and is both an end in itself—a crucial kind of freedom—and a means to ensure that society and its institutions respect people's rights and meet their needs. Active citizens provide vital feedback to state decision makers, exert pressure for reform, or solve their problems themselves, bypassing state systems altogether.

Such 'social capital' is often as valuable as cash or skills. World Bank research in Indonesia found that membership in local associations had a bigger impact on household welfare than education.[4] By one estimate, voluntary associations the world over have become key providers of human services (especially health and welfare), and now constitute a $2.2 *trillion* industry in just the forty countries that were sampled[5]—sixteen times the global aid budget.

The local organizations people form, known in development jargon as civil society organizations (CSOs), complement more traditional links of clan, caste, or religion. Coming together in CSOs helps citizens nourish the stock of trust and co-operation on which all societies depend.[6]

Of course, citizens' groups can also reinforce discrimination, fear, and mistrust; called 'uncivil society' by some, their activities can sometimes spill over into violence, as in the case of religious or racist pogroms, football hooligans, or paramilitary organizations. At the time of Rwanda's 1994 genocide, the country had the highest density of voluntary associations in sub-Saharan Africa.[7]

---

[4] Michael Edwards, *Civil Society*, 3rd edition (Cambridge: Polity Press, 2014), p. 92.

[5] Michael Edwards, *Civil Society*, 3rd edition (Cambridge: Polity Press, 2014), p. 13, footnote 15.

[6] Jude Howell and Jenny Pearce, *Civil Society and Development: A Critical Exploration* (Boulder, CO: Lynne Rienner Publishers, 2001), p. 31.

[7] Michael Edwards, *Civil Society*, 3rd edition (Cambridge: Polity Press, 2014), p. 51.

Nor are CSOs immune from the wider power inequalities in society. Men often dominate them, as do individuals from powerful ethnic or caste backgrounds. CSOs of hitherto marginalized groups have often emerged as splinters from mixed organizations, when women or indigenous or HIV-positive people found that their specific concerns continually evaporated from the agenda.

CSOs' work is often local and below the media radar, pushing authorities to install street lighting, pave the roads, or invest in schools and clinics. CSOs often run such services themselves, along with public education programmes on everything from hand washing to labour rights. Even in the chaotic, dangerous world of the Eastern Congo (DRC), Community Protection Committees made up of six men and six women elected by their villages have brought new-found confidence and resilience to conflict-affected communities. They identify the main threats and actions to mitigate them. When people are forced to flee renewed fighting, these committees are often instrumental in getting people organized in their new refugee camps.[8]

For the UN, CSOs include everything from small, informal, community-based organizations to the large, high-profile, international NGOs like Oxfam.[9] Many observers distinguish between grassroots CSOs and NGOs: CSOs tend to be membership-driven and local (although some have got very large indeed), can be informal or legalized entities, and are often almost entirely voluntary in nature. NGOs tend to be run by boards and professional staff, with only limited accountability to their supporters. Crucially, CSOs work to advance the interests of their members, whereas NGOs usually do so

---

[8] Duncan Green, *Community Protection Committees in Democratic Republic of Congo* (Oxford: Oxfam GB for Oxfam International, 2015), http://policy-practice.oxfam.org.uk/pub lications/community-protection-committees-in-democratic-republic-of-congo-338435.

[9] Brian Tomlinson, *Working with Civil Society in Foreign Aid: Possibilities for South-South Cooperation?* 'Annex 1: NGOs and CSOs: A Note on Terminology' (Beijing: United Nations Development Programme (UNDP) China, 2013), www.cn.undp.org/content/dam/china/docs/Publications/UNDP-CH03%20Annexes.pdf.

in the public interest, by running projects, responding to disasters or trying to influence public policy.

Of course grassroots organizations also lobby for changes that go beyond the immediate interests of their members; and many people in NGOs work there because of their acutely personal commitment to issues such as gender injustice. But a large NGO is clearly a very different beast from a village savings group. The distinction matters partly because the relationship between NGOs and CSOs is often fraught with tensions over access to money and expertise, and issues of representation (who speaks on behalf of poor communities?). This chapter sticks mostly to grassroots CSOs, while Chapter 11 covers the influencing work of NGOs.

Citizen activism and protest

Since the 1980s, citizen activists have become prominent in the global media for leading protest movements that have ousted dozens of authoritarian regimes across Latin America, Eastern Europe, and Central Asia. They have removed dictators in the Philippines and Indonesia, ended apartheid in South Africa and most recently brought down oppressive governments in Tunisia, Egypt, and Libya. Many autocrats must live in fear that one day tear gas from the protests outside will invade the comfort of the presidential palace, as thousands of citizens gather in the square to demand justice, vowing to remain until they get it.[10]

While other factors contribute to political transitions (involvement of the formal political opposition or the military, foreign intervention, and so on), boycotts, mass protests, blockades, strikes, and other

---

[10] Thomas Carothers and Saskia Brechenmacher, 'The Civil Society Flashpoint: Why the Global Crackdown? What Can Be Done About It?', From Poverty to Power blog, 6 March 2014, http://oxfamblogs.org/fp2p/the-civil-society-flashpoint-why-the-global-crackdown-what-can-be-done-about-it/.

civil disobedience by cohesive non-violent civic coalitions have proven vital.

Protest movements exhibit a particular rhythm and structure. One historian of European social movements sees them as passing through 'cycles of contention',[11] similar to the cycles of state reform described in Chapter 4. The response to explosions of protest is often repression, but frequently laced with reform. As conflict collapses and militants retire to lick their wounds, many of their gains are reversed; nevertheless, they leave behind incremental expansions in participation, changes in popular culture and residual networks that lay a groundwork for future protest. Open conflict is a season for sowing, but the reaping often comes in the periods of demobilization that follow, by latecomers to the cause and reformers among elites and officialdom.

While many outsiders see protest movements as homogeneous (journalists and politicians often lament their lack of easily-identifiable leaders), on closer inspection, they contain smaller, more durable organizations that emerge at vital moments, and then disperse.[12] According to Oxfam's Ihab El Sakkout, the protesters in Cairo's Tahrir Square in 2011 exhibited a degree of granularity:

> On 2nd and 3rd of February, when the protestors were attacked viciously by regime thugs, the Muslim brotherhood and organized groups of soccer fans played a key role in defending the square (principally by being able to convey quick decisions via their groups, showing extreme courage and discipline under attack, quickly building barricades, managing counter-attacks, etc.), which helped to turn those in the square from a mass of individuals into a cohesive group able to defend itself.[13]

Now, whenever I read of apparently faceless blobs of protest, I look for those underlying 'grains' of organization.

[11] Sidney Tarrow, *Power in Movement: Social Movements and Contentious Politics* (Cambridge: Cambridge University Press, 1998), p. 24.
[12] Sidney Tarrow, *Power in Movement: Social Movements and Contentious Politics* (Cambridge: Cambridge University Press, 1998).
[13] Duncan Green, 'Egypt: What are the Drivers of Change?', From Poverty to Power blog, 17 February 2011, http://oxfamblogs.org/fp2p/egypt-what-are-the-drivers-of-change/.

Citizen activism and markets

Most day-to-day efforts of citizens' associations are more mundane than the overthrow of governments, but they are equally important to how change happens. Factory workers, state employees, and small-scale farmers around the world have long realized that getting organized will give them the bargaining power they need to exact a better deal out of markets. Trade unions, producer associations, cooperatives, small business associations, and the like can win fairer wages, prices, or working conditions for their members. Many of them take up lobbying for state regulation or other measures to limit the excessive but hidden power of vested interests.

Trade unions have been at the forefront of the struggle for workers' rights for over two centuries, winning huge advances regarding wages and working conditions, the rights to collective bargaining and freedom of association, holidays, pensions, and a host of other areas.[14]

In many countries unions' achievements have been rolled back in recent decades, as corporations and their allies in international institutions and government have gutted hard-won labour legislation. Worker organizations continue to face repression and violence; union leaders around the world confront harassment, rape, and murder. In 2015, almost half of 141 countries assessed had 'systematic violations' or 'no guarantee' of labour rights.[15]

In part due to entrenched attitudes in the labour movement that women are temporary, secondary, or less valuable workers, women's organizations have come to the fore in struggling to improve working conditions for the millions of women now employed in factories in developing countries, especially in export processing zones (EPZs), where unions are banned. In Nicaragua, the María Elena Cuadra

---

[14] The International Labour Organization (ILO) has so far agreed 189 Conventions on almost every aspect of working life.

[15] International Trade Union Confederation (ITUC), Global Rights Index, 2015, http://www.ituc-csi.org/IMG/pdf/survey_global_rights_index_2015_en.pdf

Movement of Employed and Unemployed Women (MEC) and its 2,000 volunteers helped to win the country's first National Health and Safety Law in 2007, with increased site inspections in EPZ factories to ensure compliance, as well as human rights training for mid-level private sector managers.[16] On export plantations where women make up most of the labourers, women's organizations have also stepped into the fray. In South Africa, the Women on Farms Project helped isolated seasonal workers form an organization to demand a minimum daily wage; after a 2013 strike, the women won a 52 per cent pay increase.[17]

Despite the efforts of women's groups and unions, approximately 90 per cent of the world labour force is unorganized, and union membership is declining in direct proportion to the growth of the informal economy. Unions have struggled to reach people working within homes or without contracts, who are determined to hang on to even meagre jobs.

In contrast, the number of independent producer organizations has mushroomed in recent decades.[18] Farmers and other producers are forming co-operatives or associations to improve their bargaining power nearly everywhere. Between 1982 and 2002 the number of villages in Burkina Faso that had such organizations rose from 21 per cent to 91 per cent.[19] In Nigeria, the number of producer co-operatives nearly doubled between 1990 and 2005.[20] By 1998 65 per cent of

---

[16] For further examples of organizing in the informal economy, see Women in Informal Employment: Globalizing and Organizing (WIEGO) website, www.wiego.org.

[17] BBC News, 'South Africa Farm Workers Get 52% Pay Rise', BBC News website, 4 February 2013, www.bbc.co.uk/news/world-africa-21324275.

[18] For an overview of the issues facing producer organizations, see Chris Penrose-Buckley, *Producer Organisations: A Guide to Developing Collective Rural Enterprises* (Oxford: Oxfam GB, 2007).

[19] Jean-Louis Arcand, 'Organisations paysannes et Développement rural au Burkina Faso', CERDI, Université d'Auvergne, France, 2004, in Marie-Rose Mercoiret and Jeanot Mfou'ou, *Rural Producers Organizations for Pro-poor Sustainable Agricultural Development*, Paper for World Development Report 2008, Paris workshop, 30–1 October 2006.

[20] Research by Leuven University cited in Proceedings Report, 'Corporate Governance and Co-operatives', Peer Review Workshop, London, 8 February 2007.

all rural households in India belonged to a co-operative society.[21] Such organizations can win better terms for credit, share the cost of expensive machinery like tractors, and process and market their produce more efficiently, thereby gaining a far greater share of the final market price.

One of India's biggest and best known independent producer organizations is the Self Employed Women's Association (SEWA), which had a million members in 2008 (the latest available figures).[22] Born in 1972 as a trade union of self-employed women, its members include everyone from street vendors, to home workers, to casual construction and farm labourers.

SEWA describes its task as 'organising workers to achieve their goals of full employment and self reliance through the strategy of struggle and development'. The 'struggle' part includes campaigns and lobbying for better services for women and against 'the many constraints and limitations imposed on them by society and the economy'; SEWA's development activities strengthen women's bargaining power and offer them new alternatives. SEWA has set up its own bank, health insurer, training schools, and childcare centres.

Civil society and the state: opponents or collaborators?

Where the political system is viewed as inclusive and legitimate, much of the activity of CSOs is channelled into the formal politics of elections or in democracy's daily 'public conversation' about laws and state policy. Many CSOs have ties to political parties, at least at election time, and can be important vehicles for marshalling votes in poor countries and rich alike.

On a visit to India in 2012, grassroots activists in the slums of the city of Lucknow told me the first stage in winning political clout is to

---

[21] Udai Shanker Awasthi, 'Resurgence of Co-operative Movement Through Innovations', *Co-op Dialogue* 11, no. 2 (2001): pp. 21–6.

[22] Self Employed Women's Association (SEWA) website, www.sewa.org/About_Us.asp.

convince the lowest rank of elected officials, known as 'corporators', that the slum is worthy of being designated a 'notified slum,' and so appear on the political and fiscal map. Corporators then distribute voting cards, which are the only identity papers many residents have.

In the eyes of slum dwellers, corporators are the most approachable, but least powerful, politicians. Above them only a few members of the state assembly are willing to talk to them. 'The officials are worse, especially the low-level ones, they ignore us or demand bribes. At least corporators listen, even if they don't do anything.' Asked why they vote, one responded, 'We're positive if our candidate wins, they will provide basic services. When it doesn't happen, we're disappointed, but then we wait five years and vote for someone else. What else can we do?'[23]

But CSOs are seldom mere pawns in politicians' games. They have set up crowd-source websites, such as 'ipaidabribe.com' in India,[24] to expose corruption by corporate lobbyists, clientilist political networks, and the like. Many now monitor government spending, painstakingly analysing what is promised vs. what is delivered, and seeking to influence budget allocations. In Israel, for example, activists from different social movements set up the Adva Centre, an NGO that does research, lobbying, and outreach to promote equal rights for Mizrahi Jews, women, and Arab citizens.[25]

Lobbying government can be a disillusioning experience, as I found when talking to CSOs in South Africa.[26] 'Party hacks get parachuted into senior administrative jobs, lacking the capacity or interest to perform them properly', one activist told me. 'You look at the giant that is government and it's so difficult to navigate. You never quite

---

[23] Author visit, Delhi, 2012.

[24] 'I Paid a Bribe', India, www.ipaidabribe.com/#gsc.tab=0.

[25] Adva Centre, Israel, http://adva.org/en/.

[26] Duncan Green, 'How to Build Local Government Accountability in South Africa? A Conversation with Partners', From Poverty to Power blog, 18 March 2013, https://oxfamblogs.org/fp2p/how-to-build-local-government-accountability-in-south-africa-a-conversation-with-partners/.

know where to push—and nor do the officials! You invest hugely in building intimate relationships only to find they've moved department and you have to start all over again.'

In some countries, CSOs have built new political parties, much as trade unions did to represent their interests in the UK and elsewhere. In Bolivia and Brazil, social movements came together to found the Movement for Socialism (MAS) and the Workers Party (PT), both of which subsequently came to power and enacted major progressive reforms (discussed in Chapter 4). While crucial for policy change, links to the governing party can undermine CSOs' vitality, their leadership poached to become MPs or ministers, or their reputation tarnished by association with the inevitable compromises of political office.

Civil society also finds ways to effect change in more closed political systems, using research and demonstration projects rather than the more risky avenues of campaigns and public protest.[27] Officials in one-party systems are sometimes more willing to listen to evidence of what isn't working because they don't have to worry about adverse press coverage or buying political support. In Russia, for example, disability campaigners lobbied successfully to change badly designed laws on benefits by explaining the problems behind closed doors.[28]

Even in apparently unpropitious areas such as women's rights in Pakistan,[29] CSOs have won reforms by working at local level, where the imbalance of power between activists and the state is less extreme and relationships are easier to establish. Participatory budgeting began in villages and towns in Indonesia and Brazil before spreading more widely, and Brazil's renowned Bolsa Familia social welfare programme

[27] Duncan Green, 'How Can You Do Influencing Work in One-Party States?', From Poverty to Power blog 8 June 2011, http://oxfamblogs.org/fp2p/how-can-you-do-influencing-work-in-strong-authoritarian-states/.

[28] Duncan Green, 'Advocacy v Service Delivery in Russia: FP2P Flashback', From Poverty to Power blog, 17 August 2011, http://oxfamblogs.org/fp2p/advocacy-v-service-delivery-in-russia/.

[29] Jacky Repila, *The Politics of Our Lives: The Raising Her Voice in Pakistan Experience* (Oxford: Oxfam GB, 2013), http://policy-practice.oxfam.org.uk/publications/the-politics-of-our-lives-the-raising-her-voice-in-pakistan-experience-294763.

was first launched as an experiment under progressive municipal governments.

As noted in Part 2, effectively engaging the state means understanding its internal structures and incentive systems. Framing demands in ways that make sense to politicians can greatly improve the chances of success. Publicly congratulating officials and politicians when they do something right, rather than immediately moving the goalposts and issuing new demands, can help build trust.

A review of 200 citizens' anti-corruption projects in fifty-three countries found that success relied on identifying allies among officials and politicians who could act as champions and sources of inside intelligence.[30] An in-depth evaluation of efforts to influence state services in South Africa, Mexico, Tanzania, and Brazil agreed on the importance of champions and stressed the role of alliances with the media, academics, and other players as activists dig in for the long haul.[31]

State support for citizen activism

Civil society can help the state become more effective, and states can in turn promote citizen activism by addressing the different kinds of power discussed in Chapter 2.[32] Issuing birth certificates or other official registration to members of excluded groups (lower castes, indigenous, the elderly, the disabled, migrants) can bolster their individual identity ('power within'). So can public education on rights and discriminatory norms and values, or laws that guarantee equitable access to assets and opportunities, not to mention preventing violence against women and other forms of intimidation.

---

[30] Pierre Landell-Mills, *Citizens Against Corruption: Report from the Front Line* (Leicester: Matador, Troubador Publishing, 2013).

[31] Duncan Green, 'Ups and Downs in the Struggle for Accountability – Four New Real Time Studies', From Poverty to Power blog, 5 September 2013, http://oxfamblogs.org/fp2p/watching-the-ups-and-downs-of-accountability-work-four-new-real-time-studies/.

[32] Duncan Green and Sophie King, *What Can Governments Do to Empower Poor People?* (Oxford: Oxfam GB, 2013), http://policy-practice.oxfam.org.uk/publications/what-can-governments-do-to-empower-poor-people-305513.

The state can also help build the capacity of interest- and identity-based organizations and create an enabling environment for excluded groups to organize and represent their interests ('power with'). Affirmative action for the political representation of disadvantaged groups, as well as initiatives and reforms that promote transparency and accountability, can strengthen citizens' ability to take action ('power to').

Finally, states can play an important role in curtailing 'power over': the excessive concentration of influence and its use against excluded groups and individuals. Strengthening poor people's access to the legal system can cut across all these categories and encourage a reformist rather than a revolutionary approach to citizen activism.

Many states see civil society as a double-edged sword: useful when it delivers services and promotes jobs and growth, but threatening when it seeks a more fundamental redistribution of power. I am reminded of the words of Brazil's great radical archbishop, Hélder Câmara: 'When I give food to the poor, they call me a saint. When I ask why they are poor, they call me a communist.'[33]

In what is partly a backhanded acknowledgement of growing civil society strength, more than fifty countries in recent years have enacted or seriously considered legislative or other restrictions on the ability of CSOs to organize and operate. As Russia's Vladimir Putin chillingly explained, 'If you get permission, you go and march. . . . Go without permission, and you will be hit on the head with batons.'[34]

Models of non-democratic systems, such as China's, may inspire these governments, or perhaps cracking down on CSOs is just convenient. Foreign funding can make CSOs easy targets for accusations of foreign interference, and weak governance and accountability

[33] Personal communication with Julian Filochowski, CAFOD, 1984.
[34] Michael Stott, 'Putin Hints Will Return to Kremlin in 2012', Reuters website, 30 August 2010, quoting Vladimir Putin defending a recent crackdown on pro-democracy protesters, www.reuters.com/article/us-russia-putin-interview-idUSTRE67T2J920100830.

structures can open the door to questions about their legitimacy.[35] Governments have sought to impede or block foreign funding, or harass external aid groups offering it.[36]

How can outsiders support citizen activists?

If the rising voice and influence of civil society is widely recognized, how aid agencies should support it, if at all, is far from clear.[37] A hundred years ago, during the Mexican Revolution, President Alvaro Obregón is said to have caustically observed, 'No general can withstand a cannonade of 50,000 pesos.'[38] The same appears to apply to some CSOs. Based on research in Pakistan, Masooda Bano[39] argues that aid often erodes the cooperation that underpins CSOs. When foreign money flows in, the unpaid activists that form the core of such organizations can lose trust in their leaders, whom they now suspect of pocketing aid dollars. In Bosnia, my conversations with CSOs suggest that even their supporters view them as little more than 'briefcase CSOs', only interested in winning funding.[40]

I find such conversations painful, as they force me to acknowledge that the aid dollars that Oxfam has spent so many years advocating for can in some circumstances do more harm than good. But I think such fears are also exaggerated. Having no money can be as big a constraint

[35] Ross Clarke and Araddhya Mehtta, '5 Trends That Explain Why Civil Society Space is Under Assault Around the World', From Poverty to Power blog, 25 August 2015, http://oxfamblogs.org/fp2p/5-trends-that-explain-why-civil-society-space-is-under-assault-around-the-world/.

[36] Thomas Carothers and Saskia Brechenmacher, *Closing Space: Democracy and Human Rights Support Under Fire* (Washington DC: Carnegie Endowment for International Peace, 2014).

[37] 'Álvaro Obregón Salido (1880–1928)', http://axoquen.8k.com/biografias/obregonsa.html.

[38] Stephen Morris, 'Corrupción y política en el México contemporáneo'. Mexico, Editorial Siglo XXI, 1992.

[39] Masooda Bano, *Breakdown in Pakistan: How Aid is Eroding Institutions for Collective Action* (California: Stanford University Press, 2012).

[40] Duncan Green, 'Strengthening Active Citizenship After a Traumatic Civil War: Dilemmas and Ideas in Bosnia and Herzegovina', From Poverty to Power blog, 25 June 2014, http://oxfamblogs.org/fp2p/building-civil-society-after-a-traumatic-civil-war-dilemmas-and-ideas-in-bosnia-and-herzegovina/.

as having too much, and is much more common. By one estimate, Southern-based NGOs get only around 1 per cent of all aid.[41]

If chucking money at CSOs risks killing with kindness, there are more subtle ways that outsiders can support citizen activism.[42] In preparation for writing this book, I examined ten cases of Oxfam's work on citizen activism,[43] ranging from grassroots women's empowerment to the global campaign on the arms trade. Here are a few lessons I drew from them:[44]

1. **The right partners are indispensable:** Whether programmes flourish or fail depends in large part on the local CSOs northern aid agencies choose to work with. Good partners bring an understanding of local context and culture, have long-term relations of trust with poor communities, and well-developed networks with those in positions of local power; they will carry on working in the area long after the outside agency has moved on.

2. **Don't neglect 'power within':** Helping citizens build their power is a deeply personal process that often starts with boosting their self-confidence and assertiveness, especially in the case of women's activism.[45] Many women experience 'citizenship' very differently from men—even when they share racial, ethnic, age, or class identities. In the realm of formal politics, 'power within' is often a vital precursor

---

[41] CIVICUS, *State of Civil Society Report 2015*, http://civicus.org/index.php/en/media-centre-129/reports-and-publications/socs2015.

[42] Duncan Green, 'Can Donors Support Civil Society Activism without Destroying it?', From Poverty to Power blog, 9 September 2014, http://oxfamblogs.org/fp2p/can-donors-support-civil-society-activism-without-destroying-it-some-great-evidence-from-nigeria/.

[43] Duncan Green, 'Active Citizenship Case Studies' (Oxford: Oxfam GB, 2014), http://policy-practice.oxfam.org.uk/our-work/citizen-states/active-citizenship-case-studies.

[44] Duncan Green, *Promoting Active Citizenship: What Have we Learned from 10 Case Studies of Oxfam's Work?* (Oxford: Oxfam GB for Oxfam International, 2015), http://policy-practice.oxfam.org.uk/publications/promoting-active-citizenship-what-have-we-learned-from-10-case-studies-of-oxfam-338431.

[45] Duncan Green, *The Raising Her Voice Nepal Programme*, Oxfam Active Citizenship Case Study (Oxford: Oxfam GB for Oxfam International, 2015), http://policy-practice.oxfam.org.uk/publications/the-raising-her-voice-nepal-programme-338476.

to 'power with'; individual self-confidence lays a foundation for setting up collective organizations.

3. **Build the 'grains' of change:** Success in building citizen activism usually involves identifying and working with its constituent 'grains'— the more durable organizations within movements[46]—which are best placed to survive, adapt, and flourish in the complex and ever-changing panorama of activism and protest. These grassroots CSOs naturally adapt to shifts, grab opportunities, seek friends and allies, and frequently show remarkable courage and endurance in the face of attack. For CSO activists, this is their life, not a project or a plan.

4. **Building citizen activism takes time:** Gathering individual organizations into a social movement is painstaking work, requiring sustained investment. The timelines for the cases I examined show work stretching back over a decade or more, far longer than the typical aid funding arrangement.

5. **Think about working with faith groups:** As we have seen, many people living in poverty place enormous trust in religious institutions, which are often central to the construction of norms and values, including those that promote or inhibit citizen activism.

6. **Conflict vs. cooperation:** Serious change is seldom entirely peaceful, but conflict carries huge risks for people living in poverty. In high-risk environments, the activists opted explicitly for a less aggressive approach; elsewhere, lobbying mixed with confrontation and protest proved effective.

In applying these lessons, outsiders should think of themselves as 'ecosystem gardeners', nurturing diversity and resilience, and focusing on the 'enabling environment' (such as laws that support, rather than impede) and systemic issues (such as access to information or finance). This role implies that outsiders should stand by CSOs through thick

---

[46] Duncan Green, *The Raising Her Voice Pakistan Programme*, Oxfam Active Citizenship Case Study (Oxford: Oxfam GB for Oxfam International, 2015), http://policy-practice. oxfam.org.uk/publications/the-raising-her-voice-pakistan-programme-338443.

and thin, in an extended act of solidarity, as they cope with emerging events, no matter if they shift direction or focus. Nothing could be farther from the aid industry's standard approach today, driven by its penchant for short-term, measurable results.[47]

Conclusion

Active citizens are the unsung heroes of how change happens, putting the *demos* in democracy,[48] holding governments to account, making states and markets work better, and, occasionally, erupting onto our TV screens to drive tyrants and thieves from power. Like the other systems discussed in this book, civil society is complex, unpredictable, and fascinating. By immersing ourselves in its highways and byways, nourishing a curiosity for its endless energy, courage, and innovation, we activists will find not only inspiration but the knowledge we need to better support progressive change.

We will return to the role of outsider organizations in the final section of the book. First, let's explore the role of leadership in making change happen.

Further Reading

T. Branch, *Parting the Waters: America in the King Years, 1954–63* (New York: Pocket Books, 1989).

M. Edwards, *Civil Society*, 3rd edition (Cambridge: Polity, 2014).

J. Gaventa and R. McGee, *Citizen Action and National Policy Reform: Making Change Happen* (London: Zed Books, 2010).

S. Tarrow, *Power in Movement: Social Movements and Contentious Politics* (Cambridge, Cambridge University Press, 1998).

C. Tilly and L.J. Wood, *Social Movements, 1768–2008*, 2nd edition (Abingdon: Routledge, 2009).

L. Thompson and C. Tapscott, *Citizenship and Social Movements: Perspectives from the Global South* (London: Zed Books, 2010).

---

[47] Michael Edwards, *Civil Society*, 3rd edition (Cambridge: Polity Press, 2014),

[48] The word democracy comes from the Greek 'demos' (people) and 'kratos' (power).

10

LEADERS AND LEADERSHIP

Men make their own history, but they do not make it as they please; they do not make it under self-selected circumstances, but under circumstances existing already, given and transmitted from the past. The tradition of all dead generations weighs like a nightmare on the brains of the living Karl Marx[1]

Joseph Sungi MP is known throughout Papua New Guinea's remote Nuku district simply as 'the Member'. He is a Big Man in every sense, oozing authority and confidence, his bull neck and large frame squeezed into a dapper pin-striped suit. Joe is a man on a mission, and that mission is roads. Using the discretionary funds at every MP's disposal, he plans to build all-weather roads to every one of Nuku's eighty-four wards by the next election in 2017.

'When we went home for Christmas we had to walk the last seven kilometres to get to our villages. Our kids don't want to go back home any more. In my village I said, this is the last time I walk here—next time I'll be in a car. So I made sure the road was built, to show I am a man of my word. Then the people are convinced.'[2]

Travelling with Joe's team in Nuku, I saw plenty of evidence that his obsession is bearing fruit. The district has bought thirteen shiny yellow pieces of earth moving equipment and hired a civil engineer; work is under way.

Joe has tapped a nerve. Everyone I spoke with, from government officials to church and women's groups at ward level, is enthusiastic: roads allow farmers to get their cocoa to market, reduce the costs of

---

[1] Karl Marx, 'The Eighteenth Brumaire of Louis Bonaparte', Essay, 1852.
[2] Author Interview, Port Moresby, November 2014.

resupplying schools and clinics, help retain teachers and nurses reluctant to work in isolated locations. Of course, roads are no panacea. Women and church leaders worry about negative influences, such as drugs and disobedience, which they blame on the improved links. Women farmers say they can now get their crops to Nuku's main town, but find no buyers and end up bringing them home again.

Joe's other priority is even more ground breaking. He has handed a large wad of local funding directly over to the wards, US$10,000 each, to spend as they please. In Papua New Guinea this is revolutionary— the Big Man is handing over money *even to villages that didn't vote for him*. More traditional spending patterns are on display in the yard of the district administrator's office, where four land cruisers are parked, the first instalment of some twenty vehicles the previous MP allegedly handed out to his cronies, which are now being confiscated.

Like a giant magnet surrounding by iron filings, Joe's leadership seems to have built a sense of optimism and common purpose. At every level of society, from the village committee or women's savings group to great nation builders, leaders reinforce group identity and cohesion, and mobilize collective effort toward shared goals. Successful leaders know how to inspire and motivate, and they intuitively understand that to turn a vision and a mobilized following into a transformational force they, as leaders, must retain that difficult-to-define quality known as legitimacy.[3]

Of course leadership comes in many styles. Some leaders oppress, others empower. Some are driven by greed, others by a passion for social justice. When I talk to leaders, especially the more charismatic variety, I am always torn between fascination and suspicion that their fine words are just camouflage for corruption, arrogance, or deceit. This chapter looks at the progressive leaders, who are to be found at all levels of society and in all countries.

---

[3] Robert Rotberg, *Transformative Political Leadership: Making a Difference in the Developing World* (London and Chicago: The University of Chicago Press, 2012), p. 19.

The shelves of airport bookshops groan under the weight of homages to corporate titans, promising to distil the secrets of leadership and success for the rest of us. And the subject fascinated great thinkers of the more distant past, who analysed the use of violence, the role of luck, and whether it is better to be loved or feared.[4] Plato and Machiavelli lined up behind political expertise and the concentration of power; Aristotle, Cicero, and Montesquieu argued for constitutional limits on leaders' power. Beyond the Western bubble, few thinkers placed such unreserved confidence in leadership as Confucius, who saw it as the originating and sustaining force behind good politics: 'Let there be the proper men and their good political order will flourish; but without such men, their political order decays and ceases.'[5]

Activists and academics, however, tend to downplay the role of leaders and leadership in driving change. Development studies as a discipline has little to say about the Big Man in the presidential palace, and even less about leadership from below—that which emerges in citizens' movements, voluntary associations, trade unions, faith organizations, and indeed in every walk of life.

Ideological bias may lie behind the academy's neglect of leadership. Marxists (and, more generally, positivists and structuralists) think in terms of masses and institutions, rather than individuals. Socialist historians like E.P. Thompson proposed a 'history from below',[6] in which leaders who strut the stage, claiming to be making history, are in reality mere flotsam on a sea of political, technological, economic, and social change that makes or destroys them.

At the other extreme are rational choice thinkers such as Gary Becker, who see society and the economy as a set of 'utility-maximizing

---

[4] Nannerl Keohane, 'Western Political Thought', in The Oxford Handbook of Political Leadership, edited by R.A.W. Rhodes and Paul Hart (Oxford: Oxford University Press, 2014).

[5] Confucius, The Doctrine of the Mean, circa 500 BCE, quoted in Joseph Chan and Elton Chan, 'Confucianism and Political Leadership', in The Oxford Handbook of Political Leadership, edited by R.A.W. Rhodes and Paul Hart (Oxford: Oxford University Press, 2014).

[6] Richard Taylor and Roger Fieldhouse, 'Our History is Under Attack', The Guardian, 31 December 2013, www.theguardian.com/commentisfree/2013/dec/31/history-under-attack-ep-thompson.

individuals' with little need for leaders (or followers). Progressives uncomfortable with the elitism of a Big Man theory of human history that excludes all women and most male followers fall somewhere in between. Aid technocrats avoid discussions of leadership, because it rapidly gets political and clouds the seductive purity of 'evidence-based policy making' and 'technical assistance'.

That seems like a serious oversight. Over the years, I've been lucky enough to spend time with hundreds of leaders in dozens of countries, from ministers and senior officials to grassroots activists who galvanize their communities to work for the common good and take great risks holding corrupt officials or companies to account.

I have come to believe that leadership is central to any understanding of how change happens. Leaders operate at the interface between structure and agency, striving to leave their mark on the institutions, cultures, and traditions in which they live and work. Activists need to understand where leadership comes from and how we can best identify, support, and work with progressive leaders.

This is not just about politicians. Anyone who has worked in organizations (i.e. most of us) will have seen the critical role of leadership (or lack of it). Leadership styles vary—I have worked under 'bull-in-a-china shop' bosses trying to force their will on reluctant organizations, charismatic visionaries who inspire and motivate but leave the detail to others, and subtle backseat drivers who drip ideas steadily into the corporate bloodstream without ever taking credit. They may not be great managers (lots of them need a 'finisher' as their number two), but good leaders align the iron filings, just like Joe Sungi did, replacing the natural tendency of organizations to fragment into competing groups with a shared purpose and passion and building up alliances and coalitions for change.

A power and systems approach poses some important challenges for leadership. The bull-in-a-china shop school are usually more comfortable with command and control, than with emergent change and empowering mavericks. But both charismatic visionaries and backseat drivers can create the space needed for their organizations to 'dance with systems'. If leadership is identifying the 'what', management is about establishing the 'how'—we look at the challenges of a power and systems approach for the management of activist organizations in Chapter 12.

Understanding leadership at the top

Joe Sungi is no revolutionary. He is a 'transactional leader' trying to make the system work for his constituents, and in Papua New Guinea that is an uphill task. More than a decade of continuous high growth has raised per capita GDP by 150 per cent, yet Papua New Guinea has not achieved a single one of the Millennium Development Goals (MDGs). It shares that dubious distinction only with Zimbabwe and North Korea (the MDGs that is, not the growth); in terms of turning growth into development, Papua New Guinea is a strong candidate for the world's worst underachiever. At the heart of that failure, I'd argue, stands politics: most of Papua New Guinea's Big Men are more concerned with strengthening their own power and fortune than with building roads or other essential public goods.

Some leaders have managed to be more transformational than transactional. Nelson Mandela in South Africa, Gandhi in India, Martin Luther King in the US, or Julius Nyerere in Tanzania all emerged at critical junctures in history—moments of abrupt change, crisis, or external threat—and they seized the opportunity to alter the balance of power in their societies. When structural constraints to action are weakened, great leaders can help remake societies, rather than simply make them work a bit better.

Even in the absence of crisis, leaders in developing countries often have more potential to transform society. Where institutions are relatively weak, force of will and personality can help build national culture, laws, and political institutions, including the checks and balances on the power of future leaders. Perhaps that is why early leaders like Bismarck, Washington, Lee Kuan Yew, Ataturk, or Mandela often achieve mythic status as the founders of the nation.

Even the best of those that follow are hemmed in by compromises, institutions, and rules, and, through no fault of their own, may look like puny pen-pushers by comparison.

But that relative absence of constraints also increases the potential for damage. Some leaders enter power with the best of intentions, but cling on long after their sell-by date. In 2015 when Barack Obama told African Union that, 'Nobody should be president for life',[7] the public gallery reportedly erupted in cheers, while the front rows maintained a stony silence. At the time nine African leaders (and one monarch) had ruled for more than twenty years. (And yes, NGOs can suffer from the same syndrome.)

If strong institutions are an indicator of development, then the success of a leader can be measured by the institutional legacy he or she leaves. Effective leaders breathe life into institutions; ineffective leaders destroy or stifle them. I began writing this chapter the week a truly transformative political leader died, Singapore's Lee Kuan Yew, and the obit pages were filled with praise for his achievements (albeit laced with criticism for his record on human rights). The *Economist* glowed: 'A tribute to Mr Lee's nation-building was the absence of any flicker from the stock market on news of his death. . . . [T]hanks largely to Mr Lee, Singapore's institutions are strong, its governance honest, effective—and dull.'[8]

An article in the same edition entitled 'King Paul'[9] presented a contrasting portrait of one of Africa's most celebrated contemporary leaders, Paul Kagame, the Rwandan president: 'In history's judgment, leaders are only as good as the successors they groom. Mr Kagame has sacked or chased away just about everyone around him who could

---

[7] 'Obama to African Leaders: "Nobody Should be President for Life"', BBC News website, 28 July 2015, www.bbc.co.uk/news/world-africa-33691468.

[8] 'After the Patriarch: Singapore After Lee Kuan Yew', *The Economist*, 28 March 2015, www.economist.com/news/asia/21647333-island-state-mourns-its-founding-father-its-politics-changing-after-patriarch.

[9] 'King Paul: A Successful Man with No Successor', *The Economist*, 26 March 2015, www.economist.com/news/middle-east-and-africa/21647365-successful-man-no-successor-king-paul?zid=309&ah=8odcf288b8561b012f603b9fd9577foe.

take over. Some have fled the country and a few have died in mysterious circumstances; others went to prison.'

What makes a leader?

There are many pathways to leadership, and those pathways form some noticeable patterns. One explanation for the differences between Lee and Kagame may lie in how they came to power. Kagame, as a former rebel commander, introduced the top-down disciplines of military authority, along with its rejection of dissidence and pluralism. That path was shared by Ethiopia's Meles Zenawi, Cuba's Fidel Castro, and China's Mao Tse Tung. Lee Kuan Yew, on the other hand, was a lawyer who led Singapore's non-violent independence movement. A similar case was José Figueres, the coffee farmer who led Costa Rica's 1948 revolution that abolished the army and set the country on a democratic path. The military men were willing to use brute force to stay in control and achieve the changes they sought, while the civilians preferred the law and institutions.

The Developmental Leadership Program (DLP)[10] (through which the research for this book was funded) has examined the backgrounds of leaders from a variety of countries and found that education was instrumental in allowing them to stretch their loyalties beyond family, region, class, or ethnicity.[11] In-depth interviews with leaders of Ghana's transformation since the late 1980s revealed three common elements they learned in school: core values of moral purpose and commitment to serving the nation; ways of working such as critical

[10] The Developmental Leadership Program (DLP), www.dlprog.org/. DLP is funded by the Australian government, which also provided support for this book.

[11] Laura Brannelly, Laura Lewis and Susy Ndaruhutse, *Higher Education and the Formation of Developmental Elites: A Literature Review and Preliminary Data Analysis*, DLP Research Paper 10 (Birmingham: University of Birmingham, 2011), www.dlprog.org/publications/higher-education-and-the-formation-of-developmental-elites-a-literature-review-and-preliminary-data-analysis.php.

thinking and collaboration; and the expertise and knowledge that leaders need if they are to drive change.

Of the Ghanaian leaders who attended secondary school or higher, nearly all of them went to elite institutions that were both relatively meritocratic and residential, bringing together talented children from all backgrounds who then forged values and bonds that would shape their future roles as leaders.

A brilliant DLP paper by Sarah Phillips[12] reaches a similar conclusion regarding Somaliland, which split off from the chaos of Somalia in the 1990s. Sheekh Secondary School, set up by Richard Darlington, who in the Second World War commanded the British Army's Somaliland Protectorate contingent, takes only fifty students a year and trains them in leadership and critical thought (Darlington borrowed from the curriculum of his elite English private school, Harrow). The school stresses student intake from all clans, especially the more marginalized ones. Sheekh has provided three out of four presidents of the new nation, along with numerous vice presidents and cabinet members.

Joe Sungi's life story echoes these findings. The son of subsistence farmers, well down the clan hierarchy, he was educated at an Australian Catholic mission school, and then a boarding school for the best and brightest kids from around the country. He traces his sense of public ethics to that school. Joe laments that one of the unintended consequences of the spread of secondary education is that kids now go to high school in their own communities, rather than being forced to board with the best and brightest from around his fragmented country. He is urging the government to consider introducing elite public boarding schools based on the French lycée system to recreate the lost leadership crucible of his youth.

---

[12] Sarah Phillips, *Political Settlements and State Formation: The Case of Somaliland*, DLPResearch Paper 23 (Birmingham: University of Birmingham, 2013), www.dlprog.org/publications/political-settlements-and-state-formation-the-case-of-somaliland.php.

These are uncomfortable findings for activists. Advocating for elite boarding schools, even meritocratic ones, smacks of old English colonialism (Ghana, Somaliland, and Papua New Guinea are former British colonies) and feels distinctly regressive compared to getting every child into a primary school. So we had better pin down what aspects of elite education create more capable, publicly-minded leaders, and figure out how those can be incorporated into modern school systems.

The DLP's findings on education are important, but are only one part of the much wider story of what makes for good leaders. DLP researchers suggest a range of other factors: travel, both internal and international, broadens horizons and builds links with the wider world; religious faith is a common motivating factor; shared experiences of resistance, armed struggle, or suffering bind future leaders together. Finally, some of the most effective leaders, like Nelson Mandela, are traditional authorities with a sense of *noblesse oblige*.

What do leaders do?

The system delivers for Joe Sungi because he knows how decisions get made in the capital: which tables to bang, which favours to call in. Joe says, 'The key is you talk to people. I don't write letters, I do the talking! Most of what I do is informal, I owe it all to informal relationships.'[13]

Like many leaders, Joe gets things moving, but leaves the finishing to others. One of his key men is Kenny Myeni, a jovial, bearded engineer whom Joe managed to lure from a comfortable job with British American Tobacco to run the road-building programme. Funds are often in short supply laughs Kenny, but 'the Member knows where the money is. We provide the documentation and the Member does the talking'.[14]

[13] Author Interview, Port Moresby, November 2014.
[14] Author Interview, Nuku, November 2014.

Sungi exemplifies the two-level game that leaders have to play—building bridges among constituencies and driving bargains with those in power—while constantly maintaining and boosting followers' morale. They must lead but look constantly over their shoulder because, as a Malawian proverb has it, 'A *leader without followers* is simply someone taking a *walk*'.

Indeed, 'great leaders' are often created by their followers and by accidents of history; their rise only appears inevitable with hindsight. Churchill was revered by the British during the Second World War, but ridiculed beforehand and unceremoniously dumped at the ballot box once the war was over.

As the quote from Karl Marx at the start of this chapter argues, leaders do not get to do 'as they please'. The art of leadership lies in finding ways to move forward (or more frequently to inspire others to do so) within the circumstances of the moment, in other words within the system. They turn the legacy of history from 'weighing like a nightmare on the brains of the living' into a force for change.

Leaders understand the role of symbolism in building mass movements, a language parallel to and separate from the policy detail preferred by officials and academics. Rather than confront the British on their own terms, Mahatma Gandhi wrong-footed colonial authorities with small personal acts like collecting salt and spinning cotton on a simple spinning wheel to highlight the search for self-sufficiency and independence. The spinning wheel even appeared on an early version of the Indian flag.[15] Mandela too had a talent for the heart-stopping gesture, reaching out to white South Africans by wearing the Springbok rugby shirt or travelling to a remote Afrikaner community to take tea with the ninety-four-year-old widow of Henrik Verwoerd, a key architect of apartheid.[16] Both Mandela and Gandhi demonstrated

[15] Makarand, 'Mahatma Gandhi—The True Revolutionary', Makarand blog, 30 January 2015, https://makarandimpressions.wordpress.com/2015/01/30/mahatma-gandhi-the-true-revolutionary/.
[16] Robert Rotberg, *Transformative Political Leadership: Making a Difference in the Developing World* (London and Chicago: The University of Chicago Press, 2012), p. 63.

that humility and ethical probity can generate more political legitimacy than displays of force or expertise.

Discussions of leaders and leadership customarily fixate on the people at the top—the habits and psychologies of CEOs and presidents, be they saints or sinners. But leaders are everywhere, nowhere more than in the movements for change active in poor communities across the world.

Leadership from below

Penha was an imposing figure, a big confident woman who rose to become president of the Alagoa Grande Rural Workers' Union in Brazil's drought-prone and poverty-ridden north east. When I visited her in 1990, Pehna was trying to persuade an impoverished farming community to join the union. Pot-bellied children with skinny arms played at the feet of adults while banter and serious talk rolled easily along. Penha guided the conversation with a blend of authority, humour, and kindness, letting others speak and enjoying their jokes. The impromptu discussion developed into a full-blown community meeting about the causes of poverty in Brazil and the need to organize to demand rights to the land. As dusk fell, the meeting turned to music and dance, in honour of the visitors.[17]

Later on, she told me her life story, the words half lost in the drumming of a sudden downpour, which turned the street into a river bearing rubbish from the nearby market. A broken home, starting work at age seven, a mother who died from tuberculosis when Penha was twelve, early marriage, and the struggle to feed her six children. To that point it was the story of countless poor Latin American women.

Penha was able to turn her personal courage and determination into leadership thanks to a chance encounter with a charismatic leader

---

[17] Duncan Green, *Faces of Latin America*, 3rd edition (New York: Monthly Review Press, 2012).

named Margarida Maria Alves, who first introduced her to the union. When Margarida was murdered, allegedly by local landowners and politicians, Penha took over.[18]

Like leaders at the top, grassroots leaders are shaped by experiences of travel, struggle, and conflict, and are thrust forward by the historical moment ('cometh the hour'). In dozens of countries across several continents, I have met grassroots leaders inspired by their faith and equipped with skills by their experiences in choirs or as preachers, both Christian and Muslim. Scripture helped them form a personal narrative about the sources of their deprivation and repression, galvanizing them into action.

Unlike those at the top of society, social movement leaders have little money and few threats with which to control or reward their followers. They rely heavily on their ability to communicate understanding of the lives of others and belief in the value of collective action to address common problems. They foster their followers' sense of 'power within', buttressed by a vision of a better future that justifies taking action, even when to do so at best takes up poor people's scarce time and energy and at worst puts their lives at risk.

Strengthening community organization is often insufficient to win access to land, funding, or respect. Grassroots leaders must also play the same two-level game as Joe Sungi, building alliances with other organizations and cutting deals with people in positions of power. One of the functions of such leaders is to 'create space' for others. Chinese philosopher Lao Tzu put it this way in the sixth century BCE: 'A leader is best when people barely know that he exists, not so good when people obey and acclaim him, worst when they despise him. But of a good leader, who talks little, when his work is done, his aims fulfilled, they will all say, "We did this ourselves".'[19]

---

[18] Inter-American Commission on Human Rights, Report No. 9/08, Case 12.332 Admissibility, Margarida Maria Alves, Brazil, 5 March 5 2008.
[19] Lao Tzu, Tao Te Ching, Chapter 17, sixth century BCE.

In the recent protest movements of the Arab Spring, some observers viewed the lack of identifiable leaders as a strength, since none could be co-opted or attacked. If a movement has no head, how can it be beheaded? It seemed somehow more pure and genuinely of the masses to have no leaders instead of a grand personality who achieves celebrity status. But such 'anti-leadership' ideas have their limitations.[20] When the cycle moves on from protest and conflict to cooperation and reform, someone has to engage with those in power to maximize whatever gains have been won through protest. Headless movements cannot cut deals.

A simple dichotomy between grassroots leaders and those at the top is, of course, misleading. Intermediary organizations and leaders bridge the gap between state and citizens. Effective grassroots leaders are often well connected with those in formal power, especially in countries where national leaders have themselves emerged from grassroots activism, such as South Africa, Brazil, or Bolivia. Mandela was a civil rights lawyer and African National Congress (ANC) activist; the transformational presidents of Brazil and Bolivia (Lula and Evo Morales) started out as trade union and peasant leader, respectively. But for every household name, there are thousands of Penhas, unsung heroes organizing their fellow citizens in the struggle for change.

Women and leadership

Joe Sungi typifies a leadership style—individualistic, confrontational, public ('I do the talking!')—which seems quintessentially male. Penha's approach was altogether more inclusive; she listened as much or more than she spoke. People like her form a growing movement of women leaders around the world, at all levels of society.

---

[20] Neil Sutherland, Christopher Land, and Steffen Böhm, 'Anti-leaders(hip) in Social Movement Organizations: The Case of Autonomous Grassroots Groups', *Organization* 5 June 2013, 1350508413480254.

A study by the Overseas Development Institute identified some common factors in the backgrounds of women leaders, which echo some of Penha's life story: many are married, have some professional training and work in 'nurturing' or community-related occupations like teaching or social work. Many enjoy the psychological and financial support of close family members, as well as the encouragement of role models (women in public office or active in women's civic movements).[21]

Srilatha Batliwala draws a distinction between feminine and feminist understandings of leadership.[22] A feminine approach to leadership recognizes that women often bring a greater attention to collaboration, collective decision making, and building relationships, characteristics that fall well within the traditional gendered roles of women. In contrast, a feminist approach seeks to transform relations of power, paying close attention to 'power within' and 'power with', as well as hidden and invisible power.

In many ways, the feminist understanding of leadership seems well suited to the power and systems approach advocated by this book. At the end of a lecture in Washington a few years ago, I was rather disconcerted by my thank-you present—a copy of *The End of Men and the Rise of Women* by Hanna Rosin.[23] Hopefully I'll be retired and gardening by the time that process is complete.

Leadership, power, and systems

It's easy to forget that when Nelson Mandela was finally released from prison in the early 1990s, South Africa was teetering on a knife's edge.

---

[21] Tam O'Neil and Georgia Plank, with Pilar Domingo, *Support to Women and Girls' Leadership: A Rapid Review of the Evidence* (London: Overseas Development Institute, 2015), www.odi.org/sites/odi.org.uk/files/odi-assets/publications-opinion-files/9623.pdf.

[22] Srilatha Batliwala, *Feminist Leadership for Social Transformation: Clearing the Conceptual Cloud* (New York and New Delhi: CREA, 2010), www.uc.edu/content/dam/uc/ucwc/docs/CREA.pdf.

[23] Hanna Rosin, *The End of Men: And the Rise of Women* (New York: Penguin Books, 2012).

Fighting between Inkatha and ANC supporters threatened to tip over into civil war; fragile state status beckoned. At one early event, ANC supporters called for Mandela to 'give us weapons. No peace'.[24] Mandela reprimanded his fired-up supporters: 'Listen to me. I am your leader. I am going to give you leadership. If you are going to kill innocent people, you don't belong in the ANC.' What would have happened if he had opted for the populist route and stoked the fires?

Mandela was no King Canute, standing futilely against the tides of history. He was an expert navigator in a complex system, forging personal or political alliances with erstwhile enemies, publicly denouncing attempts to pervert or prevent the transition to black majority rule. He built unity among the different factions of the ANC, and turned it from a protest movement into a dominant ruling party. Like all good leaders, he could 'see' how power is distributed and fought over in society, and spot opportunities to seize and shape the tide of events. One can only wonder what would have occurred had Mandela died on Robben Island.

For institutions promoting change, training and supporting local leaders should be an attractive proposition. It is pleasingly tangible and puts a human face on the often amorphous process of development. But few aid agencies invest in individuals. Why not emulate the few schemes, such as the MacArthur Foundation Fellowship, that identify and back outstanding leaders?[25] Or offer work experience, internships, or teaching opportunities for students with potential to become tomorrow's progressive leaders?

Among activists, many of whom have a deep commitment to egalitarianism, words like leadership and leader elicit mixed feelings. Most of us would prefer to build the capacity of organizations rather than invest directly in individuals with high potential. Indeed, even

---

[24] Robert Rotberg, *Transformative Political Leadership: Making a Difference in the Developing World* (London and Chicago: The University of Chicago Press, 2012), p. 40.

[25] 'MacArthur Fellows Program', MacArthur Foundation website, www.macfound.org/programs/fellows/.

talking in terms of high-potential individuals can feel somehow contrary to principles of fairness and equality.

But addressing leadership much more systematically need not imply being seduced by a simplistic Big Man approach to politics. On the contrary, acknowledging and supporting the crucial role leaders play in how change happens is a vital step in amplifying the voices of groups that currently go unheard.

Now that we have looked at both the grassroots citizen activists, and the leaders that inspire them and others at all levels of society, we move on to a subject that involves both of them, and which I have been most involved with over the years: advocacy.

Further Reading

H. Lyne de Ver, 'Conceptions of Leadership' (Birmingham: Developmental Leadership Program Background Paper 4, 2009), http://www.dlprog.org.

N. Mandela, *Long Walk to Freedom: The Autobiography of Nelson Mandela* (London: Little Brown, 1995).

M.A. Melo, N. Ng'ethe, and J. Manor, *Against the Odds: Politicians, Institutions, and the Struggle Against Poverty* (London: C. Hurst & Co., 2012).

Robert Rotberg, *Transformative Political Leadership: Making a Difference in the Developing World* (London and Chicago: The University of Chicago Press, 2012).

Further Surfing

The Developmental Leadership Program http://www.dlprog.org/.

11

THE POWER OF ADVOCACY

The bacon rolls were to die for. They sat alluringly at the entrance to the 'breakfast meeting' at Number 11 Downing Street, the residence of then Chancellor of the Exchequer (i.e. finance minister) Gordon Brown. But the risks of grabbing one on my way in were too high: lobbying the number two in the UK Government was scary enough without bacon fat dribbling down my chin. I walked resolutely by. Such are the heroic sacrifices of the lobbyist.

The occasion was one of Brown's periodic breakfasts with faith groups (I was working for the Catholic aid agency, CAFOD, at the time). About thirty people were around the table, each of us given two minutes to pitch whatever was on our minds. On mine was an obscure but important issue in the nascent Doha Round of talks at the WTO: the EU (which at the WTO negotiates on behalf of the UK) was intent on adding investment to the already overloaded agenda, probably to distract attention from Europe's notorious Common Agricultural Policy. A large number of developing country governments were opposed, backed by international NGOs.

I was armed with a short summary of the arguments and academic evidence for our position.[1] As the paper made its way round the table, I used my two minutes to summarize its contents. When it reached him, Brown scribbled something and the spotlight moved on. I later discovered that as he left the room, he said to his officials 'Why are we

[1] ActionAid, Catholic Fund for Overseas Development (CAFOD), Christian Aid, Oxfam, Save the Children, and World Development Movement, 'Unwanted, Unproductive and Unbalanced: Six Arguments Against an Investment Agreement at the WTO', May 2003, www.actionaid.org.uk/sites/default/files/doc_lib/10_1_six_arguments_wto.pdf.

supporting this?' The UK subsequently distanced itself from the EU position, a small victory, but as good as it gets for an NGO lobbyist.

A couple of months later, this seemingly obscure topic was a major factor in the spectacular collapse of the WTO summit in Cancún. The media room was a shouting, shoving, frenzy of journalists on deadline, desperate to find someone to interview; some were even interviewing each other. I was in spin-doctor mode, regurgitating the same sound bite—the EU is 'chief suspect number one and number two for the collapse'—to anyone who would listen. We were hoping to pre-empt the inevitable attempt to blame either developing countries or NGOs for the collapse. My quote made The Guardian, so CAFOD was happy.[2]

Dodging bacon sarnies in Downing Street or spinning at global trade summits are hardly the kinds of activities the public normally associates with international NGOs. When CAFOD asked its youth supporters for a picture of its work, they drew cartoons of nuns throwing bags of food out of planes. But over the last twenty years CAFOD, Oxfam, and others have devoted a rising proportion of their efforts to influencing government policy through campaigns and lobbying (still amounting to only 6 per cent of Oxfam's spending, far less than long-term development and emergency response).

The turn toward policy work came partly as a result of hard lessons learned during the 1980s and 1990s heyday of World Bank structural adjustment programmes, when it became apparent there was little point in constructing islands of project success only to see them swept away by a tidal wave of bad public policy decisions. Growing size, capacity, and self-confidence no doubt also played a role.

The rise of campaigns and lobbying has produced a proliferation of training manuals and toolkits, some of which can be found on this book's website. Organizations such as Oxfam now also provide

[2] Larry Elliott, Charlotte Denny, and David Munk, 'Blow to World Economy as Trade Talks Collapse', The Guardian, 15 September 2003, www.theguardian.com/world/2003/sep/15/business.politics.

considerable support to local groups to develop their advocacy skills—generally known by the rather condescending term (to my ears, anyway) of 'capacity building'. This chapter will steer clear of the fine detail, and instead sketch in the broader nature of the beast, as well as addressing some of the dilemmas it poses for activists who want to bring about change.

First, some definitions: 'Advocacy' is the process of influencing decision makers to change their policies and practices, attitudes, or behaviours. 'Campaigning' usually refers to mobilizing the public or influencing the public's attitudes and behaviours. And 'lobbying' is going directly to policy makers to get them to do something in particular. For simplicity, I will use 'advocacy' as an umbrella term for both campaigning and lobbying.

The tactics employed usually fall somewhere along a continuum from sitting down with those in power to help sort out a problem (at the 'insider' end) to mayhem in the street (at the 'outsider' end). One study defined five points on that spectrum: cooperation, education, persuasion, litigation, and contestation.[3]

Advocacy typically involves a combination of these elements, and the balance shifts over time. One reason Gordon Brown was willing to listen to me prattle on about trade rules was the public pressure and media coverage generated by campaigners in the Trade Justice Movement, a large, noisy, and media-savvy civil society coalition. Often a public campaign is required to get an issue onto the table, at which point a more insider approach can help move it towards a decision on policy or spending. And public action may be needed at any stage to prevent backsliding and foot-dragging.

When it comes to campaigning, the playbook was pretty much written two centuries ago, after a dozen people met in a print shop in London's East End, brought together by Thomas Clarkson, a twenty-seven-year-old Quaker. Thus began a campaign to end slavery that

[3] Valerie Miller and Jane Covey, *Advocacy Sourcebook: Frameworks for Planning, Action and Reflection* (Boston, MA: Institute for Development Research, 1997).

lasted fifty years, brilliantly captured in Adam Hochschild's *Bury the Chains*.[4] The abolitionists invented virtually every modern campaign tactic, including posters, political book tours, consumer boycotts, investigative reporting, and petitions. Fast forward two centuries, and today's energetic activism on issues from climate change to disabled people's rights, corruption, or same-sex marriage is built on the foundations laid by Clarkson and his colleagues.

The abolitionists combined immense stamina and courage with an inspirational moral vision and a deep understanding of power and systems. Over their fifty-year campaign, they adapted to massive critical junctures, in the shape of the French Revolution, the Napoleonic Wars, and Caribbean slave revolts; they combined insider-outsider tactics between street petitioners and parliamentary debate; they recruited 'unusual suspects' as allies, such as repentant slaver John Newton who wrote 'Amazing Grace' to work alongside freed slaves and Christian ministers.

How advocacy works

Advocacy typically targets the institutions described in this book, be they formal (states, courts, political parties, corporations, and international bodies) or informal (norms and public attitudes). During my brief spell as a civil servant at the British aid agency DFID, I witnessed good and bad advocacy in action in the space of a morning spent shadowing the Secretary of State, Hilary Benn. The Minister's first visitor was an NGO that seemed content to bask in the presence of power, with no clear asks beyond 'We hope you will take a strong position on labour rights'. Benn was charming and kind, small talk took up most of the time and nothing was agreed.

A few hours later, the Fairtrade Foundation bustled in, led by its dynamic boss Harriet Lamb. She politely curtailed the introductions,

[4] Adam Hochschild, *Bury the Chains: The British Struggle to Abolish Slavery* (London: Pan Macmillan, 2012).

gave the Minister some of the Foundation's new products to play with and moved on to a series of specific asks: since Asda's headquarters were in his constituency, would the Minister kindly sign a letter asking them to do more on Fairtrade? She would of course be happy to draft something for him. As she left the room, Benn turned to me and said we should definitely fund them, a promise we 'civil serpents' subsequently managed to turn into a £750,000 grant.

Harriet's half hour was well spent because she followed the rules of good lobbying: know what your targets can and can't deliver; treat them like human beings; persuade by appealing both to altruism and self-interest.

Often advocates are unable to reach decision makers themselves, and instead reach out to those who do have access. These 'influentials' might include journalists, members of parliament, donors, faith and business leaders, public intellectuals (usually academics), and key people in other government departments or trade unions. And celebrities, of course—even world leaders love a selfie with Bono or Angelina Jolie.

Perhaps the most impressive (if disturbing) exercise I ever witnessed of 'influencing the influentials' came during an internal British government seminar in the run-up to the 2009 climate change summit in Copenhagen. The Foreign Office hired former Greenpeace campaigners to help it identify a hundred individuals from the Indian elite best placed to influence India's climate change policy; for each of them, they put together a dossier on how best to persuade them to act.

Retired influentials, sometimes known as 'grey panthers',[5] can make great advocates. The Amnesty International Business Group was founded by a classic old-man-in-a-hurry, Sir Geoffrey Chandler, a former senior manager at Royal Dutch/Shell who was more than willing to march into boardrooms and unleash his cut-glass accent

---

[5] Duncan Green, 'Are Grey Panthers the Next Big Thing in Campaigning?', From Poverty to Power blog, 2 November 2010, http://oxfamblogs.org/fp2p/are-grey-panthers-the-next-big-thing-in-campaigning/.

to promote human rights in the private sector. Such people understand how to get around internal obstacles and spot management
excuses for inaction, but the brand risk posed by a bunch of stroppy
pensioners doing their own thing would challenge any organization.[6]

When the advocacy target is the public at large, star power can draw
massive attention to an issue. I have worked with some great 'celebrities' over the years, like Bill Nighy (Robin Hood Tax) and Gael García
Bernal (global trade rules), who lent themselves to the cause with
dedication and humility. In Peru, celebrity chefs have been at the
forefront of changing public attitudes towards the merits of traditional
Peruvian foods, challenging the burger culture that is depressingly
omnipresent in Latin America.[7]

The range of possible advocacy tactics is limited only by the
imagination of the advocates: street protest, litigation, insider persuasion, media campaigns, demonstration projects, and many more. Key
considerations include the appropriate balance of conflict and cooperation, the risk of cooptation or dilution, impact on alliances and the
nature of the message.

In his delightful book *Blueprint for Revolution*, Srdja Popovic, a leader
of the Serbian uprising that overthrew Slobodan Milosevic, surveys
tactics from non-violent protest movements around the world and
concludes that food is one of the best entry points. Activists have built
movements around cottage cheese (Israel), rice pudding (Maldives),
and, most famously, salt (India) and tea (US). 'Food has a special way
of getting people to come together', he writes, and is low-risk in
dangerous places.

But there are other small starters too: in San Francisco, future City
Supervisor Harvey Milk's political career took off when he switched

---

[6] The Amnesty group was wound up in 2007, partly because, as one insider told me, 'a
semi-autonomous group of grey eminences was rather more than [NGO managers] were
prepared to accept'.

[7] Leila Nilipour, 'Even Peru's Top Chefs Are Addicted to Fast Food', Munchies website,
13 October 2014, http://munchies.vice.com/articles/even-perus-top-chefs-are-addicted-to-
fast-food.

from campaigning for gay rights to campaigning against dog excrement in city parks. The trick is to learn what people really care about, even if it's not top of your priority list. If you don't, you will only rally the people who already believe in what you have to say—a great way for coming tenth at anything (as Harvey Milk initially did).[8]

Tone and language matter too. I find that a combination of tactical self-deprecation and humour can disarm critics expecting a bout of self-righteous NGO finger-wagging. The British comedian Mark Thomas specializes in the subversive use of humour. Dressed as cartoon character Shaun the Sheep, he recently protested against the privatization of public space by walking up and down outside the London Stock Exchange in the square owned by Mitsubishi. Baffled security men ended up wrestling a cartoon character to the ground on camera, before frogmarching him from the square, bizarrely addressing him as 'Shaun' throughout.[9]

Humour can add an edge even in altogether riskier protests. In Aleppo, Syrian protestors buried loudspeakers broadcasting anti-regime messages in smelly dustbins, so the police would make themselves look ridiculous, and less scary, rummaging around to find them.[10]

Often, however, protest movements succeed by provoking repression from the authorities, which acts as a catalyst for further protest and can motivate reformers within government. In 1967, US police beat demonstrators demanding national civil rights legislation. Martin Luther King Jr commented 'Sound effort in a single city such as Birmingham or Selma, produced situations that symbolized the evil everywhere and inflamed public opinion against it. Where the

---

[8] Srdja Popovic, *Blueprint for Revolution: How to Use Rice Pudding, Lego Men, and Other Nonviolent Techniques to Galvanize Communities, Overthrow Dictators, or Simply Change the World* (New York: Spiegel & Grau, 2015).

[9] Mark Thomas, 'Trespass', Edinburgh Fringe, August 2015.

[10] Srdja Popovic, *Blueprint for Revolution: How to Use Rice Pudding, Lego Men, and Other Nonviolent Techniques to Galvanize Communities, Overthrow Dictators, or Simply Change the World* (New York: Spiegel & Grau, 2015).

spotlight illuminated the evil, a legislative remedy was soon obtained that applied everywhere.'[11] Provoking violence from the system is, of course, a dangerous game, especially when there are few checks on the state's power.

Because getting new laws onto the statute books is so difficult, many campaigns zero in on enforcement of laws and policies that already exist. Decision makers have a harder time publicly opposing things they have themselves approved. Getting down among the weeds of existing legislation and policy can be unattractive to campaigners seeking more fundamental 'transformative' change and it can be highly technical. But done right, it can set the stage for larger changes.

One example comes from India's new state of Chhattisgarh, home to marginalized traditional communities that make a living from forest products. Despite the protection of the 2006 Forest Rights Act, their livelihoods were under threat from mining and other commercial activities. An impressive local NGO, Chaupal, launched an advocacy campaign based on this 'implementation gap'. After negotiations, petitioning, and community protest, backed up by solid research, dozens of villages gained the forest and grazing rights promised under the Act.[12]

Research is often an effective weapon in the advocate's armoury. Pleas to Gordon Brown over the Downing Street breakfast table would have had little impact without credible analysis to back them up. My colleagues Ricardo Fuentes, Deborah Hardoon, and Nick Galasso have hogged headlines and shaped the policy discussion at recent Davos

[11] Quoted in Mark Engler and Paul Engler, 'When the Pillars Fall – How Social Movements Can Win More Victories Like Same-Sex Marriage', Waging Nonviolence blog, 9 July 2014, http://wagingnonviolence.org/feature/pillars-fall-social-movements-can-win-victories-like-sex-marriage/. Original source: Martin Luther King Jr, *Where do we go From Here* (Boston, MA: Beacon Press, 2010).

[12] Duncan Green, 'The Chhattisgarh Community Forest Rights Project', India, Oxfam Active Citizenship Case Study (Oxford: Oxfam GB for Oxfam International, 2015), http://policy-practice.oxfam.org.uk/publications/the-chhattisgarh-community-forest-rights-project-india-338434.

business summits with 'killer facts' on the extreme levels of inequality in the contemporary world. At last count (it keeps falling), the sixty-two richest individuals on earth owned as much wealth as the poorest half of global population—3.5 billion people.[13]

That said, in democracies decisions are made rather more often on the basis of power, institutional inertia, received wisdoms, and vested interest than by a dispassionate review of the evidence. As noted in Chapters 4 and 9, good research may be more persuasive in closed political systems like China's, Russia's, and Viet Nam's, where government technocrats and political leaders are more insulated from political pressures.

In the ideas ecosystem, new approaches and concepts bubble up all the time. Many remain on the fringe, but some start to have real influence. I find the image of a 'policy funnel' helpful.[14] At the broad, open end, are ideas that are only starting to make it into public debates and onto decision makers' radars. An example would be the impending threat of climate change in the 1990s and 2000s. Broad general messages on such ideas are more important than detailed policy proposals. In the early years, the climate change debate was dominated by its impact on Arctic wildlife. Oxfam's first, and to my mind still most effective, contribution was to dress activists up in polar bear outfits, carrying placards that said 'save the humans'.

Once ideas start to move down the funnel and be incorporated into policies, laws, and spending decisions, activists' task is to build alliances, target blockers, and win over waverers. We also need to find ways to express our concerns in ways that fit the policy process underway. 'Stop the world and start again' is unlikely to get much

[13] Deborah Hardoon, Sophia Ayele, and Ricardo Fuentes-Nieva, *An Economy for the 1%: How Privilege and Power in the Economy Drive Extreme Inequality and How This Can be Stopped* (Oxford: Oxfam GB for Oxfam International, 2016), http://policy-practice.oxfam.org.uk/publications/an-economy-for-the-1-how-privilege-and-power-in-the-economy-drive-extreme-inequ-592643.

[14] Duncan Green, 'The Policy Funnel—A Way to Sharpen Up Our Advocacy?', From Poverty to Power blog, 3 August 2011, http://oxfamblogs.org/fp2p/the-policy-funnel-a-way-to-sharpen-up-our-advocacy/.

traction, whereas 'change the agreement on agriculture by adding this paragraph to allow governments to protect small farmers' is more likely to get a hearing.

At the tip of the funnel, when negotiations over policy changes are well advanced, we need to grapple with the fine details, pushing for very particular demands, which requires working closely with allies inside the institution, all the while maintaining public pressure to prevent backsliding.

Advocacy has lifted much from the field of advertising, since it is, after all, a form of salesmanship. An essential lesson is to craft the message to fit the audience. What we say to a finance minister may not work for a parliamentarian or allies like health professionals, and certainly would not suffice for the general public.[15]

We activists need to stand in the shoes of the people we are trying to influence, and view the world as they do. Empathy is critical if we are to build a bridge to people who see the world very differently from ourselves. I have seen government ministers visibly turn off when preached at by finger-wagging activists more interested in 'speaking truth to power' than building a relationship.

The messenger is often as important as the message. African activists speaking about the challenges of development carry far more weight with most people than European academics, however long their publications list. Government ministers listen to other government ministers, the World Bank, or their supervisor from university days. Captains of industry are likely to listen to (and believe) something from a fellow master of the universe (like Amnesty's Sir Geoffrey) or a leader of their church, rather than a nerdy researcher or zealous campaigner.

---

[15] The impressive NGO WaterAid features a good example of crafting the message for different audiences (finance ministers, parliamentarians, health professionals, broadcast media and the press, and the general public) on p. 50 of its 'Advocacy Sourcebook', http://www.wateraid.org/~/media/Publications/advocacy-sourcebook.ashx.

Advocacy and systems thinking

Advocacy has been my natural habitat for most of my working life, whether in think-tanks and NGOs or government departments. The way I have presented advocacy up to this point fits well with the central argument of this book regarding how change happens. But what led me to write the book was partly my dissatisfaction with the way advocacy was practiced in the 2000s by northern NGOs and others.

My doubts began while lobbying on the WTO for CAFOD. I was on a roll, generating press coverage and loving being on the inside track. Then my colleague Henry Northover burst my bubble by asking why I thought global trade rules were more important to people on the ground than his area of work, helping civil society organizations in Africa counter the 'structural adjustment' policies imposed by the World Bank and IMF that were slashing public spending and causing serious hardship. I had no answer.

My disaffection grew when I joined Oxfam in the middle of a massive global campaign, 'Make Poverty History'. The campaign's implicit premise was that increasing aid, forgiving debts, and making trade rules fair could end world poverty. But I was becoming increasingly convinced that real change happens at the national level, and that such a campaign was aiming at the wrong target.[16] I remember standing in Trafalgar Square listening to Nelson Mandela declare in his magnificent way to an overwhelmingly white, European crowd: 'Sometimes it falls upon a generation to be great. You can be that great generation.'[17]

---

[16] My book, *From Poverty to Power*, was, in many ways, an implicit critique of Make Poverty History. Duncan Green, *From Poverty to Power: How Active Citizens and Effective States Can Change the World* (Oxford: Oxfam International, 2008).

[17] Nelson Mandela, speech at event organized by the Campaign to Make Poverty History, Trafalgar Square, London, 3 February 2005, http://news.bbc.co.uk/1/hi/uk_politics/4232603.stm.

All I could think was, 'Right generation, wrong audience'. Henry had been right. In my lobbyist's hubris, I had lost sight of what really matters. Not only had the campaign mistakenly (in my view) drawn attention and resources away from the national arena, it had arrogantly imposed its analysis on affiliated national campaigns around the world.

In many ways, this book is a response to my doubts about Make Poverty History. Allow me to conjure up a caricature of an old-style advocate: he would be arrogant, sure that he knows best both what poor people need, and how to bring it about; he would know in advance who to work with (probably people just like him); he would concentrate on generating media coverage and speaking 'truth to power', even if power wasn't listening. And no matter the problem, he would know the solution lies with the great global powers. A caricature, certainly, but not without some ring of truth.

Alex de Waal argues compellingly that Western campaigners tend to dumb down the complex realities of messy conflicts into simple narratives of good and bad to be remedied by simple solutions (preferably deliverable by the west).[18] Such narratives squeeze out the more nuanced views of local people and the deeper, underlying causes of conflict, and end up promoting superficial victories rather than real change.

Exhibit A is 'Kony2012', a campaign by a US NGO for military intervention by the US to defeat Ugandan warlord Joseph Kony, which went viral. The 'hashtag activism' of #BringBackOurGirls (for the return of 200 Nigerian schoolgirls abducted by Boko Haram in 2014) also showed the limits of outsider outrage with no insider links or understanding. Both campaigns made a huge splash in Western media and activist circles, but had little or no impact on the ground. Make Poverty History was certainly not as misguided, but still it downplayed the crucial arena of national politics.

[18] Alex de Waal, *Advocacy in Conflict: Critical Perspectives on Transnational Activism* (London: Zed Books, 2015).

When I got to Oxfam, I was told that good campaigns require three things: a problem, a solution, and a villain (heroes are largely optional, it seems). It is a remarkably good guide to which campaigns succeed and which flounder.

Systems thinking, on the other hand, suggests problems are multiple, interrelated, and complex, solutions are unknowable in advance and likely to emerge through trial and error, and at least some villains are likely to also be indispensable allies in bringing about change. When I say this to campaigners, their eyes have a tendency to roll: you really want us to launch a campaign by admitting we don't have a solution? What should the media team say to journalists who ask what we're recommending to fix the problem we've highlighted?

By becoming more attuned to power and systems, do we risk losing our edge as advocates, able to distil complex issues into simple, powerful demands for change? I don't think so. Acknowledging the lessons of systems thinking obliges us to reflect deeply about what issues are truly ripe for campaigning and what proposed changes might address the problem. It means we look in more places for those ideas—history, positive deviance, the lived experience and ideas of people on the sharp end. It keeps us alert to any unintended consequences of a victory. It should sharpen our edge, make our campaigns more compelling, even as it makes us suspicious of dumbed-down slogans.

Fortunately, the world of advocacy has moved on since the hubristic heights of Make Poverty History, shifting away from global summitry and toward a much greater emphasis on national influencing, as well as away from a 'command and control' campaigning style and toward nimble, locally generated strategies and tactics.

An acknowledgement that social and political changes are largely driven by internal forces and players may place international agencies like Oxfam on terrain that is just as treacherous as global campaigning. Is it right for organizations to try to influence affairs in a country that is not their own? Is there truth in the accusation frequently levelled by developing country governments that aid workers are stooges of a foreign power?

Think back to the example of ex-Greenpeace campaigners advising the British Foreign Office. However laudable their intentions, how would the effort to change India's climate change policy be seen by Indian politicians and activists? How would Her Majesty's government (let alone the British press) react if the Indian government used similar tactics to change UK policy on, say, migration?

In my experience, most international organizations doing advocacy in developing countries think very hard about these issues of legitimacy and what to do about imbalances of power between them and their local partners, despite the alarming exceptions noted above.

I have come round to thinking that global campaigns still have their place. They can't solve an entrenched national dilemma, but they can stop an international activity that is clearly causing harm. A good example is the Arms Trade Treaty discussed in Chapter 7. Campaigns can tackle global problems that require concerted action by several or all countries to succeed, like climate change or ending the 'race to the bottom' when countries try to undercut each other to attract investment by lowering taxes.

Foreign organizations can also be an asset in national campaigns where the levers of change are susceptible to outside pressure. To improve wages and conditions for workers in Indonesia's vast network of sportswear factories, the Indonesia Labour Rights Project (ILRP) provided support to local trade unions and others and managed to broker conversations between them and companies making brand-name sports gear for export. When the talks were only getting workers suspended or dismissed, the project mobilized its supporters in the countries that were buying the factories' shoes. Under pressure from consumers, in 2011 the companies signed an industry-wide Protocol on Freedom of Association, which also had the happy side-effect of improving communication between the brands and the unions.[19]

---

[19] By exposing the vulnerability of Nike's brand, the Indonesia campaign played an important part in the company's 2011 decision to reduce exposure to toxins (toluene) in all its factories and in 2012 (along with Adidas) to limit the use of short-term contracts.

Organizing exchanges between activists working on similar issues in different countries is another useful role for international organizations. Oxfam's Raising Her Voice programme promotes visits among women's rights activists in seventeen countries to swap notes and ideas.[20] The 'We Can' programme discussed in Chapter 2 was born as an Indian adaptation of work on violence against women in Uganda.[21]

I'm not sure if a power and systems approach requires us to abandon the old ways, or just treat them with caution, but it certainly has a number of implications for activists wishing to get better at 'dancing with the system'. Let's explore a few.

Critical junctures

In Chapter 1 we discussed 'critical junctures'—windows of opportunity provided by failures, crises, changes in leadership, natural disasters, or conflicts. At such times decision makers and the public may become painfully aware of the inadequacies of the status quo and cast around for new ideas. A well-prepared advocacy campaign can spot and respond to such moments, with striking results.

In 1972, Nobel laureate economist James Tobin suggested introducing a small tax on all financial transactions between different currencies, which, he argued, would curb short-term speculation and raise a lot of money for good causes, such as development assistance. The idea got nowhere, but continued bubbling on the margins of political debate for over three decades.

Duncan Green, 'The Indonesian Labour Rights Project', Oxfam Active Citizenship Case Study (Oxford: Oxfam GB for Oxfam International, 2015), http://policy-practice.oxfam.org.uk/publications/the-indonesian-labour-rights-project-338442.

[20] Duncan Green, 'The Raising Her Voice Global Programme', Oxfam Active Citizenship Case Study (Oxford: Oxfam GB for Oxfam International, 2015), http://policy-practice.oxfam.org.uk/publications/the-raising-her-voice-global-programme-338444.

[21] Duncan Green, 'The 'We Can' Campaign in South Asia', Oxfam Active Citizenship Case Study (Oxford: Oxfam GB for Oxfam International, 2015), http://policy-practice.oxfam.org.uk/publications/the-we-can-campaign-in-south-asia-338472.

It took the global financial crisis of 2008 and some inspired advocacy to bring the Tobin Tax in from the cold. Crushed by debt repayments, finance ministers were desperate for new sources of revenue for their cash-strapped governments, while the banks and currency traders who opposed the tax had suddenly become political pariahs.

A coalition of trade unions, church groups, and NGOs cleverly rebranded the Tobin Tax as the 'Robin Hood Tax'[22] and waged public campaigns across Europe featuring a series of hilarious, hard-hitting videos by top filmmakers and actors.[23] By 2011, the European Commission had proposed a Europe-wide tax on financial transactions. Though whittled down to eleven countries it was scheduled to come into force in 2016 and represents a historic breakthrough as the first truly international tax.[24]

Spotting and responding to critical junctures is just as important at national level. In 2002, the Malawian chapter of a regional women's rights NGO, Women in Law Southern Africa (WILSA), proposed and drafted legislation on violence against women, but got nowhere promoting it to government. Three years down the line, the media reported a spate of incidents of violence from across the country, ranging from wife-killing to grievous bodily harm and rape. Oxfam's Malawi team put out a press statement condemning the violence and calling on key leaders to take action. A range of different groups echoed Oxfam's message, most strikingly the Blantyre police, who drove up to Oxfam's offices in a van with loudspeakers on top broadcasting messages against gender-based violence. Following a very difficult debate in parliament, with opponents accusing the bill's supporters of attacking Malawi's culture, it passed.[25]

[22] Robin Hood Tax website, http://www.robinhoodtax.org.uk/.

[23] 'The Banker', video, https://www.youtube.com/watch?v=qYtNwmXKIvM.

[24] European Commission, Taxation and Customs Union, 'Taxation of the Financial Sector', http://ec.europa.eu/taxation_customs/taxation/other_taxes/financial_sector/index_en.htm.

[25] Duncan Green, 'Seizing the Moment: A Successful Campaign on Domestic Violence in Malawi', From Poverty to Power blog, 23 June, 2009, http://oxfamblogs.org/fp2p/seizing-the-moment-a-successful-campaign-on-domestic-violence-in-malawi/.

Coalitions and alliances

One of the skills of a good advocate is knowing how to construct effective alliances—and to distinguish powerful engines of change from soul-sapping talking shops. Similar organizations sometimes ally effectively, especially in the initial stages of building 'power with'. But interesting things happen when unusual suspects join forces.

The press conference organized by developing-country delegates to the 2001 WTO ministerial was a disaster. Not only was it scheduled late in the working day, long after all the European and American journalists had filed their pieces and retired to the bar, it had a dull technical title that belied the importance of the issue—how to protect poor farmers from being crushed by an avalanche of cheap, often subsidised food imports. Hardly anyone showed up.

After a hurried discussion, the policy and media teams from inter-national NGOs offered to rerun the event. The 'alliance of food insecure developing economies' was rechristened 'the G33' (no jour-nalist wanted to be blindsided by a new 'G'), a suitably eye-catching title and news release was bashed out, and NGO press officers fanned out to round up their contacts in the media room. The next day's event, on exactly the same topic, was standing room only. The dele-gates purred with satisfaction and gave barnstorming presentations.

Activists working alongside government delegates in the WTO is just one example of the uncomfortable alliances that seem to work in complex systems. We NGOs were worried about supporting govern-ments with questionable human rights records, and the governments were highly suspicious of NGOs that had criticized them in the past. But both sides saw potential in a tactical alliance on an issue they agreed on.

Unorthodox alliances can involve an element of holding your nose. After the BP Deepwater Horizon disaster in 2010, Oxfam and its local partners were determined to seize a classic critical juncture to ensure the reconstruction effort benefited the poor coastal communities disproportionately affected by the oil spill. Big prizes require big compromises. Oxfam worked closely with private companies and conservative evangelical church leaders, and even spent $120,000 on lobbyists who had access to Republican politicians. Campaigners had a hard time swallowing it, but they won investment in vulnerable communities and preferential hiring of local people.[26]

Insiders vs. outsider tactics

An enduring tension exists between 'outsider' and 'insider' activists. Suppose you uncovered some dirt on a corporate target and have written a hard-hitting briefing on it. You need to give the corporate a chance to see it before publication. The outsider would hand it over the day before the launch, so that the company is caught all but unaware and a good press story is assured. The insider, on the other hand, would do so several weeks in advance, hoping the company would take action to clean up the problem and avoid a public scandal. The outsider prizes the opportunity to build public awareness of the wider issue, while the insider favours maintaining good relations and sorting out a specific problem.

Systems thinking suggests that both play important roles. Outsiders keep important issues alive and fight to get new ones onto the table. They work in public, where mass mobilization often needs stark, unchanging messages. Insiders, on the other hand, take issues forward into the necessary fudges involved when turning ideas into policies.

In what are euphemistically termed 'closed political spaces' (dictatorships, autocracies, or countries where raising particular subjects is impossible due to the workings of hidden power), outsider tactics can be dangerous and counter-productive. A study of coalitions working

[26] Duncan Green, 'Advocating for Gulf Coast Restoration in the Wake of the Deepwater Horizon Oil Spill: The Oxfam America RESTORE Act Campaign', Oxfam Active Citizenship Case Study (Oxford: Oxfam GB for Oxfam International, 2015), http://policy-practice.oxfam.org.uk/publications/advocating-for-gulf-coast-restoration-in-the-wake-of-the-deepwater-horizon-oil-338441.

on gender rights in Egypt and Jordan concluded that the most effective advocacy engaged in 'informal backstage politics' often based on activists from elite family backgrounds networking with old friends and classmates. An acute understanding of the degree of political space (which opens and closes over time) was an essential skill.[27]

Unsurprisingly, outsiders often think the insiders are sell-outs who muddy the waters through compromise or hijack their issues, while insiders often view outsiders as politically naïve purists, but recognize that the threat they pose often drives decision makers into their arms.

The balance between insider and outsider tactics often varies over the course of a campaign, imposing real strains on activists, because of the very different tactics and language each uses. In the conflict phase, these are often polarizing and confrontational, and the alliances are likely to be among similar groups. By contrast, in the cooperation phase, the language and tactics are more propositional, and alliances need to be forged with actors in other spheres. Messy compromises replace clarion calls for revolution.

Individual activists tend to prefer one or the other of the two mindsets, and find it hard to change gears. Many tacitly opt for a division of labour, specializing in either the conflict or the cooperation phase. I am a co-operator: conflict makes me anxious and I like ambiguity; yet I have friends and colleagues who much prefer the clarity and adrenaline of a good punch-up.

Such tensions become particularly acute when the disagreement is between 'outsiders' in the South, and 'insiders' in international NGOs. In 1999, on the eve of an historic victory, winning debt relief for dozens of developing countries, the international Jubilee 2000 movement dissolved in acrimony, with Southern activists accusing Northern lobbyists of losing sight of politics in their obsession with

[27] Mariz Tadros, 'Working Politically Behind Red Lines: Structure and Agency in a Comparative Study of Women's Coalitions in Egypt and Jordan', DLP, February 2011.

policy. It brought home to me how divisive 'success' can be—what looks like victory to a reformist can easily appear as betrayal to a more radical mindset.

These tensions echo a more fundamental (and to my mind largely insoluble) dilemma: expediency versus long-term transformation. Does signing off on limited reforms legitimize the current distribution of power, forestalling deeper change? My own view is that a reform that expands the 'freedoms to be and to do' of poor and excluded people is almost always worth pursuing. I am too old and impatient (and perhaps too European) to hold out for 'all or nothing' approaches, which sadly often end up with the latter. If anything, systems thinking should improve our capacity for understanding just how much we are likely to win at a given time in a given situation, and therefore when we should bring one campaign to an end before we regroup for the next.

Conclusion

Many of my advocacy colleagues will look askance at this chapter. Too much self-doubt, too much navel-gazing. Why not just get out there and change the world?

I believe introspection is both warranted and necessary. Advocacy can backfire when campaigners become stuck in a hubristic bubble of tactics and media hits, and lose touch with the views and needs of the supposed 'beneficiaries' of their frenetic activities. Advocates need to be acutely conscious of their own power and position in the system, and the biases and behaviours those induce. We need deep connections with local communities.

Getting advocacy right requires political maturity, the right combination of tactics and allies, and making the most of windows of opportunity as they come along.

More subtly, good advocacy requires a mindset that finds each different context fascinating, that embraces ambiguity and complexity, empathizes with how different people see the world, and learns from mistakes and responds to changing events. All that, while maintaining the passion and energy needed to win.

Further Reading

D. Brockington, *Celebrity Advocacy and International Development* (Abingdon: Routledge, 2014).

A. Hochschild, *Bury the Chains: The British Struggle to Abolish Slavery* (London: Pan Macmillan, 2012).

S. Popovic, *Blueprint for Revolution: How to Use Rice Pudding, Lego Men, and Other Nonviolent Techniques to Galvanize Communities, Overthrow Dictators, or Simply Change the World* (New York: Spiegel & Grau, 2015).

A. de Waal, *Advocacy in Conflict: Critical Perspectives on Transnational Activism* (London: Zed Books, 2015).

PART IV

PULLING IT ALL TOGETHER

12

A POWER AND SYSTEMS APPROACH TO MAKING CHANGE HAPPEN

Commenting on an early draft of this book, Masood Mulk, who runs a large NGO in what he calls 'the badlands' of the Pakistan–Afghanistan border, provided this memorable example of what can go wrong:

> I will never forget a Princeton graduate who was brought in to undertake a change programme within an educational institution in a remote region. He started by throwing out 'inefficient people.' But he started moving those who represented the tribal balance in the region out of their jobs, the people from the mountains descended and surrounded him in his house. He was a virtual prisoner for days. I remember going to meet him and he kept shaking his head: 'They never taught me this at Princeton, they told me the villagers were simple people.'[1]

Such stories of failure to understand culture and context are unfortunately common in the world of aid and development, and among activists more broadly. Diagnosing what went wrong is always a lot easier than suggesting what we activists should do differently. This chapter offers a more theoretical sketch of the nature and dynamics of change portrayed so far in this book, a methodology of sorts, which I call a Power and Systems Approach (PSA).

The lexicon of aid and development is a bubbling morass of buzzwords and fuzzwords (like buzzwords, only more fuzzy). One of the more recent additions is 'theories of change'. In meetings and

---

[1] Masood Mulk, personal communication, email, January 2016.

documents, people earnestly enquire 'what's your theory of change?' You're in trouble if you don't have an answer, although I find replying 'I don't know, what's yours?' can induce a satisfying fit of spluttering and panic in my tormentor.

PSA is one such theory. Theories of change locate a programme, project, or campaign within a wider analysis of how change comes about. They articulate and challenge our assumptions and acknowledge the influence of wider systems and actors.

The concept originated from two very different disciplines: evaluation, (which seeks to clarify the links between project inputs and outcomes) and social action (which seeks to encourage a group of individuals to work together toward a common goal). Evaluation experts have led much of the innovative thinking on systems, probably because the task of assessing impact forces them to look much harder at how change really happens, including how systems and power derail the best laid plans of activists. Social activists, who spend their days navigating complex systems, also realize that linear thinking (if we do x then we will achieve y) is often a wild goose chase.

Confusion arises when we activists conflate how change happens in the system with how we intend to change it—a subject that might better be called a 'theory of action'. In my experience, activists spend much more energy talking about their own strategy than about the wider world—the dynamic context that should determine their intervention. A theory of change should contemplate both the context and the theory of action.

Theories of change can provide a more flexible alternative to conventional planning tools, such as logical frameworks (logframes), especially for complex programmes and contexts.[2] Viewing a theory of change as a compass not a map, a dynamic process rather than a static document, allows for assumptions to be regularly challenged

[2] Craig Valters, *Theories of Change: Time for a Radical Approach to Learning in Development* (London: Overseas Development Institute, 2015), www.odi.org/publications/9883-theories-change-time-radical-approach-learning-development.

and updated. It encourages a greater focus on learning through a continual back and forth between emerging evidence from the changing local context and the theory on which the programme is based.

From what I have seen so far, a theory of change is best used when individual activists are ready to acknowledge their own cognitive constraints and challenge their adherence to particular ways of thinking. In other words, we need to be willing to ask fundamental and sometimes awkward questions, and the organizations we work for must be prepared to alter the direction of the programme. Few institutional cultures are well adapted to such questioning—a challenge I discuss at the end of this chapter.

Three ubiquitous forces in the aid business and other sectors stand in the way of widespread adoption of a theory-of-change approach. First is the lure of the top-down, whereby philosopher kings (or at least consultants) from universities and think-tanks contemplate a political and economic system and, like Hermione and her Elf Liberation Front, derive the perfect theory of change without actually talking to anyone on the ground. Rarely it seems do experts show interest in poor people's own theories of change (after all, it might do them out of a job). The ever-more elaborate 'political economy analyses' they produce for aid donors seem to pay more attention to the economy than the politics,[3] and thus induce a helpless acceptance of the status quo in their readers.

Second the 'toolkit temptation'. Activists are busy, stressed people who need support. Most do not take kindly to being told 'every situation is different—go study yours, and come up with some stuff to try'. They want an idea of where to begin, what questions to ask, what success looks like. This natural instinct has prompted a proliferation of 'toolkits' and best-practice guidelines that, while better than a single 'right' answer, are often incompatible with the kinds of

---

[3] David Hudson and Adrian Leftwich, *From Political Economy to Political Analysis*, DLP Research Paper 25 (Birmingham: University of Birmingham, 2014), www.dlprog.org/research/from-political-economy-to-political-analysis.php.

systems thinking I believe underpins effective activism. At least to some extent, the best activists make it up as they go along. But making it up as you go along requires a considerable degree of self-confidence and chutzpah, a level of intellectual independence our educational systems do not always prepare us for (not to mention a degree of flexibility that few organizations will tolerate).

Good toolkits should provide a cookbook, to extend the cake metaphor on linear thinking from Chapter 1, leaving it to the activists to select promising recipes to try out in any given situation. Other tools (including the logframe) started out with the same noble intentions, only to be boiled down in the crucible of bureaucracy and time pressure into largely uniform checklists. At the time of writing, some promising guidance to working in a more flexible, iterative way is beginning to appear.[4] Let's hope that trend continues, to keep theories of change from becoming little more than logframes on steroids.

The third force is the demand for evidence of quick results and value for money. While accountability is necessary—it justifies aid spending to funders or taxpayers and promotes learning and improvement— the top-down pressure for results can have some deeply negative consequences for the way theories of change play out in practice. It is much easier to 'prove' results by assuming the world is linear, reinforcing the 'if x, then y' mindset. In complex systems, on the other hand, it makes more sense to be accountable for what you have learned and how you have adapted to it, than for results against a pre-set plan, but that can be a tough sell with traditional funders.

The need to demonstrate results in order to obtain funding also pushes activist organizations to work on issues where such 'islands of

[4] See, for example, Aruna Rao, Joanne Sandler, David Kelleher, and Carol Miller, *Gender at Work: Theory and Practice in 21st Century Organizations* (Abingdon, Oxford: Routledge, 2016); Matt Andrews, Lant Pritchett, and Michael Woolcock, *Doing Problem Driven Work*, Center for International Development (CID) Working Paper No. 307 (Cambridge, MA: CID at Harvard University, 2015); David Hudson, Heather Marquette, and Sam Waldock, *Everyday Political Analysis*, DLP (Birmingham: University of Birmingham, 2016), www.dlprog.org/publications/everyday-political-analysis.php.

linearity' are to be found (distributing bednets, registering voters, vaccinating kids), rather than ones that may matter more (women's empowerment, fighting corruption) but are harder and more expensive to measure. I would even blame the results agenda for skewing aid towards autocracies, because they are better equipped than democracies to provide the certainty donors crave.[5]

A power and systems approach

With these caveats in mind, I will now sketch out the elements of a theory of change based on the concepts outlined in this book, which I have dubbed the 'power and systems approach'—PSA. Unlike the conventional toolkit, with its typologies and checklists, I have settled on a combination of questions and case studies (lots of them scattered around this book and collected on its website). Together these can act as an engine of imagination, because though it may seem contradictory, a theory of change should expand the range of potential approaches rather than narrow them down.

I use the PSA in two main ways. The first looks backwards— exploring past stories of change, such as the Chiquitanos (see pp. 69–73) or Paris Agreement (see pp. 171–175). There the PSA helps broaden the kinds of questions to ask, and avoids the tendency to think that whatever changed was 100 per cent down to the activists concerned. One of the main lessons I drew from researching ten case studies in 'active citizenship' in preparation for writing this book is the importance of unpredictable events and accidents:[6] the arrival (or loss) of champions in positions of power, unexpected changes in laws and policies, crises, and scandals.

---

[5] Rachel Kleinfeld, 'Current Aid Design and Evaluation Favour Autocracies. How Do We Change That?' From Poverty to Power blog, 30 June 2015, http://oxfamblogs.org/fp2p/best-practice-and-linear-thinking-favour-autocracies-so-what-do-we-do-instead/.

[6] Duncan Green, 'Promoting Active Citizenship: What Have We Learned from 10 Case Studies of Oxfam's Work?', Oxfam Active Citizenship Case Study (Oxford: Oxfam GB for

The second, and perhaps more important, use of a PSA is in looking forward. A PSA acknowledges that we can't anticipate those critical junctures, so it is essential to 'expect the unexpected' by putting good feedback and response systems in place.

The PSA suggests characteristics that activists should cultivate in order to flourish in complex systems, like curiosity, humility, self-awareness, and openness to a diversity of viewpoints. People become activists not to analyse the world, but to change it. We are impatient of anything that smacks of navel-gazing (one Oxfam head of advocacy dismissed my job as head of research as 'beard stroking'). Consequently, we often fail to understand the history that lies behind the system we are facing, and thus we fail to 'dance with' the system. A PSA encourages us to nurture a genuine curiosity about the complex interwoven elements that characterize the systems we are trying to influence, without abandoning our desire to take action. We need to be observers and activists simultaneously.

There is a scene in one of my favourite TV series, *The Wire*, when Bunk, a dissolute but brilliant detective, advises a new recruit that the key to success is cultivating 'soft eyes', learning to spot the important clues that lie in your peripheral vision or that you weren't looking for.[7] Being a good observer is harder than it sounds. It's easy to see what we are looking for, but much harder to notice and register the unexpected, or the evidence that contradicts our assumptions.

Curiosity about the system needs to be laced with humility and self-knowledge. We don't—can't—have all the answers; we can't predict events; what works in one place won't work in another. We need to become comfortable with (maybe even enjoy) messiness and uncertainty, and give weight to local knowledge and feedback. We need to include a more diverse range of people and viewpoints in any

Oxfam International, 2015), http://policy-practice.oxfam.org.uk/publications/promoting-active-citizenship-what-have-we-learned-from-10-case-studies-of-oxfam-338431.

[7] *The Wire*, 'Soft Eyes', Season 4, Episode 2, aired 17 September 2006.

discussion, and (however busy we are) take regular time-outs to assess what is or isn't working and change course accordingly.

We need to recognize that 'we' are not lofty, disinterested observers. We make decisions at least partly based on our default models of the world and assumptions not based on evidence. We are wielders of power in our own right as are the organizations we work for. Power flows within our networks, influencing our relations with partners and allies. Let's recall Robert Chambers' question from Chapter 2: 'Am I an upper or a lower in this conversation?'

A PSA suggests questions we should ask (and keep asking) regarding the system, our theory of action, and our method for learning.

What kind of change are we talking about? I find it helpful to begin by asking where the change we are seeking sits on a 2x2 chart,[8] which was developed for work on women's rights and empowerment. It locates change processes according to the nature of the institution in question (on a scale from informal to formal) and the locus of that change sought (ranging from individual to systemic). The authors of the framework find that activists typically neglect the left hand side— the informal world. By reminding us to look at change in terms of all four quadrants, the framework stresses the need for work to happen at all levels (individual, community, formal politics, etc.) and it helps activists map who else is working on a given issue and identify gaps in the collective effort.

To use the framework, think about how the different aspects of the change process that you are considering fit into the different quadrants (see Figure 12.1, on the next page). Aspects of individuals' access to resources, such as credit, or jobs, or health and education, belong in the top right quadrant; what is going on inside their heads—issues of awareness, confidence and 'power within', belong on the top left. At a systemic level, visible power exercised through laws and policies goes on the

---

[8] Aruna Rao, Joanne Sandler, David Kelleher, and Carol Miller, *Gender at Work: Theory and Practice in 21st Century Organizations* (Abingdon, Oxford: Routledge, 2016).

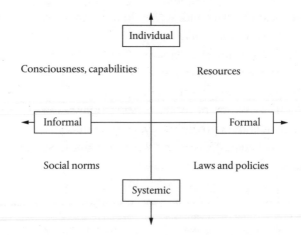

Figure 12.1 Domains of change

Source: Rao, Sandler, Kelleher and Miller, Gender at Work: Theory and Practice for 21st Century Organizations, (Routledge), 2016.

bottom right, but often, as we have seen, more informal institutions such as social norms play a significant role, and belong on the bottom left.

Change processes will flow between the different quadrants, and activists' attention may move from one to another. Taking the Chiquitanos in Chapter 3 as an example, change began on the left with individual consciousness and social norms, and then moved to the right to press for resources (land) and policies (indigenous rights). Victories in these formal spaces in turn fed back into and helped boost identity and awareness on the left. The many facets of power permeate each quadrant, influencing how change happens.

What precedents are there that we can learn from? Before cooking up our own change strategies, we ought to look around. Are the positive changes we seek already happening somewhere in the system (positive deviance)? Are there precedents from local history that we can draw upon? Are existing tides in the local political and economic context likely to help or hinder the desired change? Working from precedent rather than importing 'best practice' from outside makes it more likely that whatever we do or suggest will be compatible with the local system.

Who are the stakeholders and where do they stand? Whatever the issue we are thinking about and seeking to change, everyone involved will be linked by a subtle and pervasive force field of power. A good power analysis should identify the players (both individuals and organizations), how they relate to each other, who or what they are influenced by (peer persuasion or rivalry? evidence and example? protest?) and the different kinds of power in play (conventional visible power, or something more behind-the-scenes, like the invisible power of ideas or the hidden power of 'old boy networks'?).

A power analysis should stimulate ideas for strategies for engaging with the main institutions that drive or block change. It should dissolve the monoliths of 'the state' or 'big business' or 'the international system' into turbulent networks full of potential allies as well as opponents. A power analysis should also help us understand how those allies and opponents perceive the change, and why change *doesn't* happen—the forces of inertia and paradigm maintenance.

A power analysis disaggregates power, exploring the role of 'power within' (empowering individuals to become more active), 'power with' (collective organization), or 'power to' (action by individuals and organizations). That helps move the focus to those people who are often excluded from decision making (women, poor communities, indigenous groups, those living with disabilities) and whose empowerment often lies at the heart of long-term change.

What kind of approach might make sense for this change? Now it's time to examine the 'how', as well as the 'what'. Here I'd like to suggest the second and last 2x2 diagram in this book. Although designed by international aid policy people at a recent USAID workshop,[9] I think it is relevant to local activists as well. I like it because it acknowledges

[9] Duncan Green, 'Doing Development Differently: A Great Discussion on Adaptive Management (No, Really)', From Poverty to Power blog, 4 November 2015, http://oxfamblogs.org/fp2p/doing-development-differently-a-great-discussion-on-adaptive-management-no-really/.

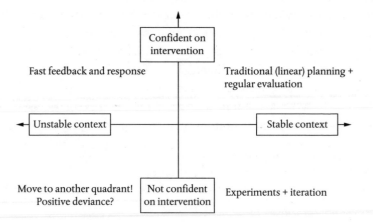

Figure 12.2 Adapting your change strategies to the system
Source: Adaptive Management workshop, NESTA, November 2015.

that not every situation is complex—sometimes you should just vaccinate kids, build roads, or distribute voting registration forms.

To use the framework in Figure 12.2, think about both the context and your proposed strategies. If you are operating in a stable or predictable context with a well understood change strategy (in the upper right quadrant), it may be entirely appropriate to use a traditional linear planning approach. In the end, some change processes are relatively straightforward, and there, KISS ('keep it simple, stupid') is not a bad approach. But remember the need for humility—too many interventions assume certainty exists, only to find things are much messier than anticipated. So you need to put in place ways to continually gather evidence to check that things are indeed as predictable as you initially thought.

If the context is stable, but you are not sure what kind of change strategy might work (bottom right quadrant), then experiment with several different ones, and iterate according to the results. If you are fairly sure about the strategy but not about the context (upper left quadrant), the emphasis should include setting up fast feedback systems to detect and respond rapidly to sudden changes.

Finally, if you are not confident of either your understanding of the context or your change strategies (bottom left quadrant), you clearly have a problem! It may be worth adopting a positive deviance approach, as discussed in Chapter 1. Alternatively, you can look for a simpler, or more tried-and-tested intervention to get you into the top left quadrant, or spend time understanding the context much better, so you can move to the bottom right.

What actual strategies are you going to try? This is where most manuals and toolkits start generating lists of options. I'm not even going to try, because the list of potential strategies is as great as your imagination: a basic list would include delivering services (like health, education, or credit); improving the broader 'enabling environment' (women's empowerment, producer organizations); running demonstration projects; and convening and brokering or forming multi-stakeholder groups to address particular issues. The tactics for achieving these various strategies can be equally varied: building alliances; seeking quick wins to gain momentum (e.g. by targeting implementation gaps); dividing and neutralizing opponents; winning over agnostics.

Since no amount of upfront analysis will enable us to predict the erratic behaviour of a complex system, a PSA interweaves thought and action, learning and adapting as we go. The purpose of these initial exercises is to enable us to place our bets intelligently. Crucial decisions come after that, as we act, observe the results, and adjust according to what we learn. Robert Chambers calls it the 'Ready? Fire! Aim!' approach.[10]

How will we learn about the impact of our actions and changes in the context? A power and systems approach encourages multiple strategies, rather than a single linear approach, and views failure,

---

[10] Robert Chambers, *Managing Canal Irrigation: Practical Analysis from South Asia* (Cambridge: Cambridge University Press, 1988), p. 230.

iteration, and adaptation as expected and necessary, rather than a regrettable lapse. How else are we going to learn?

Learning as we go requires good feedback systems, which could include anything from regular time outs to take stock on what has changed in the context, and what is/isn't working, to more technological approaches such as using 'big data' to detect changes in the political or economic environment.[11]

Dancing with complex systems is like navigating through traffic—success depends on fast feedback to detect new situations and having the ability to respond quickly (a pedestrian has stepped out into traffic—hit the brake!). If I tried to drive across London with a pre-planned route and velocity, and no adjustments according to feedback, I would be lucky to get to the end of the street. We have to spot new windows of opportunity, learn from failure, develop useful rules of thumb to guide decision making, and take multiple small bets until we find something that works. Analysis of the system, then, is not a one-off upfront engagement, but a continual process of analysing and reanalysing the context in which the programme or campaign operates.

And that's as far as I'm prepared to go, toolkit-wise. Even going this far has made me anxious that I am losing touch with the essential lesson of working in systems and thinking about power: that we have to make it up as we go along. For more guidance of this sort, check out the links on the How Change Happens website.

Implications for activist organizations

One of the most common responses from activists when I present the PSA is 'great, but they will never let me do this', 'they' being anyone

---

[11] Duncan Green, 'Big Data and Development: Upsides, Downsides and a Lot of Questions', From Poverty to Power blog, 23 July 2014, http://oxfamblogs.org/fp2p/what-is-the-future-impact-of-big-data/.

from a line manager, to the whole organization, to 'the funders'. That needs to change.[12]

For organizations serious about adopting a PSA, the first step is recruitment. Have we got the right proportion of risk-taking, rule-defying mavericks, or are we recruiting only planners whose skills lie in implementing a pre-agreed campaign project strategy? An organization made up entirely of mavericks would be dysfunctional, but my fear is that many have gone too far in the opposite direction. We need to inject more excitement and unpredictability into the mix. That also means getting serious about diversity: from India to the UK, too many activist organizations are dominated by members of the elite. Even if they have renounced elitist values, as many have, that kind of institutional monoculture slows the rate of evolution of new ideas and approaches.

Once activists are in position, do the incentives they work under, both moral and material (but mainly moral, in my view), encourage a power and systems approach? Will experiments, risk taking, and the inevitable failures be applauded or criticized? Do people get promoted on their ability to conform, or to disrupt?

Fear of losing grants from donors and governments, or donations from the public, drives many activist organizations to micro-manage every operation. While they should be held accountable for how they spend donors' money, 'command and control' will stifle the creativity needed to succeed. In a complex system a more productive approach may be 'don't control unless there is good reason to'. Local staff or junior staff and partners should have a fairly free rein to apply their deeper understanding to the programme. The job of head office should be to create the space for them to experiment, adapt and learn, and to negotiate that leeway with funders.

---

[12] This section draws on Duncan Green, 'Fit for the Future? Development Trends and the Role of International NGOs', Oxfam Discussion Paper (Oxford: Oxfam GB, June 2015), http://policy-practice.oxfam.org.uk/publications/fit-for-the-future-development-trends-and-the-role-of-international-ngos-556585.

Relinquishing 'command and control' opens the way to other PSA ideas, some of which are outlined in this book. Not insisting on slapping your brand on every project or document makes it easier to engage in multi-stakeholder initiatives and 'convening and brokering' exercises that bring together unusual suspects in search of new ideas and solutions. It also facilitates spinning off successful innovations: the hugely successful independent magazine *New Internationalist* began life as an Oxfam/Christian Aid project. Spin-offs can innovate and experiment, free from the constraints of being part of a large bureaucracy. The McDonalds burger chain may not be an obvious place to look for inspiration, but one option already showing signs of success is 'social franchising', where an NGO develops a basic 'project in a box' that individuals and local groups can pick up and adapt.[13] Spin-offs could be one way for international NGOs to maintain the momentum of an exciting project innovation, even though it carries organizational costs in terms of 'losing' success stories.

The opposite of spin-offs are mergers and acquisitions (M&As). Major tech companies snap up emergent start-ups, and something similar, but less systematic, happens in development. When I was a lobbyist at CAFOD, persuading the much larger Oxfam to steal my ideas was one of the surest ways to increase my impact. Of course I don't really mean stealing, but borrowing, collaborating, and so on. Why not make that a deliberate policy, with 'what have you stolen this year' as a performance metric?

Fast feedback and response are often neglected by activist organizations. Yet operating in the uncertain world of systems means putting processes in place to continually pick up signals about the local context, including our own impact, and to respond to those signals. Are we flexible enough to adapt or even shelve the previous plan if events so require? Advances in information and communications

---

[13] Kate Wareing, 'What Can Aid Agencies Learn from McDonald's?', From Poverty to Power blog, 1 August 2012, http://oxfamblogs.org/fp2p/what-can-aid-agencies-learn-from-mcdonalds/.

technology should facilitate such capacities, but activist organizations have been slow to change business models. Where is the equivalent of TripAdvisor for the development sector?[14]

Mike Edwards likens civil society to a diverse ecosystem.[15] Yet international support for civil society more often resembles monoculture—finding and funding partners that 'look like us' in terms of their institutional structure and way of seeing the world. Edwards argues that international supporters ought to see themselves as 'ecosystem gardeners', looking for vigorous local plants, whatever their origins (civil society, faith-based, private sector, none of the above). They can focus on the 'enabling environment'—the fertility of the political and institutional soil in which those organizations grow. Large aid agencies, for example, could fund ecosystem intermediaries, which in turn could administer hundreds of small grants. They could provide equity for spin-off organizations or seed money for groups to raise resources locally (an echo of governments' shift away from aid to 'domestic resource mobilization' such as taxation and natural resource revenues).

Finally, organizations need to review how they treat failure. Rather than attempt to hide failures, which occur in almost every programme or change process, the important thing is to identify elements within a programme that are not working and fix them en route. Some brave organizations have advocated talking explicitly about failure,[16] but in my experience that isn't the best way to approach the issue. Why not ask 'what have you learned?', and make 'accountability for learning' as important as accountability for results? It covers much the same ground in a less stigmatizing way.

---

[14] Duncan Green, 'Do Aid and Development Need Their Own TripAdvisor Feedback System?', From Poverty to Power blog, 10 April 2015, http://oxfamblogs.org/fp2p/do-aid-and-development-need-their-own-tripadvisor-feedback-system/.

[15] Michael Edwards, *Civil Society*, 3rd edition (Cambridge: Polity Press, 2014).

[16] 'Engineers Without Borders', Failure Reports, http://legacy.ewb.ca/en/whoweare/accountable/failure.html.

Innovation is one of those words that entrances senior managers; cynics advise people to acquire 'Innovation Tourette's', to impress their bosses by randomly sprinkling the word around their sentences. Happily, a PSA really does encourage innovation, which is essential to success in complex, fast-changing systems, where today's 'best practice toolkit' is likely to become tomorrow's redundant fax machine. A premium on innovation presents something of a conundrum for large aid organizations replete with procedures, reporting requirements, and accountability chains.

Activist organizations could create spaces free from standard organizational procedures to encourage 'intrapreneurs'. Google allows its employees 20 per cent time for personal projects (although only about 10 per cent of employees use it, and critics say it is actually more like 120 per cent time, i.e. on top of your day job).[17]

As suggested in Chapter 10, there may be a case for investing more in spotting, nurturing, and promoting individuals, rather than funding only projects (which individuals are then obliged to devise). Besides identifying potential grassroots or national leaders early on, activist organizations could promote an enabling environment in which more and better leaders are likely to emerge. Options to be tested could include influencing syllabi, university partnerships, scholarships, competitions, leadership training, and mentoring.

But overall, and despite its allure for managers, I am not convinced that 'innovation' is a terribly helpful concept. James Whitehead, Oxfam's 'global innovation adviser', has found that those who truly are 'innovators' don't see themselves as such and don't label what they do as 'innovation'. They just carry on working with others to solve problems. Innovation is a by-product of the process of collaborative problem solving, not the destination.[18]

---

[17] Jillian D'Onfro, 'The Truth About Google's Famous "20% Time" Policy', *Business Insider UK*, 17 April 2015, http://uk.businessinsider.com/google-20-percent-time-policy-2015-4?r=US&IR=T.

[18] James Whitehead, 'Unlocking Innovation: Enabling and Blocking Factors in Developing Innovative Programmes in Oxfam GB', Oxfam Research Report (Oxford:

Implications for funders

Activism costs money, and money is power. Funders can exert significant influence over the ability of activists to adopt a power and systems approach. Of course, funders are often activists themselves, both through the way they allocate cash and negotiate with recipients and through their own role as influencers. Nevertheless, there are a few additional points funders need to consider if they are to get behind a PSA.

The first, discussed earlier, is their standards regarding results and reporting. Is a funder willing to accompany a grant recipient as the organization navigates a complex change process, with changes in both direction and expected results, or does it insist, 'This is the plan we funded, stick with it'?

Funders, even more than individual activists, should think of themselves as ecosystem gardeners. They should sow diversity to encourage innovation and resilience, rather than institutional monoculture. Funders must embrace the fact that giving an activist organization $10 million may be more damaging than not giving it anything. Can they find ways to break up their funding into numerous small grants?

The good news is that although activists are often pessimistic about funders' readiness to work in new ways, many of the innovative examples of a PSA in this book actually grew out of 'good donorship'. In Tanzania, DFID was willing to fund a 'venture capitalist' theory of change involving multiple parallel experiments and the expectation that many of them would fail.[19] In Tajikistan, the Swiss Development Agency supported Oxfam with a ten-year grant to convene and broker

Oxfam GB, June 2015), http://policy-practice.oxfam.org.uk/publications/unlocking-innovation-enabling-and-blocking-factors-in-developing-innovative-pro-558453.

[19] Duncan Green, 'The Chukua Hatua Accountability Programme, Tanzania', Oxfam Active Citizenship Case Study (Oxford: Oxfam GB for Oxfam International, 2015), http://policy-practice.oxfam.org.uk/publications/the-chukua-hatua-accountability-programme-tanzania-338436.

national and global institutions working on water and sanitation, described in Chapter 2.[20] I hope activists working for funders and their grantees will collect and publicize such examples to make the case for wider change.

More broadly, some of the big funding bodies are in the vanguard of new ways of thinking about change, particularly in the area of governance. The networks 'Doing Development Differently' and 'Thinking and Working Politically' are made up largely of aid donors.[21,22]

How international activist organizations might adapt

Can you take a supertanker white-water rafting?[23] The agility of 'guerrilla' organizations like Global Witness, and the single-issue focus of institutions like the Ethical Trading Initiative, make them prime candidates for adopting the new ways of thinking and working discussed in this chapter. In contrast, large organizations, whether NGOs or government departments, feel very cumbersome. As one Australian government aid worker complained, 'We have to be like the incredible elastagirl, stretching between what our political masters demand and what communities need and want.'[24]

But size brings advantages too, in the form of large knowledge bases and economies of scale, which allow organizations to experiment and exchange ideas between countries and programmes. And when it comes to influence, small is seldom beautiful: governments

[20] Duncan Green, '"Convening and Brokering" In Practice: Sorting Out Tajikistan's Water Problem', From Poverty to Power blog, 17 January 2013, http://oxfamblogs.org/fp2p/convening-and-brokering-in-practice-sorting-out-tajikistans-water-problem/.

[21] Doing Development Differently website, http://doingdevelopmentdifferently.com/.

[22] David Booth, Thinking and Working Politically, GSDRC Professional Development Reading Pack no. 13 (Birmingham, UK: University of Birmingham, 2015), www.gsdrc.org/professional-dev/thinking-and-working-politically/.

[23] Jo Rowlands, 'Do We Drive a Supertanker or Go White-Water Rafting? A Brief Exploration of Complexity in Change Strategies/Types: Plugging a Gap', unpublished paper for Oxfam GB's UK Poverty Programme, 2005.

[24] Personal communication, December 2015.

are more likely to listen to bigger players, particularly when they have 'skin in the game' (programmes and staff on the ground). What kind of hybrid combination of scale and subsidiarity provides the optimal blend of flexibility and clout?

One option might be a 'conscious uncoupling' in which a large international organization transitions from a supertanker to a flotilla, with a medium-sized mother ship and a fleet of small, independent spin-offs and start-ups. As noted above, the smaller, more nimble crafts could include individuals in addition to projects. A flotilla structure could potentially conserve the advantages of scale while fostering the agility and innovation that is essential to success.

Large international organizations will continue to have the ears of Western donors, but the real arena for advocacy in national and local development will increasingly be the interaction between developing country states and diverse domestic players. Big agencies should take care not to usurp that space, adopting a supporting role rather than the star part.

That leaves several important roles for international activist organizations, noted in Chapter 11. They could choose to focus on the growing number of collective action problems that have so far stymied the chaotic institutions of global governance, like climate change, the narcotics trade, and restrictive intellectual property rules.

When they spot new trends and successful innovations, thanks to their on-the-ground presence in developing countries, they can give them greater exposure and place the ideas behind them at the open end of the 'policy funnel'. And they can raise the alarm when necessary, such as when governments crack down on civil society organizations.

The Washington-based Center for Global Development has made a virtue out of lobbying for policy improvements in rich countries as a way to promote development.[25] In areas such as aid policy or tax havens, there is certainly scope for international NGOs to expand their

---

[25] Center for Global Development, http://www.cgdev.org/.

engagement, as well as for taking on new and pressing topics such as migration.

Up to now international organizations have had a fitful engagement with debates on social norms and citizen rights. Although measuring effectiveness is a challenge, striving to accelerate normative shifts that enhance the rights of groups currently facing discrimination is an important activity that lends itself to an international approach.

International organizations are also well positioned to help activists link up across national borders, for example, via multi-stakeholder initiatives in global supply chains, such as the Ethical Trading Initiative.[26] On the new generation of health challenges in developing countries, such as obesity, tobacco, and road traffic accidents, international organizations could facilitate contact and exchanges between Southern and Northern campaigners who have a track record of success.[27] A Northern presence could also enhance South–South exchanges between activists.[28]

Conclusion

Contrary to the standard rhetoric of management gurus, the status quo probably is an option for activists and their organizations. It's just not a very good one. If we stay stuck in logframe linearity, we will become ever less effective. New, disruptive organizations and approaches will eventually take our place, or at the very least, take part of our turf.

Thinking more deeply about how change happens should change everything: the way we think and work, the things we try to change, and the structure and activities of our organizations.

---

[26] Ethical Trading Initiative website, www.ethicaltrade.org/.

[27] John Gaventa and Rajesh Tandon, eds., *Globalizing Citizens: New Dynamics of Inclusion and Exclusion* (London: Zed Books, 2010).

[28] Oxfam, 'Raising Her Voice' programme, Oxfam website, http://policy-practice. oxfam.org.uk/our-work/citizen-states/raising-her-voice.

It certainly won't be easy. Examples of the PSA can already be found in the work of many activists from local to global level, but rarely do they catch on and spread. One of my biggest frustrations at Oxfam has been how seldom great new approaches and ideas (including many described in this book) have been picked up, replicated, and adapted elsewhere. Harking back to the 3i's explanation of inertia, I suspect the problem lies not in interests or ideas, but in institutional culture: activist organizations need to change if they are to make the PSA work.

The prize for doing so is potentially enormous. It could unleash a wave of energy and creativity among activists at all levels, as they both dance with the system and change it utterly.

Further Reading

M. Andrews, L. Pritchett, and M. Woolcock, 'Doing Problem Driven Work', CID Working Paper No. 307 (Cambridge, MA: Center for International Development at Harvard University, 2015).

D. Green, 'Fit for the Future? Development Trends and the Role of International NGOs', Oxfam Discussion Paper (Oxford: Oxfam GB, June 2015).

D. Hudson, H. Marquette and S. Waldock, *Everyday Political Analysis*, Developmental Leadership Program (DLP) (Birmingham: University of Birmingham, 2016).

A. Rao, J. Sandler, D. Kelleher, and C, Miller, *Gender at Work: Theory and Practice in 21st Century Organizations* (Abingdon, Oxford: Routledge, 2016).

C. Valters, *Theories of Change: Time for a Radical Approach to Learning in Development* (London: Overseas Development Institute, 2015), www.odi.org/publications/9883-theories-change-time-radical-approach-learning-development.

Further Surfing

Doing Development Differently, http://doingdevelopmentdifferently.com/.
Thinking and Working Politically, http://twpcommunity.org/.

CONCLUSION

Congratulations, we're nearly done. What you have read thus far (assuming that you haven't skipped to the end, as I often do) is an attempt to make some sense out of the many things I have done, seen, read, talked about, and thought about for decades.

The story of how change happens is an inspiring one, filled with little-known heroes. And it is a story that never ends. As long ago as the sixth century BCE, the Greek philosopher Heraclitus noted, 'Everything changes, and nothing stays still.'[1]

But before you throw down the book and rush out to make change happen, some caution is advisable. Progressive change is not primarily about 'us' activists: it occurs when poor people and communities take power into their own hands; shifts in technology, prices, demography, and sheer accident can be far more important than the actions of would-be change agents. The first lesson for activists is humility.

That said, activists do play a crucial role. We put new questions into the endlessly churning stream of public debate, and we can help those on the sharp end raise their voices, shifting some degree of power from those who have too much to those who have too little.

Such work is a joy, a privilege, and a responsibility. We need to study the systems in which we operate, immersing ourselves in the complexities of the institutions (states, private sector, international system) that shape the pathways of change. We must get to know the players, both our targets and fellow activists, whether they work for the state, the private sector, or civil society organizations: how they

---

[1] Quoted in Plato's Cratylus (dialogue).

see the world and how we can work with them. We have to understand the underlying force field of power that links them in all its varied manifestations.

We will have more impact if we are prepared to take risks, try new, uncomfortable things, question our own power and privilege, and acknowledge and learn from our failures, all the while continuing to work with the zeal and commitment that characterize activists everywhere.

That goes for organizations every bit as much as for individuals. Researching and writing this book has convinced me that my organization, Oxfam, along with many others involved in promoting progressive change around the world, needs to change. We have to work in ways that reflect our evolving understanding of power and systems, becoming smarter, quicker to react, and more innovative. If we don't, then just like any other sclerotic company that resists change, new, bolder start-ups will enter the fray and eat our lunch (which may be no bad thing, of course).

Finally, I want to go back to what this is all about: human development, so brilliantly captured by Amartya Sen's definition, 'the freedoms to be and to do'.[2] Despite setbacks and the grim filter of the evening news, that story is overwhelmingly positive. The expansion of those freedoms over the last century has been unprecedented: millions, even billions of human beings leading healthier, better educated lives, freeing themselves from poverty and hunger, expanding their rights, living richer, more rewarding lives. For me, nothing gives life more meaning than being an activist, doing what we can to support that historic struggle.

---

[2] Amartya Sen, *Development as Freedom* (Oxford: Oxford University Press, 1999).

INDEX

Note: Figures and notes are indicated by an italic *f* and *n* following the page number.

INDEX

citizen activism
  definition 180–3
  growth of 179–80
  how outsiders can support 192–5
  importance of 195
  and markets 185–7
  and protest 183–4
  and state support 190–2
Citizens UK 112, 113, 118
civil society organizations (CSOs)
  definition 181–3
  distinguished from NGOs 182–3
  as drivers of change 116
  and government 187–90
  how outsiders can support 192–5
  and a power and systems approach 249
civil society protests 87
Clarkson, Thomas 214–15
climate change
  and advocacy 216, 220, 225
  contextual drivers for 171–3
  Copenhagen Summit (2009) 172, 175, 216
  and international organizations 91
  International Panel on Climate Change (IPCC) 142
  litigation 111
  obstructive powers 43, 44
  Paris Agreement (2015) 44, 91, 108–9, 171–5
  and social norms 65–7
Climate Vulnerable Forum 173
coalitions 228–9
Colombia 91–2, 110
colonization 84–5
complexity in systems 10, 15–16
'Concert for Europe' 137
consumer pressure 167
Control Arms Campaign 140–1
Convention on the Elimination of All Forms of Discrimination Against Women (CEDAW) 52–3
Convention on the Rights of the Child (CRC) 107–8
co-operatives 186–7
corporate lobbying 161, 163–4
corporate social responsibility (CSR) 166, 167
corporations *see* transnational corporations (TNCs)
corruption 118–21
Costa Rica 101, 110, 140, 202
crises, opportunities from 16–19

critical junctures
  and advocacy 226–7
  and Arms Trade Treaty (ATT) 141
  and climate change 174
  crises as 16–19
  examples of 86
  and indigenous identity 71
  and leadership 200
  and social norms 52, 86
crowd-source websites 188
culture 56–7
curiosity in a power and systems approach 240–1
customary law 102–6

democracies 90, 114–15 *see also* non-democratic systems
Democratic Republic of Congo 31–2, 182
demonstration projects 189
developing countries
  and advocacy 228
  colonization of 84–5
  and global campaigns 224–5
  and international organizations 224–6
  and leadership 200–1
  states in 89–92
  and transnational corporations 154–5
development 3–4, 28–9, 79–83
developmental states 89–90, 91
Developmental Leadership Program (DLP) 202–4
disability campaigns 189
'Doing Development Differently' network 252

East India Company 153
economic growth 82, 86, 166
economics 13–17
Ecuador 100
education
  dropout rates 25, 51–2
  gender gap in 53
  and leadership 202–4
  private 17–18
  and social norms 49
  and use of legal system 100–1
Egypt
  activism in Cairo 180, 184
  female genital mutilation (FGM) 64
  gender rights 230
  revolution 18
elections, costs of 119–20

systems
  and change 16–19
  and complexity 10, 15–16
  definition 9–10
  and indigenous identity 70–1
  and institutions 15–16
  leadership and power 209–11
  legal 109–10
  and power 15
  in state of constant change 12–13
systems thinking
  and advocacy 222–6
  and change 26–7
  and climate change 174–5
  definition and context 9–13
  and economics 13–16
  and evaluation 236
  and hybrid institutions 94
  and insiders vs. outsider tactics 229–31
  and opportunities from crises 16–19
  positive deviance 24–6
  principles for 20–4
  reflection and planning 19–24
  and social action 236
  and theories of change 235–9

Tajikistan 39–40, 251–2
  TajWSS project 23–4
Tanzania
  bajajis 158
  Chukua Hatua (Oxfam project) 22–3
  civil society organizations (CSOs) 190
  DFID funding of change 251
  media in 130
  social accountability 130–3
  systems thinking 22–3
taxation, international 227
technology
  and citizen activism 180
  and the role of the media 127–9
  and transnational corporations 165–6
television 51–2, 130
Then a miracle occurs (Harris) (cartoon) 132f
theories of change 2, 235–8, 239–46
'Thinking and Working Politically'
  network 252
Thomas, Mark 218
Tobin Tax 86, 226–7
tone, and advocacy 218
tourism 1–2, 47–8
Trade Justice Movement 214
trade negotiations 107, 135–6

trade unions 166–7, 185–6, 225
traditionalism 1–2
transnational corporations (TNCs)
  behaviour 167–8
  change in 164–7
  driving change 157–9
  history 153–7
  as influencers 151–3, 159–64
  power of 169–70
transparency, and accountability
  initiatives 130–3
Transparency International Corruption
  Perceptions Index 93
Treatment Action Campaign 163
trust, and the evolution of states 87
Turing 164
Twitter 129

Uganda 93
  'Kony2012' campaign 222
Unilever 157–8, 159–60, 173
United Kingdom
  Chartists 76
  cost of elections 120
  Department for International
    Development (DFID) 42, 126–7,
    215, 251
  dominance 144
  government spending 83
  legal system 105
  role of the state 80, 81, 84
  transnational corporations 156
  use of humour in activism 218
United Nations (UN)
  on access to justice 101
  civil society organizations (CSOs) 182
  evolution of 137–40
  and female genital mutilation
    (FGM) 62–3
  'Human Development Report' 143
  and social norms 48, 60–1, 141–2
  and soft power 145
  Sustainable Development Goals 106
  and transnational corporations 162
  UN Conference on Trade and
    Development 138
  UN Development Programme
    (UNDP) 138, 139
  UN High Commission for Refugees 138
  UN Programme of Action on Small
    Arms 141
  UN Women 138